EDUCATIONAL PHILOSOPHY

STUDIES IN THE HISTORY OF EDUCATION
VOLUME 3
GARLAND REFERENCE LIBRARY OF SOCIAL SCIENCE
VOLUME 1017

STUDIES IN THE HISTORY OF EDUCATION

EDWARD R. BEAUCHAMP, *Series Editor*

Educational Philosophy
A History from the Ancient World to Modern America

Edward J. Power

Garland Publishing, Inc.
New York and London
1996

Library of Congress Cataloging-in-Publication Data

Power, Edward J.
    Educational philosophy : a history from the ancient world to modern
America / Edward J. Power.
        p.   cm. — (Garland reference library of social science ; v. 1017)
Studies in the history of education ; v. 3)
    Includes bibliographical references and index.
    ISBN 0-8153-1971-1 (alk. paper)
    1. Education—Philosophy—History.   I. Title.   II. Series: Garland ref-
erence library of social science ; v. 1017.   III. Series: Garland reference
library of social science. Studies in the history of education ; vol. 3.
LB14.7.P68   1996
370'.1'09—dc20   95-24265
                                                                              CIP

Printed on acid-free, 250-year-life paper
Manufactured in the United States of America

To

ALLISON, KIMBERLY, WILLIAM, ERIN,
CHIP, DANIEL, AND KATHARINE

CONTENTS

Series Preface

Garland's Studies in the History of Education series includes not only volumes on the history of American and Western education, but also on the history of the development of education in non-Western societies. A major goal of this series is to provide new interpretations of educational history that are based on the best recent scholarship; each volume will provide an original analysis and interpretation of the topic under consideration. A wide variety of methodological approaches from the traditional to the innovative are used. In addition, this series especially welcomes studies that focus not only on schools but also on education as defined by Harvard historian Bernard Bailyn: "the transmission of culture across generations."

The major criteria for inclusion are (a) a manuscript of the highest quality, and (b) a topic of importance to understanding the field. The editor is open to readers' suggestions and looks forward to a long-term dialogue with them on the future direction of the series.

Edward R. Beauchamp

PREFACE

Conceding a traditional reverence for learning, the American people are disposed to invest confidence in the schools they support and the teachers they employ. This confidence, though, has sometimes been misplaced. Teachers in the middle years of the nineteenth century, often uneasy and fretful about the vacuum in dependable pedagogical knowledge, might have agreed. In any case, they were ready and eager to embrace a genuine science of education. By then plenty of illustrations were extant of science trying to speak directly to social issues. Could science speak to education too?

A litany of activity and accomplishment vis-à-vis scientific pedagogy is long. A full recitation is not needed to make the point that education as a discipline, a subject fit for scholarship and study, made its tardy appearance first in normal schools, then in teachers colleges, and finally in colleges and universities.

Over the centuries the education of the people had commanded the attention of good minds. But as an academic subject for special study, with a status recommending it as a discipline in its own right, it played second fiddle to philosophy, politics, and psychology, and to all those areas of knowledge traditionally housed in the classical curriculum. So long as education lacked credentials of a genuine science and an academic discipline, an independent scholastic record was hard to make.

The first step in education's long road to respectability lay in the ability of its proponents to demonstrate that it was worthy of collaborating with traditional disciplines in the syllabus of higher learning. The universities where this infant discipline of education was promoted should not be credited with having had either prescience or special wisdom: almost by accident they benefited from the presence of scholars who, with missionary-like zeal, engaged in teaching and research, and with unrelenting enthusiasm preached the gospel of scientific education. These schools—Teachers College, Columbia University; the University of Chicago, and Stanford University—earned a reputation for being oases from which pedagogical knowledge flowed, but they soon had imitators. Public and private colleges alike matched their stride by introducing professional academic programs for the preparation of teachers. Foremost among the subjects selected for these programs, because of its long history and the impeccable credentials of its ancient and modern expositors, was educational philosophy.

For all its cultivation in American mental soil, though, and the rich harvest that in time was reaped, one cannot be blinded by the luster of educational philosophy's twentieth-century record. American scholars unquestionably contributed to its stature, but they were not first and not alone in tilling the seeds of a discipline that germinated first in the ancient world. I will not concentrate on what happened before educational philosophy came of age in America and began to play an important role in the education of American teachers. It is nevertheless necessary, if the record is to be reasonably complete, to return to the years of educational philosophy's birth and trace its growth through the centuries preceding its emergence as a discipline worth the attention of good American scholars. Although the main thrust of this study is the history of educational philosophy in American colleges and universities, it takes into account educational philosophy's antecedents by beginning with them.

Among educational philosophy's antecedents one detects a few enigmas. At the outset, expressions of a nascent educational philosophy were buried in paragraphs of books Greek philosophers wrote on ethics and politics. The education of citizens was important to them and their community. So they sought precise, dependable answers to the important political and ethical questions that could be raised in connection with it. Yet they could hardly have imagined that extracts of their cogent discourses would some day be winnowed from their work and studied independently. Plato, Isocrates, and Aristotle, for example, knew the difference between speculative and practical knowledge and would have agreed that educational theory, if it is to be useful, must aim at the translation of principle to policy, and to practice. But they did not go very far in making this translation and would not have thought of themselves as educational philosophers. They had and expressed important ideas about education, and their work was certainly essential to the birth of the discipline. But it would be plain hyperbole to say that they created what stands now as the discipline of educational philosophy. Their work was the first step on a long evolutionary cycle.

The ancient philosophers' successors, the Hellenists, advanced the case of educational philosophy, bringing it a few steps closer to disciplinary status when they declared the school to be first and foremost a literary agency. This declaration needed justification, so Hellenistic scholars produced a body of literature to demonstrate how schools should function, what they should teach, and how teaching should be conducted. At the same time, they performed a service for educational philosophy by separating it from its parent discipline—speculative philosophy—and encouraging it to capitalize on its newly won independence and accelerate its maturity.

The Hellenists, however, were spared the need to distinguish education from erudition, a distinction of supreme importance to Roman educational theory. Although Hellenistic allegiance to moral formation matched that of the Romans, they recruited classical literature as a moral teacher, an idea repugnant to Romans. They maintained that the currency of practical experience was responsible for shaping the mind and character of citizens. The Romans undertook to elaborate a theory of education that gave precedence to knowing how to practice virtue rather than being able to define it. The virtue idealized in Rome was too harsh to suit the temperament of Christians who tried to immunize themselves and their children from the contagion they suspected infected Roman schools. This was a good reason to inquire into the nature of education and seek for a formula guaranteeing its decency. Another reason was to find a way to handle a body of literature, necessary curricular material for the schools, whose origin and perspective were pagan and thus neutralize its threat to religious faith. All the way from Jerome and Augustine to John of Salisbury, Christians theorized about education with the intention of describing its process and defining its goal. But to call their real and important accomplishments along these lines coherent and comprehensive philosophical expressions about education would be exaggeration. From the Hellenistic age to the end of the medieval era, links were added to an evolutionary chain that began with ideas about education and ended with cogent expressions about how certain issues in educational practice should be handled.

Since it is evident that a history of educational thought is a chapter in intellectual history, it might be nothing more than semantic quibbling to dwell on the difference between educational ideas, thoughts, plans, theories, and philosophies. Just as evident, however, as we study the evolution of ideas, thoughts, plans, theories, and philosophies, were the variations in emphases in different historical periods. At one time, what we now call the content of a history of educational philosophy was a collection of ideas or thoughts about education. At another time it was a theory about how to organize a curriculum with knowledge that was supposed to have most worth. At still other times it was a body of knowledge about how to organize and conduct systems of schools to support good government and ensure social, economic, and political reward for citizens. It is possible, then, to refer to a history of educational philosophy when it is recognized from the outset that educational philosophy began its long journey through history, in much the same fashion other disciplines began, with short steps betraying signs of infancy and immaturity. Over the centuries it evolved into a discipline with credentials to attract good scholars in and out of colleges, and to ensure its position as a college course in graduate and undergraduate programs of study.

An early, perhaps the first, attempt to organize and express a comprehensive philosophy or theory of education was undertaken by John Amos Comenius in *The Great Didactic*. From Comenius to John Locke to Rousseau, Pestalozzi, and Herbart we have an assembly of educational writers who articulated views on education that closely resemble the content of a later literature. Most contemporary educational philosophers seldom try to make a distinction among educational philosophy, educational thought, and educational theory. They are satisfied, even though fine points might be raised in connection with their work, that these men were pioneers who along with their predecessors and successors were engaged in building the philosophy of education. When we read their work we know we are approaching familiar precincts. Yet for all their help in instructing us about the seminal ideas in educational theory and practice, it was left largely to talented American scholars to mold educational philosophy into the mature, independent, and scholarly discipline that took its place before an intelligent audience around the first quarter of the twentieth century. Moving from age to age, the characteristics of what became educational philosophy changed and the vocabulary identifying these characteristics might have changed as well, but the character of the intellectual undertaking was immutable.

EDUCATIONAL PHILOSOPHY

CHAPTER I
EDUCATIONAL PHILOSOPHY'S ANCIENT ROOTS

The origin of educational philosophy as an academic discipline is hard to determine.[1] Neither is it easy to discover when men and women first speculated about the proper upbringing of youth, and the customs and laws to be communicated to oncoming generations. Our ancestors likely worried about the care and tutelage of their children, and turning to ancient civilizations—to Egypt, China, India, Assyria, and Persia—signs are evident that provision was made for the education of youth. But a body of knowledge either standing independently or associated with some more mature discipline to guide them in such an enterprise was almost certainly absent.

However one defines educational philosophy, it must be more than strong social yearning and fraternal urge, regardless of the source or the praiseworthy character of urge. Among the Jews, probably from the time of Moses, education was prominently displayed and seriously cultivated. But it was not a kind of education requiring a philosophy to guide and guard it. A theocentric stance with regard to all of life, along with Jewish law, custom, and fundamental communal commitment, was enough. So in following a dim track of educational philosophy's early history to find its disciplinary or subdisciplinary genesis, the best evidence is found in ancient Greece. More than anything else, the evidence suggests, the spur to a Greek intellectual investment in educational philosophy (a more precise phrase might be educational thought), although at the outset not as an independent study, was political necessity. The Greeks began to experiment with city-states and were determined to make the experiment work, both to supply sinew to government and provide opportunity for personal development. Preoccupied, some scholars allege, with vain curiosity, they were nevertheless committed to rational government, ethical standards, and personal nobility. These goals, it turned out, except in places like Sparta, were complementary rather than competing. So to come quickly to a statement about the timing of educational philosophy's disciplinary origin, one has sound bases for setting it in early fourth-century Greece. Although other city-states probably participated (for one should not forget what the Sophists brought with them to Athens),[2] its most bountiful harvest was reaped in Athens. In this connection, the statement that among all the studies associated with the general discipline of education the most ancient is educational philosophy, is persuasive.

EDUCATIONAL PHILOSOPHY IN CLASSICAL GREECE

History is unable to account for accident, although some critics contend that history is only a recording of accident and chance, and enjoys credibility by adding proper names. We can begin by conceding that when Athens's best minds considered the meaning of education, they were not victimized by a constant succession of surprises engineered by their vast and diverse deities. They were acting with purpose and reason. Although a veil shrouds what might have occurred before Socrates (469–399 B.C.) appeared on the Athenian scene—for it is entirely possible, indeed quite likely, that Socrates was not the first to consider how citizens should be readied for effective social and political life—the proposition is seductive that educational philosophy as an independent intellectual inquiry had its origin with Socrates' assertion to Protagoras (481–411 B.C.) that "I never thought human ingenuity could make men good."[3] Seen in the context of a debate about to ensue between Socrates and Protagoras, Socrates was saying that he doubted, or at least had not seriously considered, the possibility of moral virtue being communicated the same way knowledge about music, mathematics, and wrestling is taught. Before Socrates met Protagoras at Callias's house, he knew what most Sophists claimed for their teaching. Making an extravagant promise to teach political virtue in order to secure students, they were at the same time posing as teachers capable of maintaining the integrity of the city-state. Their method, they said, was novel, but their purpose wedded them to the respected tradition of conventional Athenian education.

Plato (427–347 B.C.) has Socrates challenge this sophistic pretension, because he saw the Sophists, with Protagoras in the vanguard, plunging educational philosophy into a cold bath of skepticism. And skepticism about anything, but especially about the proper formation of citizens, was bound to rot the sturdiest beam supporting the vigor of the state. Despite signs of indecision and prudent doubt in Plato's portrait of Socrates, Plato was eager to declare skepticism anathema. It was an obstacle to everything on his philosophical path. So Socrates' and Plato's systematic doubt with respect to the vexing issue of teaching virtue should not be judged as permanent skepticism, but as a temporary process by which permanently to overthrow skepticism.[4] If the dialogue *Protagoras* illustrates anything about educational philosophy's first seminal question, it `is that dependable knowledge is the hub of the wheel turning both intellectual and moral education.

Plato was educational philosophy's first architect. The citadel he constructed was both sturdy and ornamental, but there were other laborers ready and willing to plant seed in the fertile soil of the vineyard around it. Plato heads the list but Isocrates (436–338 B.C.) and the Sophists are on it too, although their contribution to educational philosophy is dwarfed by Plato's monumental stature.

An aristocrat by birth, nurture, and temperament, Plato refused to abandon the proposition that talented, highly educated persons with knowledge in their possession should hold the reins of government. So he proceeded, naturally enough, to weigh two equally important issues: What is the basis of educational soundness, and by what means is dependable knowledge obtained? He readily affirmed the possibility of achieving truth, although there is nothing in his philosophical creed allowing for the assumption that the road to truth is easy to travel, or, for that matter, that detours along the way and wrong turns are impossible. A properly husbanded educational process holds out the most likely prospect, although no guarantee, for securing truth. At the same time, while not repudiating one word in his declaration for truth's possibility, he acknowledged the inability of most persons to grasp it. Moreover, he affirmed truth's corpus to be so enormous and complex that for most prudential judgments, right opinion would have to be embraced as a worthy, albeit temporary, substitute. Truth and right opinion are friends; vulgar opinion is an enemy to both.

Plato's personal educational experience, which gave him a starting point for philosophizing about education, illustrates the care, dedication, and discipline essential to the proper formation of a mind. The Academy, his splendid school, illustrates as well a commitment to the integrity of the educational process. His tenure in it persuaded him that the finest educational opportunity should be reserved exclusively for the most talented students. It is hard to believe, although only skimpy attendance reports are extant, that the Academy ever countenanced a policy of open admission. A place in the school was hard to attain and, probably, even harder to maintain.

The temptation to believe that had Plato been able to indulge his first love he would have been a practical politician is hard to resist, but Plato could not have his way. Although never despising the profession of teacher, becoming a schoolmaster was settling for second best. Close association with Socrates led either to suspicion or charge of sedition: political expediency recommended a swift departure from Athens after the death of Socrates. Allowing almost twenty years for tempers to cool, Plato returned to his home town, but to soften old animosity—for political memory can be long—opened a school. To ensure his safety and the school's stability, he called the Academy a religious fraternity rather than an institute for the communication of a political culture.

Isocrates, nine years older than Plato, and Plato belonged to the same generation and shared many of the same aspirations for their city. Besides, Isocrates' association with Socrates, although never on the same level of intellectual intimacy as Plato's, was close enough for him to be influenced by Socratic dialectic and by Socrates' intense addiction to ethics. Isocrates, too, had an aristocratic heritage in a family with sufficient wealth to send him to the best teachers in Athens, some Sophists, like Gorgias, among them. Isocrates was preoccupied, as was Plato, with statecraft and, somewhat different from Plato, was mesmerized by the thought of making Athens the political, cultural, and economic center of the Greek world. He, too, preferred an active to a passive political career, but his temperament was unsuited to the rough and tumble of political debate and platform oratory. For about twenty years he pursued the vocation of a writer preparing speeches for others to deliver. Put directly, he was one of history's earliest ghost writers. The occupation was profitable and, if evidence ancillary to *On the Antidosis* is dependable, Isocrates became one of Athens' wealthiest citizens.

Eventually the rash of anonymity became too oppressive and, itching for attention, Isocrates decided to open a school in competition with the schools of the Sophists and Plato's Academy. Aristotle's (384–322 B.C.) Lyceum, opened about 335 B.C., was still a long way over the horizon.[5] Seeing that the current substantial issue facing education was political virtue—whether nurture could produce responsible and just citizens—Isocrates undertook to demonstrate how the instructional program in his school was different from the schools with which his was competing. Although settling for declaration rather than demonstration, the basis for asserting the superiority of his school to those of the Sophists was fairly easy to illustrate, because the Sophists in making extravagant statements about the efficacy of their instruction were bound to reveal weakness and superficiality. Plato's educational program in the Academy along with his publicly stated positions, while not immune to criticism, were not such easy targets. Undaunted by the task facing him, Isocrates began by publishing a prospectus, *Against the Sophists*. The school he was about to open was intended to persuade wealthy Athenians to send their bright children to his school rather than to those of his foremost competitors.[6] Plato and the Sophists were not indicted for belonging to the same pedagogical band, although Isocrates undertook to illustrate where both educational programs were deficient.

The Sophists were vulnerable because of superficial teaching, lack of solid pedagogic technique, extravagant promise, and penchant for requiring tuition payment in advance.[7] Yet they had something that was attractive, too: their course of instruction was quick, invoked the luster of novelty, and succeeded in producing some students able to hold their own in political debate. Plato's course of study in the Academy, while far shorter than anything recommended in the *Republic* and the *Laws*, required students to defer entry into public life for a long time, and even then they were not assured, as were students who went to the Sophists, of being fully equipped to meet all the exigencies of political life.[8]

Careful not to cast too wide a net and thus indict all Athens's teachers, Isocrates, first, writes about the Sophists: "If all who are engaged in the profession of education were willing to state the facts instead of making greater promises than they can possibly fulfill, they would not be in such bad repute with the lay public."[9] What facts should be stated? He wants Sophists to abandon their bold boast of being able to teach students how to prepare written and oral compositions capable of complying with the requirements of all occasions. These were vulgar Sophists who habitually elevated eloquence over content, and advanced the audacious notion that if persons speak well, they can deliver effective orations on any subject. Knowledge clearly was being bargained away at discount. Address should of course be clear and persuasive, but all speeches, Isocrates averred, had to stand on a foundation of dependable content if they were to be morally responsible. Neglect this foundation and a speech would be either perceptive and immoral or superficial and amoral.

Besides, the vulgar Sophist, being ignorant of decent pedagogic technique, was content to have students commit to memory famous orations or pet sophistic compositions. To these, students added to their storehouse of memory dialogues selected for their artistry and subtlety. If students were ingenious, they could use such ammunition to win arguments. But this kind of oratory, Isocrates declared, was both barren and dangerous, and it was an oratory that reminded Aristotle of a shoemaker who instead of training his apprentices in cobblering showed them several pairs of shoes.[10]

Isocrates might have conceded that all Sophists did not engage in such fraudulent and shoddy technique. But his goal was not to exonerate any part of sophistry, for in one way or another it violated his pedagogical commitment to careful study of a standard curriculum, and to long and intensive sessions of written composition before any introduction was made to platform oratory and rhetoric's arsenal of rule and regulation. At the same time, although deploring the sophistic employment of oratorical model, Isocrates never meant to demean the use of the model in any program of study. Hyperbole is barely discernible in the assertion that in the history and theory of teaching, no one, not even Cicero (106–43 B.C.) or Quintilian (A.D. 35–97), superseded Isocrates in an idealization of model and imitation.

Isocrates could hardly charge Plato with vulgar sophistry; such a charge would have been frivolous, although he meant to tar Plato with the brush of sophistry. His objection was to Plato's optimism, and to the pedagogy associated with it, about the possibility of arriving at truth. Isocrates grieved over the years wasted in pursuit of a truth too elusive to grasp, and then went on to inquire why, if Plato and his students were in possession of truth, were they no more successful in the political arena than those who affirmed the dependability of experience on a common-sense basis? Plato, Isocrates conceded, was unquestionably sincere in believing that certitude is possible. But studying on into old age with a vague hope of rescuing knowledge from an uncooperative cosmos is nothing short of intellectual arrogance. Isocrates' dispute with Plato's pedagogic theory had its genesis in a total rejection of Plato's epistemology.

Responsible oratory is at the heart of Isocrates' declamation, and responsible oratory depends upon three things: a decent grasp of knowledge—and here Isocrates is content to accept as knowledge what most people believe to be true—which, of course, separated him from Plato; a command of the art and science of eloquence; and a character natively disposed to virtue. It is the latter ingredient, character, where Isocrates makes a huge departure from both Plato and the Sophists. He reports his doubt about the ability of the Sophists to teach their students how to be good, honest, and noble. He knew the hazard in trying to translate virtue from the order of wisdom to the order of prudence: knowing what ought to be done is not the same thing as doing it. He distrusted, moreover, any affirmation with respect to discovering the ultimate meaning of virtue. Still, he wanted oratory to be responsible, so it was essential for it to be grounded upon a foundation more stable than whim or convention.

With this as preamble, Isocrates declared that persons have an innate knowledge of what is good and true, what is responsible and what irresponsible. The meaning of justice, indeed all the virtues if they can be identified, and the difference between right and wrong action do not need the mediation of a teacher: such knowledge is a common human possession. Yet this common possession is unequally distributed: some persons have more, others less, and some have none. It is, therefore, the burden—and the ominous responsibility—of teachers to attend to youth who possess the most virtue and instruct them well. Being good persons and benefiting from a good education, they can contribute to the betterment of society. At the same time, it is the responsibility of teachers to winnow from their classes students lacking virtue: evil well-educated men are capable of doing society much harm. In the last analysis, then, Isocrates promoted a novel creed making nurture essential to the development of mind, where knowledge and skill are lodged. But nurture is powerless in connection with the soul whose reservoir holds all the virtue any person will ever have.

With this background of educational dispute and the attention it visited on virtue, Plato relates a debate between Socrates and Protagoras that has won enduring fame. Before the debate began, Plato had made his position clear with respect to virtue,[11] so there is little mystery about what Socrates is going to say.[12] Plato maintained that knowledge of virtue is essential if persons are to practice it, but he demurred from any declaration that knowing what is right and just will lead to correct and honorable behavior. At the same time, he found little to recommend in what he was sure was a naive proposition advanced by Isocrates: that virtue is an original datum. Thus is the stage set for the encounter which resulted in identifying the original disciplinary credential for educational philosophy.

It all begins when Hippocrates, a wealthy, talented young man, rushes to Socrates' house with news that Protagoras has come to town. Protagoras's reputation preceded him and Hippocrates, exhibiting youth's attraction to novelty, expresses his intention to become Protagoras's student. Socrates displays mild enthusiasm, not wanting to be an impediment to curiosity, but at the same time undertakes to elicit from his young friend what he expects to learn from Protagoras. Were the great Sophist a physician and Hippocrates wanted to become a doctor or a sculptor, and the young man wanted to become an artist, this choice might be prudent. But Protagoras is a Sophist and unless Hippocrates expects to be a Sophist, Socrates wonders whether he should select a different teacher. Hippocrates, having heard that Protagoras is a man of learning and letters, well versed in the arts of mind and expression, and entirely capable of preparing students for the profession of a public man, is unpersuaded.

Hippocrates is repeating hearsay. He lacks firsthand knowledge whether the liberal culture Protagoras claims to purvey is genuine or a crude camouflage for technical knowledge. Socrates wants his young friend to be more critical and cautious. Protagoras, he declares, has come to Athens promising to teach any subject for pay. He is a salesman of sorts, but what students buy is a mystery: they know neither its substance nor effect. Purchases from commercial salesmen can be examined and used, so almost at once buyers know whether value has been received. In the case of Protagoras's instruction, says Socrates: "You are going to commit your soul to the care of a man whom you call a Sophist. And yet I hardly think that you know what a Sophist is; and if not, then you do not even know whether your are committing your soul to good or to evil."[13] The way to unravel this conundrum, Socrates and Hippocrates agree, is to seek out Protagoras to elicit from him a clear statement about the nature of his instruction. They go to Callias's home, where Protagoras and several other Sophists are guests.

Socrates introduces Hippocrates to Protagoras, a sign that Socrates and Protagoras are acquainted. He tells Protagoras that his young friend comes from a noble, wealthy family, is ambitious and capable, aspires to a political career, and wants to be Protagoras's student. He is, Socrates knows, just the kind of student Protagoras wants. It would be well, though, Socrates adds almost as afterthought, for Hippocrates to have an aperçu of Protagoras's educational theory and practice. The great Sophist assents; he knows an attentive audience when he sees one and is eager to advertise his wares. Socrates, hoping to define the boundary for the debate, takes the lead: "I will begin again at the same point, Protagoras, and tell you once more the purport of my visit: this is my friend, Hippocrates, who is desirous of making your acquaintance; he wants to know what will happen to him if he associates with you. That is all I have to say."[14] Protagoras's answer is both quick and bold: "Young man, if you associate with me, on the very first day you will return home a better man than you came, and better on the second day than on the first, and better every day than you were the day before."[15]

The unanswered question of earlier dialogues is repeated: How can education make persons better? Moreover, how can sophistic education accomplish this ambitious goal? And Socrates' interpolation hinders Protagoras: if a person wants to be an artist and apprentices himself to a great painter, everyone would understand in what way he wants to be better; or if one wants to be a flutist and studies with a master player, it would be easy to discern the student's purpose. The issue Socrates raises is fairly simple and straightforward. What is the Sophists' special art or knowledge that can be communicated so certainly and so directly? Protagoras shows a sign of wariness and makes an ambiguous response. Unable to speak for all Sophists, he says the art he professes is political; its purpose is to teach students how to be good citizens. To clinch the point, he summarizes the Athenian educational tradition to supply evidence supporting his assertion that virtue can indeed be taught. Why, otherwise, would parents, teachers, and public officers invest time and talent to lay a foundation ensuring that students embrace right conduct? Anyone, he declares, who transgresses the rule of right conduct is to be "corrected or, in other words, called to account, which is the term used not only in your country, but also in many others. Now when there is all this care about virtue private and public, why, Socrates, do you still wonder and doubt whether virtue can be taught? Cease to wonder, for the opposite would be far more surprising."[16]

Protagoras's assertion reveals the fundamental difference between sophistic educational pretension and Plato's educational conviction. Socrates wants analysis, not declaration, so he presses on. Were he responsible for establishing the law of nature, he says, teaching political virtue would indeed be possible. But reality imposes a stricter standard and illustrates the common experience that political prudence, rather than being a science subject to the direction of dependable knowledge, is opinion and, moreover, cannot be taught. Protagoras bridles at this, thus underlining a basic principle of sophistic pedagogy: the boundary of educational achievement is limitless. The Sophists' popularity and success depended upon persuading prospective students that instruction could elevate their social station and substitute for the advantage of heritage, privilege, and wealth, so Protagoras resists any challenge to the efficacy of nurture in making minds and forming souls. Had he toned down his extravagant claim, limiting it to teaching what can be taught, Socrates would have assented. But asserting an essential relationship between intellectual and moral virtue was too much for Socrates to swallow. Besides, it put Protagoras in the unenviable position of unraveling the pedagogic riddle of how to teach moral virtue. At this point in the debate, Protagoras, unaware that he is in jeopardy, plunges on to declare that what he calls social science can establish the essential goals of ethical and political instruction. He is, he declares, a teacher of social science,[17] and then launches into a long oration illustrating his mastery of the art of eloquence and his command of a sophistic pedagogy capable of delivering on all its promises. His effectiveness is evident; he has the audience, apparently convinced of the merit of his argument, on his side. Even Socrates seems to appreciate Protagoras's eloquence. But if others in the audience are converted, Socrates is not.

He poses what on its face appears to be a harmless question: Is virtue one, and are justice, prudence, and piety parts of it, or are they different names for the same thing?[18] If we possess virtue, must we have all its parts? Can we have some virtues and not others? And are the virtues similar and related, or are they distinct? Protagoras thinks the virtues are different and distinct, but his explanation lacks both clarity and persuasion. Exhibiting distress, he complains of Socrates' tactics and threatens to withdraw from the debate. But Socrates with a hook baited has no intention of letting his prize escape. Protagoras is coaxed back to the encounter when Socrates agrees to allow him to direct the course of the debate.

The discussion turns to a critical examination of poetry and its place in sophistic education. Cleverly and skillfully, however, Socrates reintroduces the question of virtue by misinterpreting the meaning of a poem to demonstrate a method for proving anything, and then adds a clinching point: no one errs willingly.[19] Socrates then asks Protagoras to assess the status of reason and knowledge. Protagoras says that of all the human abilities, they are the highest. But the point to Socrates' inquiry is whether knowledge can help persons act virtuously. Does knowing what is good insulate them from evil action? Protagoras thinks not and this is a concession of enormous significance because it pared away the general sophistic idealization of the power of knowledge. Embarrassed, Protagoras tries again to withdraw from the debate because he believes Socrates has cleverly tricked him into making a damning admission. To hold him, Socrates promises to shift the discussion to something more to Protagoras's liking: What are the imperative standards for living a decent life?

All the time Socrates has maintained, while concealing his conviction to the contrary, that what is pleasant is good: pleasure is the principle whereupon human behavior rests. When he repeats this assertion, the Sophists in the audience express their agreement. Protagoras, wary of acknowledging the point, decides to accept what in earlier arguments he had rejected. Socrates has saddled the Sophists with two burdens: hedonism and uncertainty about the art they purvey. Hedonism was unacceptable to the intellectual community of Athens, so Protagoras's confused admission that it is the basic principle governing human behavior was bound to put sophistry in a bad light. More damaging still was the abject ambiguity in Protagoras's stance about whether virtue can be taught. First affirming that it can, he ends up denying such a possibility. What better evidence could be mustered to demonstrate the undependability of sophistry? Who would sit at the feet of teachers ignorant of what they pretend to profess? And who can depend upon an educational philosophy and a pedagogy wedded to it that refuse to trust in truth?

EDUCATIONAL PHILOSOPHY'S INDEPENDENCE

The time came—about the beginning of the third century B.C.—when the vigor of the classical age began to flag, but cultural monuments that had been created by philosophers and literary artists over several centuries remained as a cherished heritage in Greece and were preserved as a living tradition. History reports a Greek ambition that, spurred by the adventuresome spirit of Alexander the Great (356–323 B.C.), sought to extend its influence to adjacent lands. The Greeks had no urgent intent to export their culture to those places subjected by Alexander's legions, because their interest was mainly commercial and political. Yet, gratuitously, parts of the classical heritage made their way into sections of Asia and Africa, and were embraced with a surprising fervor. Clever people were quick to perceive treasure in the classical inheritance. So they embraced it with a zeal illustrative of religious conversion and undertook to master the classical bounty now unexpectedly at their disposal.

Zeal and ambition aside, the burden of absorbing a heritage for which they had little or no linguistic and cultural affinity was both huge and difficult. Before anyone could open an antique book and hope to reap the treasure in it—a treasure confidently assumed to be the highway over which the supreme ideals of the classical age would pass—it was essential to master the humble auxiliaries to language and literature. Hellenistic converts to culture had no choice but to enlist schooling in their cause. Almost at once, and fully aware of the consequence of their action, they commissioned schools as agencies for cultural transmission. But there are preliminaries to reading and understanding the classics. Before cultural heights could be scaled, Hellenistic schools had to offer competent instruction in those subjects—grammar, rhetoric, and logic—capable of bearing the weight of more advanced study of language and literature.

Confidence in an education canalized toward citizenship was high in the classical age. Culture was something to be nurtured by the vast and various activities in the city itself. In the Hellenistic world, however, the political policy shaped by Alexander and maintained by his successors declared the people inhabitants, not citizens. And the political education promoted in a classical city-state to prepare persons for an active role in political affairs was suppressed. Moreover, cultural yearning could not be satisfied by the commerce of life in the Hellenistic municipality where none of the vestiges of the ancient city could be found. It could be satisfied only by determined effort, by going to those parts of the classical heritage most capable of preserving culture from obliteration by erosion and decay. Any share of classical culture had to be bargained for in school, and schools for the first time were equipped to transmit a precious heritage. These conditions and expectations prompted clever persons to reconsider the role of education in their lives; they were led inevitably to philosophizing about it.

Early Hellenistic educators were aware of the philosophical disquisitions of their Athenian forebears, and they knew, too, of the scholastic activity of the Sophists. They had a base upon which to build, but this left plenty for them to do. Commissioning schooling as an instrument of cultural transmission was an important factor in accelerating the maturity of educational theory, but there were others. Persons in the ancient city-state were in the habit of subordinating their individuality to the common good, so they cultivated a collective spirit and lived according to its code because the city's environment affected everything in their lives. There is no exaggeration in the assertion that Athens was one great school. The Hellenistic world was different: persons absolved from any political duty that went beyond civic housekeeping were easily persuaded that their first duty was to themselves. This indifference to political idealism allowed education to sever its bond to politics. So with education no longer melded with corporate life, the time was ripe for educational theory to direct its attention to the perfection of personality rather than public service. If self-perfection were worthy of complete devotion, unsurprisingly scholars began to think more profoundly about education as a desirable means to realize it.

In consequence of these shifts, ideas about education became a common currency of intellectual exchange. Besides, it was one of the few areas wherein intellectual effort could be spent without fear of reprisal. For some curious reason the leaders of the Hellenistic empire were indifferent to what was going on either in educational theory or in the schools. Earlier, educational speculation had spent energy on clarifying the relationship between education and politics; in Hellenistic towns and cities discourse centered on how to create educational opportunity for a citizen of the world. An imposing array of thinkers turned attention to education, and began to publish views on teaching, learning, pedagogic technique, and schooling's service to culture. Their audience was eager and attentive. A sample of these educators and their contribution to educational philosophy's maturity and independence is worth our attention.

Aristippus[20] of Cyrene (435–350 B.C.), Chrysippus[21] (281 or 227–208 or 204 B.C.), Theophrastus[22] (c. 370–286 B.C.), Clearchus of Soli (third century B.C.), Cleomenes (second century B.C.), Aristoxenus[23] (third century B.C.), Cleanthes (c. 331–232 B.C.), and Zeno of Citium[24] (336–264 B.C.) marked the best trail, but they were not alone. As a cadre, they began with a belief that schools should be literary agencies committed to transmitting antique culture. They ended with a reasonably precise and fairly coherent philosophy of education. It is not too much to say that they, along with Cicero, were instrumental in helping the great Quintilian shape his views on the education of an orator. In concentrating on literature, they were following

Isocrates' literary humanism. But this emphasis, one neglecting science so much that it was in an academic hinterland, is easy to misinterpret if the assumption is adopted that in antiquity there was a general discipline with the same methods and the same lines of distinction as modern science.

The picture was far more complex. Some of the divisions of modern science existed in the ancient world as fairly distinct disciplines—for example, medicine (with a relationship to biology) and mathematics (with kinship to geometry, arithmetic, music, and astronomy). But there was nothing corresponding to modern science as a whole or to such of its branches as physics, chemistry, geology, zoology, and psychology. The content of these modern subjects belonged to natural philosophy and was cultivated by philosophers. Even when distinction was made, as was sometimes done in the case of natural philosophy and mathematics, the distinction was unimportant because the two fields were usually tilled by the same person and did not represent any professional affiliation or social role. Such a person, moreover, would have called himself neither a natural philosopher nor a mathematician, but a teacher. And his teaching would have ranged over a broad intellectual arena displaying a unity and coherence in connection with a variety of philosophical issues that were not divided sharply into separate disciplines. But this explanation tells only part of the story.

Hellenists were mesmerized by the cultural potential of rhetoric, a potential not immediately evident in philosophy to which science was necessarily and inevitably subsumed. Rhetoric was attractive, promised to pay a cultural dividend and, though hard, was an easier academic route to follow than philosophy.[25] Students flocked to schools that were committed to a transmission of a literary culture and shunned schools of the philosophers whose instruction was perceived as being culturally arid and unbearably abstract. Adopting the dogmatic assumption about the worth of literature and rhetoric, no argument was strong enough to tempt Hellenistic educators to make a large investment in philosophy and science.[26]

Aristippus deployed an educational program in *On Education* and five other books,[27] so it seems right to credit him with having raised the curtain on an issue that was to permeate Hellenism. Close enough to the tumult over educational purpose wherein Plato, Isocrates, and the Sophists were leading actors, Aristippus chose to identify with Plato's educational goal of wisdom rather than the practical efficiency of Isocrates and the Sophists. But he demurred from traveling the whole way with Plato. The kind of analysis Plato displayed in the dialogues, an analysis aimed at revealing meaning and truth, was prized, but its purpose was mental exercise.[28] Besides, where Plato idealized the curricular status of science and mathematics, Aristippus only tolerated them, and decided instead to stress literary objectives with poetry and language having pride of place. He promoted literature's ability—he must have meant Homer's epics—to ensure moral formation, but left untouched the question of whether knowledge is virtue, or even whether any moral lessons are buried in Homer's poetry. Because of his unvarnished affection for the classics, he justified the worth of studying them for their own sake. This made him a friend of liberal learning and, if one can depend upon inference, an enemy of technical training.

Chrysippus, a Stoic, the author of 705 books,[29] and a favorite of Quintilian, was eloquent in promoting education for personal fulfillment. He could think of no better way to accomplish this objective than by making literature the centerpiece of the curriculum. He anticipated Quintilian's recommendation about nurses being children's first teachers, stressing both their qualifications of morality and purity of speech.[30] And at a time when few doubted age seven was the right time to go to school, Chrysippus recommended three.[31] Boys were thought to be curious, but sometimes curiosity failed to keep them at their studies, so punishment was approved, although with the proviso that it be stripped of brutality.[32] Homer was embraced: his poetry should be taught with nothing expurgated or revised. All of Homer was assumed to have meaning for Greek culture, so mastering Homer, Chrysippus declared, should be a continuous effort to understand him even when all the resources of dialectic had to be used. This overburdened the schools, yet it gave them a precise commission. The work of instruction was to excavate meaning from classical literature, so the study of grammar was essential. In following Chrysippus's advice, the schools made a brave beginning and tried to give grammar core status in the school's curriculum. Besides grammar, Quintilian reports, rhetoric was to be taught in a way that its arsenal of rule and regulation could not be neglected. Chrysippus defined rhetoric as "the science of speaking properly,"[33] or an art "that . . . concerns the embellishment and order of a set speech."[34]

As headmaster of the Lyceum, and a popular teacher,[35] Theophrastus's comprehensive scholarship allowed him to write and speak on a variety of subjects ranging from astronomy to rhetoric. He worked hard, as well, to establish the independent credentials of educational theory and tried to shape it as an inquiry without leading strings to politics and ethics. This approach ran counter to Aristotle's, for whom educational theory was a footnote to politics and ethics, and helped Theophrastus secure a reputation as an original thinker rather than a mere foot soldier in the camp of his famous teacher.[36]

The author of four books on education (none extant) and a dozen on rhetoric, he undertook to supply a theoretical justification sturdy enough to make oratory the ornament of a curriculum. Besides, the shadow he cast on educational practice extended all the way to Quintilian, who declared that "after him we may note that the philosophers, more especially the leaders of the Stoic and Peripatetic schools, surpassed even the rhetoricians in the zeal which they devoted to the subject."[37] Despite zealous effort to elevate rhetoric to a scholastic pinnacle, Theophrastus was unable to restore the old oratory distinguished for its political significance. The Hellenistic world might have profited from a revival of deliberative oratory, but such oratory was outlaw in an imperial political climate. Hellenists were careful to deliver orations on safe topics with political meaning purged, and the man most responsible for showing them how this could be done, and at the same time preserving rhetoric's artistic integrity, was Theophrastus. He could not have been the inventor of display oratory, but he gave it an unbreakable lease on Hellenistic education.

With Theophrastus's counsel to support them, speakers exercised their skill on artificial subjects, the more fanciful and fantastic the better, with the intention of keeping the tradition and the technique of classical oratory untarnished. This required an employment of classical vocabulary if the oratorical tradition were to be kept pure. So, in the last analysis, while securing the place of rhetoric in the curriculum, although admittedly a literary rather than a judicial or deliberative oratory, he refused to discount the contribution literature could make to oratory. Good speaking is essential for an educated person, but an oration is inelegant and empty without the content, range, and charm supplied from a mastery of the classical poets. Reading the poets, he declared, "is of great service to the orator."[38]

Following in the theoretical footsteps of Theophrastus and contributing stylistic but not substantive amendment to his program idealizing rhetoric as the only dependable route to educational decency, we have Clearchus and Cleomenes. In their books[39] and teaching practice both promoted literary and oratorical instruction, for which rhetoric and grammar are essential, and added, perhaps out of a sense of nostalgia, ephebic training. Aristoxenus's *Rules of Pedagogy* hewed to the party line in extolling rhetorical skill as a superior sign of culture, declared education to have a special commitment to transmitting culture, and then added something novel. Chrysippus had made a fetish out of the law of gesture, but Aristoxenus pressed on to introduce rhythm and melody for application to gesture, word arrangement, and vocal inflection. His rhetorical innovation made a euphonious combination of sounds as necessary in speaking as in singing or reciting poetry. Years before, Plato had complained about rhetoric's lack of a theoretical foundation. Aristoxenus's bold work helped to blunt Plato's charge, and where he stopped Cleanthes started. This prominent Stoic, for a time president of the Poecile, is credited with five books on rhetoric's essential position in education.[40] He, in fact, made oratory education's goal.

Rhetoric, Cleanthes declared, is the art of speaking well, and art is inevitably sustained by theory. Proof that rhetoric is an art is supplied quickly, although not necessarily persuasively: "Art is a power reaching its ends by a definite path, that is, by ordered methods,"[41]and no one can doubt the significance of method and order to good speaking. The definition that art consists in perceptions agreeing and cooperating to the achievement of some useful end, though weak, sustained rhetoric and tended to silence Plato's criticism. But this was because rhetoric's champions were so eager for it to have a monopoly in education that they closed their eyes to flawed reasoning. Right or wrong about rhetoric, Cleanthes' proof persuaded Quintilian. That Quintilian made rhetoric the kingpin of the curriculum is beyond dispute.

Zeno, a Stoic and the last of the prominent Hellenistic educational philosophers on our list, was probably the best, because in *The Usual Greek Education* and *Handbook of Rhetoric* he codified, likely finalized Hellenistic educational theory, and infused it with a status enabling it to stand as an independent discipline. Zeno repeated the common theme of Hellenistic educators: education has a primary responsibility for transmitting culture and rhetoric has a major role in helping education to fulfill it.[42] Unstinting in his praise of rhetoric and eschewing conventional Stoic theory, he pressed on to broaden its scope by endorsing the charm, grace, and force of purple passages.[43] Meanwhile he asked teachers to remember that despite their luster and appeal, rhetorical embellishment and flourish cannot substitute for an oration with profound meaning. In this way he tried to cement a theoretical affinity between rhetoric and dialectic, thus deflecting Plato's harsh statement about rhetoric, like cooking, being only knack.[44]

Although Zeno's place in educational history does not rest upon his having been an original thinker, he nevertheless summarized a Hellenistic theory about pedagogy, learning, and curricula, and molded it into a scholastic model. When this model was almost universally adopted, as in time it was, it succeeded in making the mature, educated person a standard for educational accomplishment. Teachers were of course expected to start at their students' level, but they were not supposed to teach them as children or to give credence to their special interest and need. The goal was to start children down the cultural path and see to it that they followed it without wasting time worrying about other pedagogic technique promoted as being more appropriate to the age, talent, and motivation of youth. Zeno, and after him Hellenistic educational philosophy, refused to recognize any approach to instruction wherein children were taught as children rather than as prospective adults.

Learning is learning: it adheres to the same principles and follows the same processes for all. Despite appearance of rigidity in pedagogy, Zeno led his colleagues in extolling the imperative need of total personal formation. Contemporary educators are often tempted to believe that holistic education is their invention, but a careful analysis of Hellenistic intent reveals the worth our ancient ancestors attributed to the education of the whole person. They failed to reach their goal probably more often than they succeeded, but nevertheless are entitled to some credit for having recognized the important investment education should make in a comprehensive development of human personality.

With a large portrait of educational purpose before him, Zeno was careful to adopt a central principle in Hellenistic educational philosophy regularly giving primacy of place to moral formation. The formation of the whole person could not be gainsaid. Yet among many complementary purposes, moral education was cultivated with a vigor illustrating that the ideal way of life paraded in classical literature was a model Hellenists should be eager to embrace. Educational practice was supposed to revive the past in such a way that it would come to life in students' minds as a personal possession. Literature was a huge reservoir from which moral lesson might be drained. In this way, Zeno and his confreres believed, the moral objective of teaching might be achieved and persons benefiting from such an education would become responsible citizens of the world. Finally, Zeno read the signs of his educational day as they idealized the classical legacy to declare technical education inferior (although not inconsequential) to liberal learning. Its utility should not be ignored. But because technical skill is incapable of bearing the weight of classical value, an almost unanswerable case could be made to diminish its worth.

Toward the end of the Hellenistic period, probably as late as the first decades of the third century A.D., educational philosophy was able to stand alone as a subject worth the attention of good minds. Its connection with general philosophy, with politics and ethics especially, was spared complete severance, because careful, sober scholars were too intelligent to abandon their sources. But the sources were used to support, not replace, a discipline whose independence was finally and fully secured. Independence and maturity, though, despite common impression, are not the same. So educational philosophy, while having found equilibrium from the exertions of the

Hellenists, had a long way to go before its expositors could assert and justify a claim for its disciplinary maturity.

THE ROMAN LEGACY

Roman educational practice and theory owed a huge debt to the Hellenists. And signs can be found pointing, as well, to the influence of classical Greece. But for a long time Rome did its best to keep faith with a long, honorable, and indigenous educational past. Nowhere is this better illustrated than when Cicero, thinking of Athens, wrote in the *Republic*: "Our institutions are opposed to any detailed universal system of public education, obligatory by law."[45] An aperçu of an Athenian system of public education able to stand the test or meet the definition of contemporary public education would be hard to draw. But Athens had laws, and customs with the force of law, making an award of citizenship dependent upon success in a conventional scholastic program. Hellenistic practice was less demanding; schooling never led to citizenship, and in the Hellenistic world the meaning of citizenship was changed: its purpose was cultural rather than civic. Add to this a principal plank in Hellenistic educational doctrine where schooling could be made responsible for the formation of the whole person. And then try to reconcile Athenian and Hellenistic policy with the Roman conviction that education was a lifelong process with comprehensive human formation as its goal, while school instruction was assigned the modest objective of communicating knowledge necessary for meeting the practical obligations of life. No social institution had custody of education, whereas instruction was work proper for schools and teachers. If more ammunition is needed to sustain this view, a quick glance at the way Romans treated their schoolmasters should suffice. More often than not, slaves, or freed slaves, they seldom found it easy to persuade their clients to pay for service rendered. Athenian schoolmasters, of course, neither commanded social esteem nor were regarded as important persons, but their work was considered essential. This alone afforded a modicum of respect. Hellenist teachers fared better, but Romans, although often adopting Hellenistic practice, chose to ignore the higher status teachers were accorded in Hellenistic society.

By Cicero's time it was evident to the perspicacious that the rusticity traditionally preferred in Roman formation was an expensive luxury in need of drastic amendment. If Rome were to govern the world, as it expected to, the intellectual and social refinements that only a decent program of instruction could supply were imperative. But Romans, and Cicero chief among them, were wary of adopting the technical, abstract, and philosophical educational program of the Greeks. They were not seeking systematic instruction in the art of civilization but an educational program equipped to supply sympathy, courtesy, and kindness, and combine these virtues with practical means for doing what is useful and necessary.

Whether Cicero was ever certain that these objectives should be assigned to schools is a fine point, but at the height of his intellectual power, with Scipio speaking for him, he tended to deflate the worth of scholastic experience: "As a Roman citizen who, thanks to his father's care, has received a good education and has been fond of study since boyhood; and who, none the less, owes more to experience and the lessons of home life that to the study of books."[46] This is certainly less than a disavowal of the worth of schooling, but only a careless reader would interpret it as an unambiguous endorsement. Yet for all this nostalgia about the good old days, Rome needed better instruction than its schools were in the habit of delivering. Cicero was dissatisfied with teachers imported from Greece. He was unfriendly to a philosophy of education unable to distinguish the national aspirations of Rome from those of Greece, and an instructional practice substituting Greek for Roman history. He set out to promote change by writing *De Oratore*.

Various stories have been told by scholars trying to plumb Cicero's motive for writing the book. Most are plausible and all are practical, but it is easy to conclude, taking into account the mature ideas *De Oratore* contains about the status of Roman literature, philosophy, and politics, that he wanted most of all to generate educational reform. He was, Aubrey Gwynn correctly concludes, appealing to youth to imitate his scholastic example by offering them a cultural objective superior to the one exhibited in contemporary Roman society.[47] Roman education was in confusion: many of Cicero's confreres were hardly better schooled than boys who had just finished elementary study. Others, passing from one to another school, had combined superficial scholarship with practical experience. A few, like Cicero, had capped early schooling with an intense immersion in higher study and a long internship in the courts. This was educational anarchy that Cicero was eager to redress.

De Oratore is silent about elementary schools, so it is hard to be sure whether Cicero approved their course, was unwilling to tinker with a tradition leaving the early years of instruction and education in the hands of parents, or that this was a side to the educational process unworthy of his attention. In any case, his evident interest in education begins with what we call secondary schools. He commissioned them to make an investment in the liberal arts. Philosophy, mathematics, music, literature, rhetoric, geometry, and astronomy are the subjects in the curriculum.[48] Yet all the arts were not shown the same affection nor did they enjoy the same level of cultivation: music and mathematics (a subject Horace called a special Roman art when it concentrated upon addition and subtraction) were taught superficially, while literature and rhetoric occupied leading instructional roles. The language of instruction is not mentioned, and Cicero might have preferred Latin, but the status of the Latin language and, at the time, the condition of Latin literature were too low for anyone to believe that Latin could carry the weight of instruction. This must have displeased Cicero, because from the outset his reconstruction of Roman education was meant to revive the neglected practical aspects of oratory, and public men in Rome would certainly have to use Latin.

Secondary-school teachers were directed "to comment on the poets, to teach history, to explain the meaning of words, [and] to impart correct accent and delivery."[49] They were in the business of schooling public men who could take their place on a public platform, in the courts, or in the Forum, and deliver a genuine political speech. Most of the erudite abstractions of Greek rhetoric were abandoned, although literary style and oratorical display were retained. Cicero never meant to discredit style, as his own work amply illustrates, but he wanted speakers so well versed in their subject that persuasion would be a natural outcome of logical analysis. Greek rhetoric had its faults and Cicero was unable to remove all of them, but his program of education was meant to rescue oratory from its Hellenistic literary shackles and restore to it deliberative, demonstrative, and judicial elements. Rhetoric was an essential instrument for genuine political life but, while its cultivation should begin in the secondary school, secondary education could not possibly be responsible for teaching everything about it. Its finishing needed the attention of advanced schools and teachers who, themselves, were experienced in the courts.

The educational program Cicero outlined in *De Oratore* is easy to misconstrue, especially if read as a course of study meant for all students. It was intended for the cream of the crop and from the cream were skimmed those students prepared to make a commitment to oratory. Unless *De Oratore* is so interpreted, Cicero's ringing declaration "that no man has ever become a great orator unless he has combined a training in rhetoric with all other branches of knowledge"[50] is hardly more than elegant hyperbole. Add the following and the matter would seem to be settled: "In my opinion no one can hope to be an orator in the true sense of the word unless he has acquired knowledge of all the sciences and all the great problems of life."[51] Such language has led careful students of Cicero to argue against finding in *De Oratore* any clear definition of an educational theory. Its idealism, they say, adumbrates realism. Yet there are footprints of educational theory on the trail, and it may be worth our while to spend some time following them.

Cicero's affection for literature, rhetoric, history, law, and philosophy was deep; he could not imagine anyone being a successful orator without them in his repertoire. Safe to say, any curriculum winning his endorsement would be filled with them. History had his full support as a school subject, but he was severely critical of teachers who neglected Rome's national history and tried to sharpen students' historical sense by introducing Greek myth. Such neglect violated a principle eloquently expressed in the *Orator*: "To be ignorant of what happened before you were born is to live the life of a child for ever. For what is a man's life, unless woven into the life of our ancestors by the memory of past deeds."[52] Literature had plenty of patrons, but most of them, because there was no good alternative, stayed close to the Greek classics. Cicero's recommendations on literature were in step with this practice: Who could dispute the literary worth of Greek literature? But Cicero wanted Roman literature, too, and he predicted that it would some day rival or even surpass the Greek classics.[53] In any case, Roman literature should be taught in the schools alongside the stories of the Greeks. Rhetoric, although never an end in itself and without too much attention to literary ornamentation, was a staple in the curriculum. "Abundance of matter will give abundance of words,"[54] is good counsel and Cicero means what he says. But he means, too, to pay careful heed to the art of expression, and this was enough to secure for rhetoric a permanent place in the school's curriculum.

Law is important because orators would be close to helpless without the knowledge of a jurist. But is law a separate subject or is it part of rhetoric? No final answer can be found in *De Oratore*, but the tone of the work implies that Cicero did not want oratory and jurisprudence to be handled as separate sciences.

Finally, there is philosophy. Clearly Cicero is enamored of it and frequently attributed his eloquence more to the "groves of the Academy" than to the schools of rhetoric. But it is not a philosophy that investigates abstract theses or ultimate causes; it should possess a personal and practical character implying wisdom, and wisdom comes, if it comes at all, from studies proper to culture: "We are all called men, but only those of us are men who have been civilized by the studies proper to culture."[55] Cicero's educational theory is summarized in this phrase.

Cicero's influence on education in Europe turned out to be permanent: a condition that would have obtained without Quintilian. But Quintilian supplied a pedagogical dimension to Cicero's theory that added luster to Cicero's reputation and established his own. Quintilian's *Educa-*

tion of an Orator, sometimes called the greatest book ever written on education, adopts Cicero's theses making oratory the culmination of educational endeavor in the formation of social and political leaders. Quintilian defines the orator as a good man skilled in speaking, but this definition sells Quintilian short and makes it easy to misinterpret his educational theory. *The Education of an Orator* is considerably more than a handbook on rhetoric; almost every page reflects Cicero's ideal of the perfect orator. And Quintilian is at pains to inform his readers of his debt to Cicero: "M. Tullius, our one incomparable model of oratory and oratorical theory, has shed most light on the rules of eloquence as well as on eloquence itself."[56] Why, if Cicero is so thorough, must Quintilian write a book on a subject Cicero has handled so well? Because, Quintilian says, Cicero has deliberately omitted some of the topics that are of lesser import in the education of orators, and the usual Roman textbooks on rhetoric are silent on them as well. Quintilian takes as his commission the topics Cicero has left alone and thus completes Cicero's educational theory by filling *The Education of an Orator* with advice to schoolmasters of his own day and, as it turned out, to generations of schoolmasters thereafter.

Who is this orator to whom both Cicero and Quintilian are so ready to pay solicitous attention? He must speak well, of course, but he must have something to say, too. Most of all he must possess all the moral virtues. When school days are over, what can be expected of him? He should, Quintilian declares, be a "true citizen, fit for the administration of private and public business, and capable of guiding cities by his counsels, establishing them by his laws and reforming them by his judgements."[57] Clearly, neither Cicero nor Quintilian is writing about the formation of an ordinary citizen who will perform day-to-day civic duty. The true citizen, the orator, the public man is a leader, chosen for his talent and prepared for his role by an education that would hardly befit the ordinary person.

Comprehensive in scope, *The Education of an Orator* starts with birth and ends when excellence in oratory is achieved. Beginning with the care of the child by capable nurses, Quintilian moves quickly to elementary schools. Primary masters were common in Rome and their role in instruction was not open to dispute. Yet they were seldom if ever praised by anyone, and Quintilian does not praise them either. Their character, he says, should be flawless and they should be able to teach Greek. Quintilian's idealization of Greek language and literature and, perhaps, Greek educational theory and practice, was greater than Cicero's, so he reserved the first four years of language instruction to the study of Greek. Orators would have to know it.[58] In addition, the elementary curriculum included handwriting, copying poetry from dictation, spelling, and exercises to cultivate memory.[59] Latin was the language of the home and the street, so its study could be deferred.[60] On all school levels the ultimate goal was excellence: "Those whose aspirations are highest, will attain to greater heights than those who abandon themselves to premature despair of ever reaching the goal and halt at the very foot of the ascent."[61] Boys are quick to reason and eager to learn is a statement betraying Quintilian's optimism, but he is careful to add that faulty pedagogy can blunt the natural curiosity of youth. Almost at once two dogmatic educational assumptions are jettisoned in *The Education of an Orator*: for as long as any Roman could remember, schooling began at age seven, but Quintilian recommended that instruction commence when students are ready. "Though the knowledge absorbed in the previous years may mean but little, yet the boy will be learning something more advanced during that year in which he would otherwise have been occupied with something more elementary."[62] The second assumption was that public schools threaten the morals of youth; boys would be safer in the company of private tutors. In rejecting this assumption, Quintilian declared that neither morality nor learning is jeopardized in the public school.

Almost every sentence of Quintilian's great book underscores education's primary purpose of creating and encouraging mental activity; phrases are frequent throughout about sharpening intelligence and native capacity. Sounding contemporary, Quintilian wanted the curriculum of all schools to accommodate the intellectual acumen and interest of students. Individual differences had to be taken into account. His educational outlook must have been affected by an optimism allowing nurture to correct nature's deficiencies. Talent is essential, but good instruction will embellish and improve it. To accomplish this, however, teachers must make haste slowly and leave nothing out. The faculties of memory, imagination, and sense perception, Quintilian confidently declares, can be strengthened by study.[63]

When elementary instruction is complete, boys should pass to the grammar, or secondary, schools where teachers should be selected with special care. These teachers, even more than their elementary counterparts, are responsible for starting students down the road to excellence when they teach correct speech and introduce literature. Studies in grammar and literature take on added significance because both are basic to eloquence, but eloquence needs help from music and mathematics. A good case could be made for music. It contributes to refined modes of expression, to the development of vocal patterns, to rhythm of gesture, and to grace and harmony of speech and movement. Besides, music is close to literature and could help to illustrate its meaning and stimulate emotion. Mathematics were not so easy to justify, although Quintilian is ready to praise geometry and affirms the need orators have for a command of number.[64] When one examines Quintilian's curriculum, though, it is hard to square his ringing endorsement: "no mathematics, no orator," with their almost total neglect.[65]

Schools of rhetoric began where grammar schools stopped, but teachers in these schools were warned to articulate their instruction with that of the lower schools in order to avoid redundancy. Their primary responsibility was to teach the theory of eloquence and to offer students abundant opportunity for practicing scholastic oratory. The objective of schools of higher learning (schools of rhetoric) was to produce effective orators, but the realization of this objective made imperative the mastery of rhetorical rule and theory. Reciting a vast network of rhetorical rule and regulation took Quintilian the better part of nine books. When he was finished, he added a list of orators and historians whose books should be studied.[66] Only the best authors were on it, and those recognized for their transparency of style and lucidity of expression were preferred. Livy was better than Sallust; Cicero was in a class all by himself.

Quintilian's *Education of an Orator* completed the work so well begun by Cicero and is a landmark in the history of Roman if not in all of Western education. Besides, it had no successor. Later writers produced books on grammar and rhetoric, but none wrote with the authority of Quintilian. None had as great an influence on the development of education in Europe, an education that succeeded in linking educated Europeans with the intellectual and literary treasures—the civilization—of antiquity.

The central educational theories of the classical age have been recounted and we have seen how Hellenistic aspiration—with the help of talented Romans—applied them to education in the hope of reviving the cultural ideals of the past. Faced with the fact that so many cultural monuments are highly perishable, our Hellenistic ancestors took what they had—mainly literature—and for the first time turned schools into literary agencies. Their view of education stressed content and their successors—the Christians— were faced with the ominous responsibility of melding classical literature with a Christian vision of men and women, and reality. This, as it turned out, was a heavier burden than the first Christian educational writers and thinkers imagined. But they, along with colleagues who followed them, succeeded in supplying a formula that was used to guide education for the next thousand years. We are ready now to cross the threshold to an era when an impressive effort was made to translate educational principle to policy and practice, all the while being careful to ensure its consistency with religious faith.

1. That it had intellectual standing long before it became a college course is evident. It might be true, as some scholars have asserted, that educational philosophy's academic placement in the college curriculum dates from the early twentieth century in the United States.

2. Except for Antiphon, who was an Athenian, the composition of the sophistic cadre, although mainly Greek, was not Athenian.

3. Plato *Protagoras* 319b. In *The Dialogues of Plato*. 5 vols. Translated by Benjamin Jowett (New York: Oxford University Press, 1892).

4. Gregory Vlastos, *Socrates, Ironist and Moral Philosopher* (Ithaca: Cornell University Press, 1991), 13–14.

5. John Patrick Lynch, *Aristotle's School: A Study of a Greek Educational Institution* (Berkeley and Los Angeles: University of California Press, 1972), 68–75, gives an incisive account of the circumstances surrounding the origin of Aristotle's Lyceum.

6. Admitting to tenuous evidence, *Against the Sophists* seems to have been the original scholastic prospectus and the earliest forerunner of contemporary college catalogues.

7. There was nothing extraordinary about Athenian teachers on all levels charging tuition for instruction. But the Sophists, guaranteeing to teach virtue and wanting payment in advance, were, by implication at least, exposing doubt about the efficacy of their instruction: virtuous persons will surely pay their debts. Sophistic critics were quick to catch this anomaly. Suspicion lingers that of all Athens's stationary schools, Isocrates' was the most expensive.

8. An analysis of Plato's educational program in the *Republic* and the *Laws* allows for a reconstruction of the long course which, without all the detail here, began at age seven and, for students with exceptional talent, ended at fifty.

9. Isocrates *Against the Sophists* 1. In *Isocrates*. 3 vols. Translated by G. Norlin and La Rue Van Hook (Cambridge: Loeb Classical Library, Harvard University Press, 1928–1945).

10. Aristotle *Against the Sophists* XXXIV, 7. In *The Complete Works of Aristotle*. 2 vols. Edited by Jonathan Barnes (Princeton: Princeton University Press, 1984).

11. The following dialogues provide ample evidence: *Apology, Crito, Euthyphro, Charmides,* and *Lysis.*

12. Did Socrates hold the views on education Plato attributed to him? Lynch (*Aristotle's School*, 43) says it "would be digression and perhaps fruitless, even if desirable, at this point to define a position on the complicated 'Socratic question.'"

13. Plato *Protagoras* 313a–314b.

14. Ibid., 318.

15. Ibid., 318b.

16. Ibid., 326.

17. Ibid., 319.

18. Ibid., 329c.

19. Ibid., 345e.

20. Klauss von Döring, *Der Sokratesschuler Aristipp und die Kyreniker* (Stutgart: Franz Steiner Verlag Wiesbaden, 1988), 62–7; and Aristippus, *Aristippi Et Cyreniacorum Fragmenta*, edited by Erich Mannebach (Leiden: E.J. Brill, 1961).

21. On his life and reputation, Josiah B. Gould, *The Philosophy of Chrysippus* (Leiden: E.J. Brill, 1970), 7–14; and Emile Brehier, *Chrysippe et L'Ancien Stoëcisme*, 9th edition (Paris: Presses Universitaires de France, 1951). Gould declares that Brehier, without sufficient evidence, attributes to Chrysippus the philosophical positions of Stoicism.

22. Konrad Gaiser, *Theophrast in Asso* (Heidelberg: C. Winter

Universitätsverlag, 1985), 24–27.

23. Consulted now more for his theory of music than for his positions on education. See Aristoxenus, *Aristoxenus Elementa Rhythmica*. Edited by Lionel Pearson (Oxford: Clarendon Press, 1990).

24. Zeno, *The Fragments of Zeno and Cleanthes*, edited by A.C. Pearson (London: C.J. Clay, 1891), 1–2.

25. See George A. Kennedy, *Classical Rhetoric and Its Christian and Secular Tradition From Ancient to Modern Times* (Chapel Hill: University of North Carolina Press, 1980

26. While not dealing directly with Hellenistic education, Samuel IJsseling, *Rhetoric and Philosophy in Conflict: An Historical Survey* (The Hague: M. Nijhoff, 1976), 26–33, illustrates, nevertheless, the disdain rhetoricians had for philosophy and the low esteem in which philosophers held rhetoric.

27. Diogenes Laertius, *Lives of Eminent Philosophers*, with an English translation by R.D. Hicks, 2 vols. (London: W. Heineman; New York: G.P. Putnam's Sons, 1925), 2:85. Although fragments of his work remain, none of Aristippus's books on education has survived.

28. Ibid., 91–93.

29. Gould, *Philosophy*, 8. If this number is to be believed, the word book must have had an unconventional meaning.

30. Quintilian, *The Education of an Orator*. 4 vols. Translated by H.E. Butler (Cambridge: Loeb Classical Library, Harvard University Press, 1921–1926), I, i, 4.

31. Ibid., I, i, 16.

32. Ibid., I, iii, 14.

33. Ibid., II, xv, 34.

34. Plutarch, 2: 297.

35. According to Diogenes Laertius, 2:36, Theophrastus lectured regularly to as many as two thousand students. Even if this figure is greatly inflated, he must have had an audience large enough to give his educational opinions wide circulation.

36. William W. Fortenbaugh and Peter Steinmetz, eds., *Cicero's Knowledge of the Peripatos* (New Brunswick, N.J.: Transaction Publishers, 1989), 41.

37. Quintilian, *The Education of an Orator* III, i, 15.

38. Ibid., X, i, 27.

39. Clearchus, *On Education*; Cleomenes, *The Schoolmaster*.

40. *Of Education, Of Usages, Of Dialectic, Of Moods or Tropes* and *Of Predicates*.

41. Quoted in Quintilian, *The Education of an Orator* II, xvii, 41.

42. See Armand Jagu's brief monograph, *Zenon de Cittium* (Paris: J. Vrin, 1946), for a general exposition of Zeno's moral philosophy

43. Aldo D. Scaglione, *The Classical Theory of Composition* (Chapel Hill: University of North Carolina Press, 1972), 8–9.

44. Plato *Gorgias* 456ab

45. Cicero *Republic* IV, 3.

46. Ibid., I. 36.

47. Aubrey Gwynn, *Roman Education from Cicero to Quintilian* (London: Oxford University Press, 1926; New York: Teachers College Press, 1966), 81.

48. *De Oratore* i. 8–12; i. 187; iii. 127.

49. Ibid., i. 187.

50. Ibid., ii. 5.

51. Ibid., i. 20, 72.

52. *Orator* 120.

53. *De Oratore* i. 13–15; iii. 95.

54. Ibid., iii. 125.

55. Cicero, *Republic* i. 28.

56. Quintilian, *The Education of an Orator* III, i, 20.

57. Ibid., i, 4–5.
58. Ibid., i. 1, 15–19.
59. Ibid., I, i., 36.
60. Ibid., I, iv, 22.
61. Ibid., I, i, 20.
62. Ibid., I, i, 18.
63. Ibid., I, x, 34–49.
64. Ibid., I, x, 35.
65. Ibid., I, i, 1.
66. Ibid., X, i, 72–81.

CHAPTER 2

CHRISTIAN EDUCATIONAL THEORY

The gulf separating the pagan from the Christian world was wide and deep, but intellectual bridges sometimes spanned what otherwise would have been a chasm too forbidding to negotiate. Alongside their hatred for paganism, Christians put value on a culture that was steeped in it; they could bring themselves neither to repudiate nor embrace the classical legacy.[1] Any way they turned this conundrum loomed before them. Tertullian's (A.D. 160?–230?) exclamation, "What indeed has Athens to do with Jerusalem?,"[2] might have been understood as an assertion rather than a question by the Gentiles and Hellenized Jews who had converted to the Christian faith. But neither they nor Tertullian, who can be interpreted as being less harsh in his rejection of philosophy than conventional accounts relate, were representative of the entire Christian community.

Christianity, a religion that from the outset was embraced by the poor and oppressed, could attract highly educated men familiar with Greek philosophy and sacred writing. The kind of knowledge contained in the philosophical classics was of little use, and perhaps of less interest, to members of this new sect until internal doctrinal dissent and external threat to faith from pagan enclaves made a return to the intellectual tradition imperative. The usual classical education was important for any profound understanding of Christian belief and unquestionably essential for promulgating it. A renewed respect for traditional education occurred about the middle of the second century, but was accompanied by a sensitivity on the part of Western Christians to the danger lurking in pagan literature seldom matched by their Eastern counterparts. More familiar with the classics than their Western confreres, Eastern Christians feared them less.

For these early Christians, both East and West, the mainstream of intellectual endeavor carried a deposit of faith sustained by belief, but there was a tributary they could not afford to ignore: full participation in social and political life. And to sail this tributary with any assurance of staying afloat, a certain level of literary education was essential. Whatever these early Christians might have wanted in the way of an educational decency that would have immunized them from spiritual contamination, their range of choice was severely limited. They could send children to the schools flourishing in the Roman world—schools that were pagan in outlook and classical in content—or they could trust to the Christian institutes just coming over the horizon: catechumenal and catechetical schools. Given their zealous religious commitment, this amounted to no choice at all. They had either to send their children to the pagan schools and hope for the best, or sentence them to illiteracy and thus forsake any chance for them to lay claim to full citizenship. Fear and hatred of paganism were matched by a determination to be good and successful citizens. A huge dilemma weighed them down. What were they to do?

Less well-known Christian figures grappled this dilemma, but the first major Christian scholar to meet it face to face was Justin Martyr, born in Samaria near the beginning of the second century, and martyred in Rome sometime around A.D. 162. After long years studying Greek philosophy, especially Plato's idealism, Justin converted to Christianity and began to assert the fundamental compatibility between Christian doctrine, Platonic philosophy, and Stoic ethics. All in all, he tried to allay the fear of his fellow Christians toward the classical legacy and to stress instead the power of reason, a divine gift, in coming to a fuller understanding of the Christian message. Justin's "optimism about the harmony of Christianity and Greek philosophy"[3] survived in the work of Athenagoras,[4] Theophilus of Antioch, Clement of Alexandria (ca. 150–215),[5] and Origen (ca. 185–254).[6] Although these men approached the dilemma in different ways, all were familiar with Greek philosophy, endorsed parts of it, and counseled the use of reason and those appurtenances to the classical heritage that could contribute to understanding and spreading divine truth. To call them champions of classical knowledge would be exaggeration, but they engaged in an enterprise to help rescue Christianity from the charge of obscurantism. Even Tertullian, when studied with care and interpreted generously, was not opposed to philosophy but to heresy, and the kind of philosophy leading to it.[7]

Yet it was not these early apologists, whose effort to minimize the collision between faith and reason was by no means inconsequential, who set the stage for the development of education in the Christian West. Two prominent church fathers—Jerome (331–420) and Augustine (354–430)—took the lead in forging a compromise allowing Christian education to profit from the classical model and in welding a permanent bond between antique culture and European civilization.

Jerome's scholarship stood as a model for Christians to admire and emulate. His knowledge of classical sources was respectable and his insight into Christian doctrine was thorough. Besides, he had produced the great Latin version of the Bible, the *Vulgate*. But this is only one side to the portrait of a great man. When he spoke to the Christian community, endorsement was absent for a conventional classical education and the ancient authors whose words filled the curriculum of the pagan schools were never recommended. Anxiety about spiritual poison in the classics tempted him to repudiate them.[8] But then he relented. There was no way to escape the obvious need Christians had for a knowledge of grammar and rhetoric, if they were to understand their faith and communicate its treasure to the unconverted.

Adopting a cautious course, along with a conviction that these studies could not be mastered without going to the classics, Jerome told schoolmasters to teach the classics in a way encouraging students to concentrate on style, to cull from them the rules governing correct speech and writing, and to ignore the stories in them. Grammatical rule and rhetorical regulation were antiseptic; danger was in the story. Following Jerome's advice Christian teachers riveted attention on elements of style and swamped their students in the doctrine of use. This pedagogic technique, for all its apparent shortcoming, was good enough to survive for the next thousand years. But it had company.

St. Augustine was the beneficiary of a rich classical education obtained in the north African schools of Thagaste, Madaura, and Carthage.[9] Early religious and intellectual journeys led him to sample Manichaeanism, adopt Neoplatonism, and finally convert to Christianity. Throughout most of his life, Augustine worked to reconcile Neoplatonism and Christianity. This effort has allowed the myth to survive that Augustine substituted faith for reason and was indifferent to knowledge. But this was not his position. Philosophy, all knowledge for that matter, was not to be repudiated or replaced. It was to be Christianized. Augustine acknowledged reason to be a divine gift making human beings different from animals; it should be cultivated and used. Reason conducts the mind to truth for which faith prepares it. If reason errs it should not be shunned or detested, but corrected. Properly used, reason cannot contradict faith. Reason, moreover, is imperative if the truth of faith is to be correctly understood and defended, and if those parts of the deposit of faith that have not been revealed are to be discovered.

Did Augustine subordinate reason to faith? The answer must be yes, because ultimate authority rests with revelation. But faith is not a taskmaster to which reason must submit; it is the condition that makes genuine rational activity possible. Faith is a foundation whereupon all knowledge must ultimately stand, but it is not meant to take the place of everything that might be erected upon a foundation of faith. With this conviction uppermost in mind, Augustine turned to the question of Christian education and the part the classical corpus should have in it.

He warned schoolmasters to be prudent and selective in teaching the classics and enjoined them to excise anything dangerous to faith.[10] They should follow the example of the prince who, after capturing a comely barbarian maiden, had her groomed, bathed, and dressed, gave her time to accommodate to her new home, and then married her. Augustine put value on the liberal arts, but upon entering the schoolhouse they were to be clean and inoffensive.

Although Augustine's brush might have scrubbed away some of the classics' substance that a critical eye told him was dirt, his curricular recommendations had elements of common sense and practical pedagogy curiously lacking in Jerome's formula. Yet one page of history has victimized him with accusations that he abandoned reason and intimidated scholarship by making both abjectly subservient to religious authority and discipline. On another page, however, he is praised for having found a way to distinguish, without separating, the realms of reason and faith, and in so doing to lay an indestructible foundation whereupon Christians could engage in genuine scholarship and make a commitment to the cultivation of reason without at the same time putting their souls in jeopardy.

The scholastic side of Augustine's educational philosophy that should be stressed was his separation of the classical literary inheritance into definable parts, keeping some and discarding others. Educators were instructed to adopt a principle of selection for compiling classical anthologies: foul or unnecessary books, or parts of books, were pruned. Reading these anthologies, students were made privy to the works of the best authors. In this way the defect in Jerome's plan was eliminated: the treasure in the classic—the story—survived and with it the literary genius of classical authors. At the same time, amending without repealing the doctrine of use, Augustine told teachers to compose textbooks on grammar and rhetoric from which students could draw rule and regulation. A code of correct speech had no longer to be excavated from the classics themselves. With textbooks and anthologies on their desks, schoolboys had before them the essential ingredients to an education in the liberal arts. Should the need arise for models of style beyond what the anthologies supplied, Augustine appeared to imply that they could best be found in scripture.

Although the educational philosophy of Augustine and Jerome remained intact and almost impervious to criticism for centuries, the scholastic conditions making it useful began to change. For a long time, Christians thought they had better things to do than maintain a system of schools. So, and with some uneasiness about the pagan elements in them, they used the generally available regular classical schools. But with the demise of Rome and the disappearance of its social institutions, the Christian community faced an educational problem from which the conventional system had immunized it. If Christians wanted an education for their children, schools would have to be supplied. Old theories pronounced by respectable Christian leaders defined the character, set the ultimate purpose of education, and reminded students and teachers alike of the danger lurking in the classics. About ready to cross the threshold of the sixth century, educators had plenty of advice about the kind of learning that should be avoided; they possessed little information about how to construct a decent program of study.

By this time Capella's (ca. fifth century) *Marriage of Philology and Mercury*[11] and Boethius's (ca. 480–525) *Consolation of Philosophy*[12] recited, described, and explained the liberal arts, although neither book contained the pedagogical detail or a theoretical basis for putting them in a school curriculum. And teachers lacked the experience and skill to do the job. By happy circumstance Cassiodorus (ca. 480–575) was equipped to instruct Christian educators in the management of the classical legacy and the instructional role it should occupy in a Christian school. His *Introduction to Divine and Human Readings* turned out to be both a philosophy of education and a curricular guide for Christian educators. As one of the most important books of the early Middle Ages, it left an indelible impression on Christian schools well into the thirteenth century.[13]

Cassiodorus's *Introduction*, although friendly to liberal art, is concerned principally with religion and its author, one should remember, was nurtured on a traditional suspicion of the classics. Classical authors might be tolerated and some Christians could justify a study of liberal art for students who needed it. If there is praise for the arts in the *Introduction*, it is certainly temperate. Along with Augustine and most church fathers, Cassiodorus was sure the arts were only aids to the study of Christian doctrine and that everything in profane science was in or was implied in scripture. But any study of sacred learning, especially advanced study, had to rest on a foundation of liberal culture. Students of scripture and doctrine should be able to read the books, but they had to understand them as well.[14] So the liberal arts were recruited to do what only they could do. Despite this, the investigation of secular knowledge was kept within bounds. So when readers finished the *Introduction* they had a map to guide them along the dangerous path of secular knowledge. They traveled this path with the conviction implanted in their minds that the arts were to be used, not loved.

Cassiodorus's educational perspective—it could be called an educational philosophy—was to improve, not merely to describe, traditional educational practice and to find an efficient equivalent to instruction given in classical schools. Put another way, he offered an alternative to Quintilian's education for oratory, although at the same time conceding that much in Quintilian's prospectus was useful when directed at the practical education of Christians. The studied eloquence and the platform oratory so much prized were replaced by something teachers of this genre could understand and embrace: schooling was intended as a practical experience for solving religious and secular problems. So the scholar's study took the place of the public podium, and the disciplines of grammar and rhetoric, stripped of their ancient magnificence, became basic subjects in the curriculum of a Christian school. Contemporary educational philosophers are seldom tempted to include Cassiodorus's *Introduction* on their reading lists, and when they omit him they might be right, but his influence on education from the sixth through the tenth centuries should be acknowledged.

MEDIEVAL EDUCATIONAL PHILOSOPHY

Medieval speculation about education had both range and worth but added up neither to a coherent nor a comprehensive philosophy of education. It illustrates preoccupation with reading, one expressed succinctly by John of Salisbury (1120–1180): "There is little or nothing that lies concealed from one who is well read."[15] Attention to reading implies that books are the best teachers, but books are mute and the wisdom in them lies buried unless, first, the skill of reading is mastered and, then, what is read is understood. At the time, though, reading skills were unpolished. Books and manuscripts were written in Latin, a language not mastered easily, and from the sixth through the twelfth century reading a passage from sight would have been extraordinary for any but accomplished scholars. Books were labored over and exposing meaning was hard work only infrequently paying a dividend of understanding.[16] From the time of Cassiodorus to the outset of the ninth century, teachers had struggled with the complexities in reading. Progress was coupled with regression.

When a progressive appeared—Pope Gregory (540–604), for example—a halt to further investment in classical educational models was counseled. The past, Gregory and his confreres declared, was swamped in antique culture and any commitment to preserving the classics, classical standards in grammar and rhetoric, and the pagan ideals they contained was sheer treachery to a Christian vision of life and the literary means for representing it. Gregory could afford to be progressive. He knew Latin, was well-schooled in the classical tradition, and lived in Rome where Latin was the vernacular. Latin was a living language and holding it hostage to archaic rule and regulation curtailed its ability to represent reality in a Christian world.[17] He forgot, though, that all of Europe's Christian parts were not equal heirs to the classical legacy. By the sixth century, moreover, Christianity was a religion of the book, and Latin, the language of the church, was held by many devout Christian scholars to be a divine language created by God especially for Christian use. Despite his position of influence and his ability to persuade an inner circle of colleagues, Gregory's admonition could not be adopted. Leading strings of the classics, though badly stretched, were unbroken.[18]

If a level of decency were to be restored to raise education to a standard extant when the Roman system disintegrated, if the mischief of the Dark Ages were to be redressed, and if the citadels of scholarship were to be rebuilt, the riddle of language had to be solved. Without an accurate Latin, decency of learning would be crippled, everything would be concealed, and no one could be well read.

Teaching Latin to persons who lacked cultural affinity for it called for pedagogic technique, and theory, though ready to lend cordial support, was of little help. A complicating factor relative to techniques for language instruction loomed large: ignored by ancient grammarians, their books were barren of pedagogical clues. Such books were intended for persons who knew Greek or Latin, so any attention to method for basic linguistic instruction would have been superfluous. Ancient grammars were at liberty to speculate about language, about construction and use, and were philosophies of language or exercises in structural linguistics.

Here, at the doorstep of the Carolingian age, called by some ecstatic chroniclers the renaissance of the ninth century, we should interrupt an interpolation about sixth- to ninth-century pedagogical problems to return to medieval educational theory and the main assumptions basic to it: education's aim is civilization of intellect, the schooling of persons destined for ecclesiastical life, and preparation for eternity. No doubt medieval educators followed much in the advice of their classical predecessors and would have endorsed a great deal in the humanistic scholastic paradigm of their successors. But where classical and humanist theory gave pride of place to moral formation, medievalists centered attention upon intellectual development. Strange to say that an age so preoccupied with ecclesiastical business and with the salvation of souls should have neglected education's moral purpose.

If there was justification for this neglect, it must have been that the moral influence of the church superseded anything a school might do. Considering that a scholastic clientele was mainly clerical, the moral formation consistent with the preparation of persons for holy orders and for other occupations in religious life was so contagious that schools could be absolved from handling anything to do with nobility of character. This justification might be tempered in a rejoinder that the most certain route to morality is marked by dependable knowledge: moral virtue, in the last analysis, is guaranteed, if it can be guaranteed at all, by truth.

The twelfth century was the golden age of medieval educational speculation, but long before the advent of the twelfth century this fertile field had been cultivated by Cassiodorus, Isidore of Seville[19] (560–636), Hrabanus Maurus[20] (776–856), and Alcuin (732–804).[21] It should be said at the outset that this cultivation seldom produced a bountiful harvest, but enough was done to lay a fairly decent educational foundation. Of the four toilers in the vineyard of educational philosophy, two—Cassiodorus and Alcuin—stand out. We are acquainted with Cassiodorus, so now an aperçu of Alcuin's accomplishment is needed. Of the twelfth-century theorists—one Frenchman, two Germans, and one Englishman—Theodore (Thierry) of Chartres is remembered for *Heptateuchon* (Library of the seven liberal arts),[22] Conrad of Hirschau for *Didascalion* (Dialogue on authors), Hugh of St. Victor (1096–1141) for *Didascalicon* (Study of reading),[23] and John of Salisbury for *Metalogicon* (Defense of logical studies). Alcuin prepared the ground for them, and without him as an intelligent precursor—the right person for the right time—they, likely, would not have been able to make much progress.

Anticipating the story of medieval educational theory another interpolation should be inserted to account for what, at first, might appear to be an unpardonable omission. Why the silence about Thomas Aquinas (1225–1274)? His accomplishments in theology and philosophy, it would seem, as well as his influence on the intellectual life of succeeding centuries, should qualify him as the perfect synthesizer for the educational philosophy of the period. His absence should be justified.

The achievements of the greatest of the Scholastics are too well known in outline and too complicated in detail to be related here. They were, however, the object of an intellectual effort to handle two conflicting cosmologies, Neoplatonic and Aristotelian, in such a way as to preserve and inform Christian orthodoxy, keep reason and revelation distinct, and demonstrate the reasonableness of faith. The synthesis of Aquinas had the effect of excluding the Neoplatonic tradition along with the materialistic elements of Greek philosophical thought. To accomplish this synthesis he returned to Aristotle's original Greek text and thus set aside the Arab commentaries and translations that for so long had clouded Christians' vision as they undertook to master the mysteries of natural philosophy.[24] In the end, the *Summa* of Aquinas reconciled the metaphysics embraced by Christians with the ideas of Aristotle and succeeded in reconciling huge parts of pagan philosophy with Christian belief.

Thomas's monumental work in philosophy and theology enjoyed lasting success on the level of theory but was seldom used as a practical guide for illuminating important issues of the day. *De Magistro* (Concerning the teacher), a part of *De Veritate* (Concerning truth), was Aquinas's principal venture into teaching and learning theory, but wedded to epistemology it had almost nothing to do with the development of educational philosophy.[25] *De Magistro* concentrates upon intellectual formation and is concerned chiefly with teaching and the acquisition of knowledge. In this connection, students are certified as principal agents in the educational process: unless they perform necessary intellectual operations, nothing will happen. Teachers are secondary and have an instrumental function relative to learning, although in some cases they are indispensable. This, briefly, is Aquinas's view of teaching, and it makes important and essential points in connection with education, but, to repeat, it amounts to little more than a footnote in the history of educational philosophy.

Now back to Alcuin who, educated in Ireland and England, was summoned to Frankland by Charlemagne to be headmaster of the palace school at Aachen. Unschooled and likely illiterate, Charlemagne perceived his kingdom's need for literate laymen and well-educated clerics if it were to prosper. The palace school was projected as a model school for the empire and, moreover, was expected to introduce pedagogical technique capable of affecting learning in monastic, parish, collegiate, and cathedral schools throughout the country. The emperor was serious about improving the quality of education, so he sought the best headmaster. After several false starts with other candidates, including Peter of Pisa, Alcuin was selected.[26]

Alcuin's intention was evident from the outset: to take the program of instruction developed in the monastic school of York, with its emphasis upon teaching practical, correct Latin grammar, and introduce it to centers of teaching in Frankland. These centers could, in turn, introduce this program in their regions and, in consequence, upgrade elementary education throughout the kingdom. Once instruction in an accurate Latin was achieved, civil and ecclesiastical affairs could be conducted with assurance and the schools could expand their curricula to include subjects essential to further progress. Alcuin's service to learning was twofold: he transplanted to the Continent pedagogic techniques invented in Irish and English monastic schools to teach Latin and improved the discipline of teaching in other subjects as well. His service had the effect of whetting a medieval appetite for education.

The value of this service is easy to assess: it was a limited but competent course of elementary instruction. On it Alcuin's stature must rest. Yet, despite his affection for teaching, Alcuin did not stay always in the classroom. He prepared instructional material used almost at once by other teachers and advanced an educational theory to support his interpretation of the worth of the seven arts.

One could be persuaded that Alcuin's attitude toward the seven arts was in step with Augustine's and Cassiodorus's, and with the conventional wisdom of Christian education. But it is possible to see in it elements more progressive than anything the past had produced. Where his predecessors promoted the *importance* of the arts to education, Alcuin called them *indispensable*. When Augustine declared the arts to be alien to Christian wisdom and was cautious about admitting them to the schoolhouse, and when Cassiodorus said they were outsiders to be exploited but not loved, Alcuin claimed the arts occupied an integral position in Christian culture. Deflation of the arts was nothing more than a deflation, if not a dismemberment, of culture. They were, of course, inferior to the appurtenances to divine learning, but it was pointless to call for their decontamination because they formed an essential part in the broad syllabus of Christian education.

Had Alcuin been a more thorough scholar, he, likely, would not have played with the fire in paganism. Even Erasmus, who never skirted the classics because of the danger said to be lurking in them, supplied safeguards for students who sought to mine their wisdom. Alcuin's theory was flawed and his embrace of the arts was technically faulty; yet the luster of his reputation was strong enough to reduce the traditional fear of the pagan classics. Schools that before had shunned the arts now began to welcome them. Even so, there was a gratuitous safeguard: students affected by Alcuin's theory were on the first rungs of the scholastic ladder and could not have invaded classical lore deeply enough for it to threaten their faith. A little learning was not in this instance a dangerous thing.

Alcuin's work as a precursor of medieval education has been noted, and its two dimensions—pedagogic technique and a theory with respect to the seven arts—have been touched lightly. Yet for all their import, these achievements do not justify linking him with the renaissance of the fourteenth century or, for that matter, with any cult of antiquity. He was neither a

Petrarch nor an Erasmus. Yet his work, always thoroughly Christian in perspective, in supplying textbooks, graded readers, and pedagogic technique improved the character of education for priests and laymen. Almost always elementary, it absolved him, his students, and successors from inhaling anything more than the aroma of the classical legacy. But in concentrating on elementary instruction, especially in Latin, where concentration was imperative, it had a profound influence on the future of learning. His commitment to the seven arts, although clumsy, was clear, and he left it for others to discover the genius in classical education.

The long interlude between Alcuin's death and the advent of the twelfth century was characterized by conservatism. Scholars relied on tradition and were wary of breaking new ground, especially in theology, where innovation could land them in trouble. So they turned their attention and satisfied their curiosity by inquiring into matters of liturgy. Yet being faithful to liturgical tradition demanded a mastery of grammar, although it was a grammar concentrating on fluency with scant heed paid to elegance and eloquence in speech and writing. Grammar's code was recited in the textbooks of Donatus, Priscian, and Alcuin, and the classics were used sparingly. This scholastic preoccupation with grammar paid a steady dividend in improving the standard of Latin. But when we enter the twelfth century, with scholars' curiosity ranging beyond a corpus of knowledge with the stamp of orthodoxy, the old instructional paradigm was simply too narrow to satisfy intellectual and cultural aspiration. Established doctrine went unquestioned, but its rational support existed at best in dim outline; twelfth-century scholars craved something more. They wanted Christian doctrine to have a genuine intellectual foundation and a cultural basis.

Drill as the method and fluency as the object of grammatical study were simply not good enough, so said Bernard of Chartres (ca. early twelfth century?), when he began a crusade to elevate the standard in the study of grammar. With a reputation for original scholarship as well as pedagogical skill, Bernard, who wrote little (of which all perished), declared that because grammar is the basis of culture, students should not be rushed through it. Grammar should be studied slowly and thoroughly from the classics themselves and not from schoolmasters' manuals. And when students repair to the classics, they should know which ones are best.[27]

Bernard counseled a return to the classics and when his counsel was followed, as in time it was, grammar study was broadened and improved. With this gain in grammar, scholars were equipped to approach the Christian tradition in a different way and to arrive at different results. Their study was transformed from trying to absorb the knowledge contained in the books to its analysis. The new grammar supplied them with dialectical technique for mastering, organizing, interpreting, and applying what had been learned. Scholars were now equipped to study the Christian and classical legacy, and to profit from it in a way hardly possible earlier. Driven by extraordinary curiosity, twelfth-century scholars did their best to fill their vaults of knowledge by going to every source at their disposal. The outcome of this unusual effort at learning was an accumulation of knowledge with an almost bewildering range. What did it mean?

With only fragmentary knowledge at their disposal, earlier scholars neglected order, tried to absorb everything, and counted on personal ingenuity to discover meaning. But now, with so much more to choose from, the educational community faced a valid philosophical question: What should be studied and why? Twelfth-century theorists recognized the import of the question and did their best to answer it.

The most successful along this line were Conrad of Hirschau, Theodore of Chartres, and Hugh of St. Victor. The purpose of their enterprise was explained retrospectively by Hugh's preface to *Didascalicon*:

> The things by which every man advances in knowledge are principally two—namely, reading and meditation. Of these, reading holds first place in instruction, and it is of reading that this book treats, setting forth rules for it. For there are three things particularly necessary to learning for reading: first, each man should know what he ought to read; second, in what order he ought to read, that is, what first and what afterwards; and third, in what manner he ought to read.[28]

The opinion, later expressed by John of Salisbury, that little is concealed from the person who reads much, was taken seriously.[29] But reading, as one might suppose, did not mean either superficially skimming or indulging pleasant pastime. It was the gateway to educational decency, and what was read constituted a curriculum. When this cadre of educators finished their disquisitions on reading, they had a curricular theory that was dissatisfied with collection and classification of a mass of unspecialized knowledge. It was a theory committed to imposing order and structure on knowledge and subordinating everything to a few general ideas.

Techniques for supplying order and arranging appropriate subordination did not appear suddenly. Suitable categories had to be discovered, and in this connection the considerable advances in the discipline of logic proved to be of great help, but even at its best logic was sometimes overmatched: parts of knowledge eschewed any category. This, though, did not deter the pioneers. They began by imposing order on the parts of knowledge that would fit the categories and, as a temporary measure, ignored loose ends.

In *Heptateuchon*, Theodore compiled the accepted subject matter for the seven arts and undertook to exhibit its intention and structure. The preface contains an explanation of intention. Knowledge, he wrote, is a unity with a single purpose, and purpose is coordinated with human destiny. Wisdom, moreover, life's temporal goal, is cultivated by philosophy and almost alone the seven arts supply a foundation whereupon philosophy stands. The quadrivium—music, geometry, arithmetic, and astronomy—contains the material for thought and the trivium—grammar, rhetoric, and logic—is commissioned to cultivate expression. Theodore began with grammar and imposed an order on knowledge leading all the way to wisdom. If there is flaw in his paradigm, it was, nevertheless, a bold start that contained the germ of an educational philosophy committed to the development of thought and expression. In the end it paid a permanent dividend.

Conrad of Hirschau wrote the *Dialogue on the Authors* about 1150. In it he follows Theodore's assumption about knowledge being a unity and, in company with his confreres, regards reading as a principal means for securing an education. Unsurprisingly, the *Dialogue* is preoccupied with the nature of reading. Ancient grammarians had the same preoccupation. They had introduced students to a reading lesson by telling them something about the story they were to read, and then moved on to a kind of elementary textual criticism. This was followed by sending students to the story itself. Somewhat later, enterprising masters deciding to do something more, undertook to explain to the class the story's meaning and implication. These techniques were sometime worthwhile; too often they were exercises that, while satisfying to teachers, were meaningless to students. Yet the practice continued, was well-known, and widely used by medieval masters. It enabled them to include on their reading lists books (almost always the classics) that without interpretation would have been excluded and, in consequence, brought into the curriculum a literature that otherwise would have been neglected. By Conrad's time allegorical interpretation, although underdeveloped as a technique, was commonly employed.

Conrad was apparently uneasy with this approach to reading and especially with the way allegorical interpretation was practiced. He counseled an abandonment of the illustrative lecture on the selection read or to be read, and recommended that it be replaced by an interpretation based upon philosophical judgment. And philosophical judgment, employed effectively, would distinguish an author's intention from the book's final cause.

Final cause represented God's intention, which under any circumstance could not conflict with faith. When Conrad's formula was followed and when philosophical judgment was sound, all books could make a valid claim for a place in a school's curriculum. In attending to allegorical interpretation, Conrad was likely correct, but his justification was superficial and his method to manage it was weak. So more work had to be done before allegorical interpretation could become a common pedagogical currency.

Sometime between 1120 and 1130 Hugh of St. Victor appears on history's stage with *Didascalicon*. A native of Germany and an Augustinian monk, Hugh arrived in Paris around 1115, was attached to the Abbey of St. Victor, and shortly became master of the abbey school. His ornamental philosophical credentials, along with an intense interest in subordinating disparate scientific knowledge to wisdom, led him to retrace a path taken by Theodore. Where Theodore was a classifier, Hugh was a genuine theorist. From the outset he is ready to put all knowledge under the general heading of philosophy.[30] And he then subdivides philosophy to make room for various kinds of knowledge and to find a proper place for them: every part of knowledge should be put in its right nest.

Philosophy has four parts: theoretical, practical, mechanical, and logical. But each part has subdivisions:

> The theoretical is divided into theology, physics, and mathematics; mathematics is divided into solitary, private, and public. The mechanical is divided into fabric making, armament, commerce, agriculture, hunting, medicine, and theatrics. Logic is divided into grammar and argument: argument is divided into demonstration, probable argument, and sophistic; probable argument is divided into dialectic and rhetoric.[31]

Practical philosophy, neglected here, was defined earlier as that "which considers the regulation of morals."[32] Knowledge's boundary is set and students are left with the duty to work within it. Without further help they might have been in trouble, so Hugh supplied guidance. He lists the authors they should read if knowledge is to be mastered and tells them to be content with a little at first. But this little should be selected with care: "effort should first be given to the arts, in which the foundations stones for all things and in which pure and simple truth is revealed."[33] There is no mystery about which of the arts are to have priority in the syllabus. They are the traditional seven liberal arts.

With a curriculum prescribed for them, students are instructed how to read. Hugh begins with an acknowledgment that natural endowment, practice, and discipline are necessary for success in study, but order and method deserve attention, too. Order of study, a sequential arrangement of subject matter, is no mere detail, but it is something that can be handled quickly: "One kind of order is observed in the disciplines . . . and another kind on the exposition of a text."[34] Order in the disciplines is determined by their nature and internal logic; it must not be violated. In the exposition of a text—revealing its meaning—order means to follow the rules of logic and rhetoric. Now Hugh treats us to something new and different, although one could claim that he is operating in a field that had been plowed by Conrad.

For a long time teachers had employed two standard techniques for textual exposition. They, to which Hugh added a third, were *letter* and *sense*. Exposition according to letter meant giving attention to the author's style; sense exposition meant discovering the meaning of literary passages and, in the end, getting the story. Hugh's amendment to this formula was to add exposition according to *inner meaning*. He proffers the following explanation: "The letter is the fit arrangement of words which we also call construction; the sense is a certain ready and obvious meaning which the letter represents on the surface; the inner meaning is the deeper understanding which can be found only through interpretation and commentary."[35]

Employing allegorical interpretation to find inner meaning, every classic could be explained by moving from a literal recitation of an author's intention to an elaboration of the meaning intended by God. The technique for transcending from an author's intention to a book's final cause, timidly and literally promoted by Conrad, is firmly fixed in Hugh's theory. With more latitude for interpreting and commenting on all manner of literature, and better equipped than their predecessors to do so, medieval masters became enthusiastic about what had been regarded as the most dangerous of the classics. The schoolhouse adopted a more permissive stance and, in consequence, the range for reading became greater. Yet, in their enthusiasm to embrace what amounted to a new genre, masters sometime allowed allegorical interpretation—which in any case must be understood as a way of representing as antiseptic, or even praiseworthy, material that otherwise would be difficult to handle—to deform classical treasures and to make stories edifying when, in fact, they were not. Classical vaults were opened but their contents were sometimes spoiled by allegorical fumigation.

If Hugh's innovative disposition opened the gateway to classical study wider than at any time since Augustine and Cassiodorus, it had also the effect of directing education's purpose toward a tributary generally unexplored by medieval teachers. They acknowledged education's principal function to be informing and forming minds; homes and churches could look after moral formation and seek to inculcate a nobility of character. But part of Hugh's theory made discipline one of the essential consequences of study and coupled worthy moral behavior with knowledge. He nailed moral formation to education's mast by declaring that when teachers are drilling their students on grammar and lecturing to them on inner meaning, they must pay attention as well to building character. By restoring attention to education's moral dimension, Hugh undertook to return it to the mainstream of classical theory and practice. So he must be given some credit for breaking the hard crust of tradition to leave a path which Christian humanists of succeeding centuries could tread with some confidence that they were not abandoning the past.

Baldwin characterized the *Metalogicon* as the "cardinal treatise on medieval pedagogy."[36] The point is debatable. Yet, whatever the validity of this characterization, it is hardly possible to maintain that John of Salisbury's book was unimportant. He had ornamental credentials as a teacher and scholar, and had benefited from instruction from teachers like Abelard, Theodore of Chartres, and William of Conches. Besides, he lived in an era when schooling was becoming more popular, when the utility of knowledge was more and more recognized, when subjects theretofore unknown began to find their way into the school's syllabus, and when a philosophy of knowledge was maturing. The purpose of his book can be stated quickly and directly: he was determined to choke an anti-intellectualism that had attached itself to Christian educational perspective by eliminating hesitation and miscalculation with respect to the place logical studies should occupy in the repertoire of decently educated persons. He wanted to still voices counseling cautious compromise in approaching the liberal arts and especially the subjects in the trivium. Forebears had wavered between rejecting the arts because they were pagan and embracing them for the good they could do or, in John's day, neglecting them because they were unimportant or because there was more precious knowledge to be pursued.[37] John declared, and undertook to prove, that the arts were essential elements in the education of Christian gentlemen.

According to his own testimony, John spent twelve years studying the trivium and finished with a commitment to grammar, rhetoric, and logic that even the luster of science, philosophy, and theology could not dim. If logical studies ever had a greater champion than John, he would be hard to find in the archives of educational history. Logical studies began, as they had to, on an elementary level, but moved up the ladder of learning to become necessary components in all advanced study. At a time when it was uncommon to distinguish philosophy from theology, John called the trivium essential to the prosperity of philosophy.[38]

Grammar had undergone considerable change by the advent of the twelfth century. It remained true to a purpose explained by Alcuin—the rules of correct speaking and writing—but it went beyond this humble, though essential, function to resurrect the commission ancient grammarians had assigned to it and became the custodian of general knowledge. So when John talks about the possibility and virtue of grammar, he is referring to what we call liberal education, and the grammar course taught by Bernard of Chartres upon which John heaped so much praise would have been hard for Alcuin to recognize.

Bernard could make assumptions about the basic education of his students that for Alcuin would have been fatal. Both Bernard and Alcuin lectured to their classes, but when Alcuin's lectures were simple dictations of the rules and vocabulary of Latin, Bernard lectured to "point out, in reading the authors, what was simple and according to rule . . . . He would explain grammatical figures, rhetorical embellishments, and sophistical quibbling, as well as the relation of given passages to other studies. He would do so, however, without trying to teach everything at one time."[39] Evidently Bernard and John were prepared to heed Quintilian's metaphor that the child's mind is like the narrow neck of a bottle and that only a small amount of liquid can be poured in at a time.

When teachers' instruction was over, students wrote compositions to use what they had learned. Such "exercise both strengthens and sharpens the mind."[40] But students engaged in composition had more than teachers' instruction to aid them; they had, also, illustrations supplied by the best authors. The genius of classical pedagogy, exhibited first by Isocrates and then by Quintilian (rule and model), is evident in Bernard's teaching, and John adds his own endorsement to any method capable of making full use of imitation.

Daily, students recited the lesson of the previous day: "each succeeding day thus became the discipline of its predecessor."[41] This practice, we call it *repetition*, was characterized by Bernard and John as *the declination*. In paying their daily debt, students were exhorted to do their best, sometimes committing huge parts of their subjects to memory, but when their best was not good enough to satisfy teachers, sterner measures were taken. For a long time the advice of Quintilian in connection with corporal punishment for failure to learn was heeded, so teachers were disposed to employ competition or other devices to spur achievement. Yet failure to learn because of bad will could levy a fine exacted with a whip.

John's devotion to reading as the primary instructional means is nowhere diminished in his famous discourse. Students were expected to know the rules of grammar, and the rules were supplied in the teachers' lectures, but grammar had another side that was never subject to discount: literature. Now students were enjoined to make reading selections themselves; otherwise intellectual autonomy would be intimidated by having someone tell them what had worth and what had none. If, however, students made poor selections, they were criticized and encouraged to exercise better judgment: "To examine and pore over everything that has been written, regardless of whether it is worth reading, is as pointless as to fritter away one's time with old wives' tales."[42] The point is clear. One of the marks of a good grammarian is an ability to recognize what is unimportant and ignore it.

Reading, according to John, was to be accompanied by writing, and compositions were read by the teacher and the class, and then the teacher and the class analyzed them. John called this practice the *conference* and declared that "nothing serves better to foster the acquisition of eloquence and the attainment of knowledge than such conferences, which also have a salutary influence on practical conduct, provided that charity moderates enthusiasm, and that humility is not lost during progress in learning."[43]

John of Salisbury can be credited with an effective articulation of the place classical study should occupy in the schools. He made the same assumption that others either had made or were to make: the classics contain all knowledge most worth having. But where his predecessors, in taking this bold stance, were silent in justifying it, John was clear. He did not mean for scholars to halt with the words of the ancients; they should begin with them, build upon them, and thus come to possess knowledge. By studying the classics and adding contemporary interpretation—although hardly the allegorical interpretation promoted by Hugh—scholars could be lifted up and borne aloft on their gigantic stature:

> Accordingly the words of the authors should not be lost or forgotten, especially those which give [their] full opinions, and have wise applicability. Such words preserve scientific knowledge in its entirety, and contain tremendous hidden as well as apparent power.[44]

In their assault upon the classics, students might find some of them too difficult. So then, said John, they should consult commentaries for explication.

Objection to educational shortcuts, especially in the study of philosophy, is abundant throughout *Metalogicon*. John anticipated some of the criticism later leveled at the Scholastics, who in their eagerness to philosophize could not be bothered with the ordinary rules of grammar (reminding one of a contemporary excuse that thought counts and preoccupation with correct expression intimidates it) and were victimized by a pedantry that concealed more than it revealed when ideas were held hostage in debates about "whether the pig taken to market is being held by the man or the rope." An enemy of superficiality in study, and counseling almost limitless reading, he maintained as well that selection is a sound principle for determining the boundary of a curriculum. His friendship for the trivium is evident, but he was not blinded by its luster. Good sense should preside over the educational process and more time than necessary should not be spent on logical studies: "It is foolish to delay a long time, with much sweat and worry, over something that could otherwise be easily and quickly expedited."[45]

The day-to-day pedagogy embraced by John was to a great extent a recapitulation of the technique his own teachers had employed. Its most essential characteristics were introduced by Alcuin, but succeeding generations of schoolmasters stood on the shoulders of giants, too, and embellished their teaching with the technical insights of classical pedagogy. It is fair to say that John's educational theory was an adaptation of ancient educational theory to meet the educational requirements of the twelfth century. While it might be hard to find genuine novelty and originality in John's theory, it was one that communicated with its own time and in the end became the representative educational theory for the twelfth century. Besides, its internal vigor recommended it to schoolmasters in succeeding centuries. The way grammar and logic were taught in the universities of the thirteenth and fourteenth centuries is testimony to its influence in the schools.

In the *Metalogicon* we are introduced to an educational theory that made the training of reason the central feature of all teaching; an end most likely of achievement if Christian and classical knowledge, faith and reason, were melded in a broad and ornamental syllabus. Such an educational program was to produce analysts, dialecticians, humanists, and Christian scholars. For John and his medieval companions, they represented the fairest type of learned persons.

After many false and painful starts that began probably with Tertullian and ended with John of Salisbury, the early Christian and medieval world had come to terms both with pagan philosophy and classical literature. Western Christians had reached an educational consensus (it might be called a philosophy) allowing them to follow a path to heaven using profane means to help them along the way. They thought their most pressing educational problems were solved. It turned out they were wrong: medieval speculation and solution, despite their eloquence and erudition, were poorly suited for the temper, the taste, and the character of life in the modern age that began around the middle of the fourteenth century. We turn now to a review of the conundrums buried in the mines of educational theory that modern educators were invited to excavate.

NOTES

1. G.W. Bowersock, *Hellenism in Late Antiquity* (Ann Arbor: University of Michigan Press, 1990), 1–15.

2. Tertullian, *On Prescription Against Heretics*, translated by Peter Holmes, in *The Ante-Nicene Fathers*, edited by Alexander Roberts and James Donaldson, 10 vols. (New York: Charles Scribner's Sons, 1896–1903), 3:246.

3. Henry Chadwick, *Early Christian Thought and the Classical Tradition: Studies in Justin, Clement, and Origen* (New York: Oxford University Press, 1966), 10 and 101; and Frederick Copleston, *A History of Philosophy*, 9 vols. (Westminster, Md.: Newman Press, 1946–1975), 2:16–18.

4. Leslie W. Barnard, *Athenagoras: A Study in Second-Century Apologetics* (Paris: Beauchesne, 1972), 37–51.

5. Henry Chadwick, *Early Christian Thought*, 36–39.

6. Ibid., 103–4.

7. Timothy D. Barnes, *Tertullian: A Historical and Literary Study* (New York: Oxford University Press, 1971, 1985), 204–5.

8. St. Jerome, *Select Letters of St. Jerome*, translated by F.A. Wright, 24 vols. (Cambridge: Loeb Classical Library, Harvard University Press, 1933), 16:125–27.

9. Peter R.L. Brown, *Augustine of Hippo: A Biography* (Berkeley: University of California Press, 1967), 35–39.

10. St. Augustine, *A Select Library of Nicene and Post-Nicene Fathers of the Christian Church*, 14 vols. First Series. Edited by Philip Schaff (New York: Scribner, 1886–1889), 2:554.

11. William H. Stahl and Richard Johnson, with E.L. Burge, *Martianus Capella and the Seven Liberal Arts*, 2 vols. (New York: Columbia University Press, 1971, 1977); and Danuta Shanzer, *A Philosophical and Literary Commentary on Martianus Capella's De Nuptiis Philologiae et Mercurri* (Berkeley: University of California Press, 1986).

12. Boethius, *The Consolation of Philosophy*, translated by Richard Green (New York: Macmillan Company, 1962); Henry Chadwick, *Boethius: The Consolations of Music, Logic, Theology, and Philosophy* (New York: Oxford University Press, 1981); and Margaret Gibson, ed., *Boethius: His Life, Thought and Influence* (Oxford, Eng.: B. Blackwell, 1981).

13. Cassiodorus, *An Introduction to Divine and Human Readings*, translated by Leslie Webber Jones (New York: Columbia University Press, 1946; New York: Ocatagon Books, 1966); and James J. O'Donnell, *Cassiodorus* (Berkeley: University of California Press, 1979).

14. Cassiodorus, 1. 10. 1–2.

15. John of Salisbury, *The Metalogicon: A Twelfth-Century Defense of the Verbal and Logical Arts of the Trivium*, translated with introduction and notes by Daniel D. McGarry (Berkeley: University of California Press, 1955, 1962; Westport, Conn.: Greenwood Press, 1982), III, i, 150.

16. Pierre Riché, *Education and Culture in the Barbarian West, Sixth Through Eighth Centuries*, translated by John J. Contreni (Columbia: University of South Carolina Press, 1976), 461–77.

17. R.R. Bolgar, *The Classical Heritage and Its Beneficiaries* (Cambridge, Eng.: University Press, 1954), 56–57.

18. F. Holmes Dudden, *Gregory the Great: His Place in History and Thought*, 2 vols. (New York: Longmans, Green, 1905), 2:69–79.

19. Ernest Brehaut, *An Encyclopedist of the Dark Ages: Isidore of Seville* (New York: B. Franklin, 1912, 1964); and Jacques Fontaine, *Isidore de Seville et la culture Classique dans L'Espagne Wisigothique*, 2 vols. (Paris: Etudes Augustinienes, 1959).

20. Raymund Kottje and Herald Zimmermann, *Hrabanus Maurus: Lehrer, Abt und Bischof* (Wiesbaden: Steiner, 1982).

21. Alcuin, *Alcuin of York, c. A.D. 732–804: His Life and Letters*, translated by Stephen Allott (York, Eng.: William Sessions Ltd., 1974); and Andrew F. West, *Alcuin and the Rise of the Christian Schools* (New York: Charles Scribner's Sons, 1909; New York: Greenwood Press, 1969).

22. Thierry de Chartres, *The Latin Rhetorical Commentaries*, edited by Karin M. Fredborg (Toronto: Pontifical Institute of Mediaeval Studies, 1988), 2–3; and Thierry de Chartres, *Commentaries on Boethius*, edited by Nikolaus M. Haring (Toronto: Pontifical Institute of Mediaeval Studies, 1971).

23. Hugh of Saint-Victor, *Didascalicon: A Medieval Guide to the Arts*, translated by Jerome Taylor (New York: Columbia University Press, 1961). Jerome Taylor, *The Origin and Early Life of Hugh of St. Victor* (Notre Dame, Ind.: Mediaeval Institute, University of Notre Dame, 1957). David L. Wagner, ed., *The Seven Liberal Arts in the Middle Ages* (Bloomington: Indiana University Press, 1983.

24. William of Moerbeke, a Dominican monk, translated for Thomas's use the Greek texts of Aristotle to a Latin version in the 1260s.

25. James Collins's, *The Teacher* (Chicago: Henry Regnery Company, 1954), contains an English translation of *De Magistro*, as does Mary Helen Mayer, *The Philosophy of Teaching of St. Thomas Aquinas* (Milwaukee: Bruce Publishing, 1929).

26. R.R. Bolgar, *Classical Heritage*, 106–9.

27. John of Salisbury, *Metalogicon*, I, xxiv, 68.

28. Hugh of Saint-Victor, *The Didascalicon of Hugh of St. Victor*, 44.

29. John of Salisbury, *Metalogicon*, I, xxiv, 64–65.

30. Hugh of Saint-Victor, *Didascalicon* II, xxx, 82.

31. Ibid., III, i, 83.

32. Ibid., I, xi, 60.

33. Ibid., III, iv, 88.

34. Ibid., III, viii, 91.

35. Ibid., III, viii, 92.

36. C.S. Baldwin, *Medieval Rhetoric and Poetic* (New York: Macmillan, 1928), 155.

37. John complained, *Metalogicon*, I, x, 32–33, that students unable to read and write were attending lectures on philosophy.

38. Ibid., I, xxi, 60–62.

39. Ibid., I, xxiv, 67.

40. Ibid., I, xxiv, 68.

41. Ibid.

42. Ibid., I, xxiv, 70.

43. Ibid.

44. Ibid., III, iv, 168.

45. Ibid., I, x, 32–33.

Chapter 3
Educational Theory in the Modern World

Medieval educational practice and theory must have been thought satisfactory, otherwise a durability keeping them relatively intact until the middle of the sixteenth century is hard to explain. Yet while paralysis appeared to affect educational practice as it turned a sanguine face to the future, social, political, and religious thought was in ferment and wrestled with problems that resisted conventional solution. While the modern era agonized over social issues of genuine import, something novel was introduced that puzzled all but obtuse men and women: consideration of personal worth and noble character.

Medieval men and women led lives dominated by an order and regularity whose bases were ratified by philosophy and religion. Every condition in life was properly assessed and a correct priority was assigned. This determination for a discipline of life was translated into the everyday activity of the people. What the medieval theorists missed, however, was the human disposition to nourish the soul with experience that was not precisely intellectual and not always overtly religious. Feeling and sensitivity unaccounted for in the dialogues on discipline were not only profoundly human, they were ubiquitous. Love and hate, joy and despair, edification and meanness were never excised from the vocabulary of medieval men and women, but they were submerged in a hierarchy of knowledge and experience that could acknowledge them without ever giving them range to roam freely. Life was perhaps never stripped of all occasion for pleasure or deprived of possibility for seeking personal satisfaction. But what later generations encouraged and enjoyed as natural human disposition was underrated and, sometimes, expressly condemned. Something was missing.

An apparatus for education and schooling can hardly be expected to supply what a society at large refuses to embrace. But both education and schooling can be weaned from concentrating on intellectual acumen and find genuine delight in personal formation and temporal happiness.

At about this time, two great movements began and their wake altered the landscape of life: religious reconstruction and humanism. Education, as it turned out, became religion's handmaiden. But this had almost nothing to do with a genuine philosophy of education, although religion's influence on educational policy and practice was severe and shaking. Besides, religious formation and reformation are bound to affect the conduct of schools. Almost as afterthought, humanism introduced radical propositions about religious decorum and educational philosophy.

It would be nothing short of exaggeration to maintain that any of the humanists who now begin to appear on the pages of history were great philosophers. Few among them aspired to a career in philosophy, and those who were tempted to play on the outer fringe of philosophical scholarship could never match either in profundity or range the work of their medieval predecessors. It is fair to say, as well, that many humanists, Francesco Petrarch (1304–1374) chief among them, were never disposed to involve themselves in the enigmatic field of pedagogic technique. They thought such work beneath them.[1] Nevertheless, there were humanists who expressed penetrating thought about educational ends and means. Their expositions, if not qualifying them as main actors in the drama of educational theory, credits them with supporting roles in the cast. Without perhaps having all the qualifications of educational philosophers, their contributions to educational thought and practice turned out to be both consequential and lasting.

A NEW METHOD OF STUDY

Medieval education had maintained a permanent, though highly selective, liaison with classical literature. This is nowhere clearer than in the books studied by scholars in the great specialties of law, medicine, and theology. Yet both teachers and students in medieval schools suffered disadvantages from which their humanist successors were largely immune. The educational theory that captured and held their allegiance was fairly dominated by otherworldly perspectives, so when they tapped the classical reservoir they were reminded that some of its water was poison. Selection, winnowing safe from dangerous classical texts, was a technique available to them, and they used it. But its use inevitably narrowed the boundary wherein an acceptable antique literature could be found and cultivated.

Humanist scholars advanced a theory that played down life as merely a preparation for eternity, and accepted the temporal world as a suitable environment for exploiting every possible means for achieving human goals. And human goals stood in a different light: they were assumed to be good and noble in themselves, without any need for recasting or tempering on a supernatural forge. If this implies a rejection of religion in an age that was thoroughly religious, the implication is flawed. A litany of all the important humanists can be recited, and not one should be indicted for apostasy, heterodoxy, or heresy. They wanted to be, and for the most part were, devout Christians (many in holy orders). At the same time, they rejected monastic idealism and asceticism. Doing so, they deflated the otherworldly spirit of the medieval age.

Shifting from old assumptions to embrace novelty would likely have been a pointless exercise had humanists not engaged in scholarly expeditions into vaults of classical literature that for a long time had been left unopened. They rescued a large corpus of the ancient legacy that their predecessors, for one or another reason, had allowed to lie fallow. The consequence of this labor enriched literature in such a way that a conventional principle of selection could be employed to remove from the syllabus anything that was counted dangerous and at the same time leave a literary larder entirely capable of nourishing the human spirit. There was so much more to choose from. This rich harvest might have been left to spoil by the mold of indifference had it not been for the development of movable type, an invention of such immense significance that the whole of culture was its beneficiary.

The story of educational humanism begins with Francesco Petrarch, is invigorated by the cogent pedagogical advice of Manuel Chrysoloras (1350–1413), is given test and direction in the schools of Vittorino da Feltre (1378–1446) at Mantua and Guarino of Verona (1370–1460) at Ferrara. Its final chapters that contain both a definition and a model are written by the sensible and eloquent Erasmus (1469–1536).[2] One should not quarrel with an assertion that Erasmus bestowed his genius upon humanistic education, but it is only fair to acknowledge that the educational theory he pronounced and the pedagogic technique that he shaped did not spring suddenly from his fertile mind. He had resources in theory and practice upon which to draw.

Nothing is more characteristic of educational humanism than imitation. This criterion, idealized by Petrarch, was followed faithfully by the humanists succeeding him. But eager to adopt imitation as a guiding pedagogical principle, they too often missed Petrarch's meaning and settled for a dull, unimaginative instructional program that made a fetish out of attention to linguistic detail, and to writing, speaking, and thinking the way they supposed ancient authors had. Petrarch, though, using Cicero as a guide, nowhere recommends mere linguistic accuracy. Following Cicero, he meant for imitation to be used as a means for improving the human ability of expression. Had nothing more than literary and linguistic accuracy been his goal, it is one that likely could have been achieved with a minimum of effort by most clever students. Petrarch wanted students to use classical authors as models, so much is clear, but he wanted them, as well, to take the whole of a classic, to read and understand, and to be guided by it to refined and eloquent expression. Petrarch used imitation to make effective writing possible, and he showed almost no concern for an assimilation of classical culture. A student could read the classics and be inspired by their genius, but almost certainly when the books were closed, and depending wholly upon the unorganized functioning of memory, would retain few of the novelties they contained. If this defect were noticed by Petrarch, he neglects it.

It must have been noticed by others, though, because they were quick to enlist the advice of Chrysoloras, a man who came to Florence as a diplomat from Greece and stayed on as a teacher. He had absorbed the culture for which Greece had long been famous and was, it appears, entirely familiar with the theory and method of Greek educational practice. In any case, after surrendering the diplomatic portfolio, he began to conduct seminars for those humanists who wanted to have a firmer grasp of the Greek technical use of imitation. The story, quite likely correct, tells of the attention he was given as all manner of teachers flocked to hear him.[3]

With the exception of *Erotemata*, a school manual on grammar no longer extant, Chrysoloras left no written record of his educational ideas. But his best pupil, Guarino, who spent five years with him, supplies an account of his system of instruction.[4] It concentrated upon extensive, careful, and critical reading of classical texts. Students were to attend carefully to every "apt or colourful" expression and to impress them on their memories by constant repetition until "their use became second nature." Language was not alone in getting this attention; the same method was applied to content, "and anecdotes which described noteworthy actions or pointed remarks were to be learnt by heart whenever possible." Following this method, the ways of thought and the experiences whereupon ancient writers based their work could be absorbed until students' minds were transformed to resemble "in content and operations the mind of a fifth-century Greek." Such a method put a heavy burden on memory, and memory needed help, which was to come mainly from daily, weekly, and monthly repetitions and from a notebook wherein what was to be memorized was recorded.

Against this background and with whatever help the method of Chrysoloras could supply, Erasmus undertook to build a theory of humanistic education which had two principal components: a full recapitulation of the classical literary legacy, for evidence is lacking that he ever abandoned a conviction that all knowledge worth having can be found somewhere in the classics ("For I affirm that with slight qualification the whole of attainable knowledge lies enclosed within the literary monuments of ancient Greece"),[5] and an unshakeable commitment to a noble and Christian character. If literature is handled correctly, it can be a moral teacher, and as an outcome from such schooling students will be pious, eloquent, and trustworthy.

In *De duplici copia verborum ac rerum* (Illustrations of words and ideas), drafted in 1501, finished in 1508, and published at Colet's commission in 1512,[6] Erasmus filled in Chrysoloras's outline for teaching the classics. He showed students how to cull from them words, phrases, and ideas for a recording in their notebooks. But for all its worth, even acknowledging the extensive influence it had on the teaching of the classics in humanistic schools, the substance of Erasmus's theory is fairly well concealed in *De copia*, if it is there at all.[7] The theory was drawn from an interpretation of the meaning of classical literature and from experience, largely Erasmus's own, with the evolution and the use of language.

With careful historical interpretation Erasmus demonstrated the various ways that classical and Christian culture were melded and how, in any final accounting, rather than being hostile (though certainly hostile elements could be identified) they were complementary. And as part of the same demonstration, he was persuasive in showing the penetrating influence classical learning had on the most prominent of church fathers. There were countless times, of course, when they called upon their Christian confreres to avoid what was dangerous in the classics. Yet they were at the same time confident that properly used and thoroughly understood what was potentially contaminating to faith could be rendered harmless. There was, Erasmus understood them to say, greater danger in ostracizing the classics than in using them prudently. Sacred and profane literature do not belong to the same genre, but each in its own way illuminates the other.

The classics, Erasmus confidently asserted, can contribute to the formation of noble character. The whole of the Christian intellectual and literary tradition, he declared, supported this part of his theory. Erasmus, one should add, was not the first to find a place for classical culture in the formation of Christians and little in his argument is original, yet expression and timing count for something. The argument was strong and thorough, and Erasmus advanced it at a time in the development of educational thought when it was both most effective and most likely of being adopted.

The second part of the theory seems to have been original with Erasmus. Beginning with the proposition that the main body of classical literature is morally and ethically responsible and consistent with a Christian outlook on life if fully understood and properly interpreted, he erected a pedagogic creed on the foundation of intellectual discipline. No one, neither schoolboy nor schoolmaster, can achieve the required understanding or the correct interpretation of classical literature without an expenditure of effort. The achievement of decency in learning requires an intellectual discipline that must be fortified by a moral discipline of doing what ought to be done. Schools and scholarship have a regimen that cannot be discounted if success is to be obtained. Adhering vigorously and rigorously to this regimen implies moral discipline, and in the course of study moral discipline can be improved and strengthened. The school course, then, and especially the classical course with all its demands, contributes to the formation of moral discipline; it is a moral exercise as well as an intellectual experience.

The habit of doing what ought to be done in study does not in itself bespeak either nobility of character or an ethical disposition to do always what is right, but it is a foundation whereupon both can stand. Boys are educated morally the same way they are educated intellectually: by following a regimen inculcating habits of acting and thinking responsibly and morally. Taken together, these components form the substance of Erasmus's theory that piety and character are inculcated by achieving a level of eloquence that only a program of classical education can supply.

Still, Erasmus was a realist. He knew that any study of classical literature was hard, and he knew, too, that false starts and dangerous trails were possible in method and content for schoolboys who were at the foot of the scholastic ascent. For all the promise contained in his theory, some measures to ensure safety for immature scholars, and perhaps others as well, who were to invade the whole of Greek and Latin classical literature, had to be found and added as essential elements.

It is fair to assume, as Erasmus almost certainly did, that we are to a large extent products of our experience. What we see, hear, and read are bound to be influential. If students in schools that were to follow Erasmus's plan spent nine or ten years in intimate association with their pagan ancestors, they could not help but be affected by them. To ensure that literary influence would not turn them away from Christian faith to pagan folly, prudence alone recommended care. In a word, and Erasmus staked his reputation on this, literature is a teacher and the consequence of its teaching can be ennobling or degrading. To immunize students from the latter, certain safeguards were introduced.

The first safeguard, about which no school can do much, was a sound and effective moral formation under the direction of a good home. The roots of character formation, Erasmus acknowledged, are set early and when carefully nourished in a moral home environment are likely to be fruitful. It is hard to believe that moral formation in childhood years is capable of rendering innocuous any untoward subsequent experience, but it can be of immense help.

Benefiting from the immunity supplied by a pious upbringing, allegorical interpretation comes next. Used correctly, its expositors declared, allegorical interpretation can convert any classical phrase, allusion, or story into something edifying. But allegorical interpretation is a technique neither easily mastered nor always properly employed, and for mere schoolboys to use it for decontaminating texts that on their face reward infidelity would be expecting too much. Making the classics conform (articulating their inner meaning) to Christian taste and temperament was work for experienced scholars. With Erasmus's theory to spur them on, scholars began to sharpen their tools of interpretation for producing commentaries on the classics. Their considerable industry soon supplied a literature that was used in the schools to keep readers of the classics (students and teachers alike) on a dependable moral path.

The third safeguard was selection. Never on the side of censorship, for Erasmus wanted the full corpus of classical literature mastered, nothing was to be left out. But intellectual and moral maturity, gained as students climb the scholastic ladder, permits the study of some books by students advanced in their schooling which could not be countenanced for beginners. And with so much more to choose from, for humanist literary explorers had expanded the boundaries of the classics enormously, it was easy to keep students on a diet of good and decent books accommodated to their maturity while they were being prepared to handle good but difficult classical selections later in their academic career. Certainly, this approach had solid grounding in good sense. Erasmus's final safeguard has a strange ring: literally, the formal study of philosophy was made outlaw. Despite the logical connection that might be made between right knowledge and correct behavior, Erasmus had little or no confidence in philosophy being an effective moral teacher. Its more likely effect would be to confuse students and, in the end, to lead them astray. In matters of morality, confusion and contamination were bedfellows.

When Erasmus declaimed against philosophy in the syllabus of the secondary school, he was reacting to his own experience with its study as well as to the logical thicket wherein philosophers had corralled it. The narrow pedantry, the technical vocabulary, and the intellectual arrogance of philosophers who were still feeding on the harvest reaped by the later Scholastics gave philosophy a bad name. In any case, no humanist of this period (including Erasmus) either knew much philosophy or found it attractive. Philosophy, one must admit, never occupied a prominent place in the curriculum of any modern secondary school, but was this due to Erasmus's proscription or to the regimen consistent with its study? This question remains, perhaps forever, on probation.

How Erasmus's *pietas et litterata* managed to capture the imagination of secondary schoolmasters and, in time, came to dominate the curriculum of secondary schools is another query that awaits an answer. The theory came to full practical stature in the schools promoted by Philip Melanchthon (1497–1560), the famous Strassburg school of John Sturm (1507–1589), and the schools of the Society of Jesus (1534), and from them to schools all over Europe. Still, there is the story that it was designed especially for John Colet's school, one that served as a model for all other schools that adopted Erasmus's program. This story is worth some attention here.

For a long time, at least since the appearance of Frederic Seebohm's *The Oxford Reformers of 1498: A History of the Fellow-Work of John Colet, Erasmus, and Thomas More* in 1867, John Colet's reputation as a humanist, an orthodox Roman Catholic committed to correcting ecclesiastical abuse, and a progressive educator equipped to rival the stature of Erasmus has stood relatively unexamined.[8] A.F. Leach's *The Schools of Medieval England*[9] raised questions about humanism in English secondary schools and painted a somewhat gloomy picture of its educational worth. This was mainly because Leach cultivated an antihumanistic bias, but he skirted the issue of Colet's humanistic stature and the commitment St. Paul's made to genuine humanism.

John N. Miner's *The Grammar Schools of Medieval England: A. F. Leach in Historiographical Perspective*,[10] sees less flaw in St. Paul's than Leach alleged but, on the whole, seems not to tackle the issue of where Colet stood vis-à-vis Erasmus's program of liberal and humanistic education. But he tends to rebut Leach's thesis with respect to the influence humanism had on the great English public schools. The impressive scholarship of John B. Gleason in *John Colet* has raised doubt and rekindled lingering, but unspoken, suspicion that Colet was less a humanist than uncritical nineteenth-century admirers supposed. Instead of being a fearless champion for pristine Christianity, he was a wary divine who, at best, stayed on a safe outer fringe of any movement charting a course for internal church reform.

Gleason musters so much evidence and appears to interpret it with such good sense and attention to detail that it is hard to dispute his conclusion that Colet has reaped an undeserved benefit of fame. But the larger issues of Colet's genuine humanism and his alleged fervor for correcting ecclesiastical mistake need not detain us. An adjudication of the contradictory assertions of scholars on these points is, in any case, not part of my purpose. I want to inquire into the generally held belief that in Colet's school—St. Paul's in London, founded in 1512—Erasmus's scholastic program was put first to a test. In connection with this belief, Gleason's scholarship supports sturdy bases for what should be quite a different story.

There is little doubt that Colet and Erasmus proceeded from several common assumptions, both with respect to education and to church reform. There is a great deal to be doubted in the old allegation that Colet's agile mind supplied Erasmus with the intellectual energy to pursue the study of Greek until he was equipped to make an authoritative and definitive translation of the Greek Testament. Erasmus's humanism was clearly defined and solidly established before he had anything to do with Colet. His determination to become fluent in Greek in order to forward his biblical scholarship can hardly be attributed to Colet, who apparently knew little if any Greek and by almost any account was neither a scholar nor much interested in urging scholarship on others. Besides, the evidence is abundant that Erasmus was perfecting his knowledge of Greek, likely with scholars associated with the great publishing houses like Froben at Basle, Aldus in Venice, and the Aldine Press, a long time before he met Colet.

The common educational positions of Colet and Erasmus should be recited: both endorsed skill and correct expression in language; both wanted boys to be trained physically and morally; they wanted, besides, knowledge of truth and words. Literature and grammar should be mastered, memory should be strengthened, and pedagogic techniques involving games, plays, contests, revision, and repetition had secure places in instruction. Finally, both were certain that any decent school program should ensure that students remained firm in their religious faith. They had plenty in common, but Colet stopped while Erasmus went on.

Erasmus was captivated by the classics. They were to be studied by following an instructional regimen so demanding that only a few superior students could adhere to it. The aim was mastery of classical literature for, Erasmus believed, it held an important key to the formation of character. He seems to have followed, or discovered for himself, a position taken centuries earlier by Clement of Alexandria, that moral lessons are in the classics and do not conflict with the substance of Christian ethics. When Erasmus organized the literary syllabus, nothing was left out and nothing about the meaning therein was neglected or left to chance. The purpose of such instruction is clear: boys begin and end their studies with literature. They will know the authors, but they will develop, as well, a critical and objective approach to literature that will be ennobling. Their minds will be fortified and formed, but, more important than any wisdom they might possess, they will have a solid, moral Christian character. It must be stressed, as well, that the entire classical corpus was the object of their study; nothing was to be left out.

It would be hard to find anything in this version that Colet either supplied or, what is more, approved. Something can be said for Colet's innovative approach to school management. Undoubtedly he took the side of making teachers professional persons whose talent and accomplishment should be rewarded no less than practitioners of other professions. He lamented the tendency of giving clergymen teaching sinecures for which they were unqualified. He deplored the fairly common practice of persons becoming teachers when they lacked aptitude for doing anything else. He appears, as well, to have campaigned for the creation of a cadre of married laymen as teachers. And without having been the inventor of the practice, he followed a dimly blazed trail of putting schools under control of lay trustees rather than, as had been common, having control vested in the hands of an ecclesiastical board. None of these, however, despite their worth, bespeaks a genuine educational humanism. Colet's reputation for following in Erasmus's footsteps or matching his giant educational stride might in fact be due to the appearance of his name in *De copia* and Erasmus's generous reference to him as an ally in the promotion of classical culture. Could Colet's tardiness or refusal to pay Erasmus for copies of *De copia* be an indication "that Erasmus had let him down by showing too strong humanistic tendencies in his textbook?"[11]

When one looks for signs of humanism in a school, it is to the curriculum that one must turn. There is no better place to go. Let us see what Colet's curriculum embraced and what the 153 boys who enrolled at St. Paul's studied. Did Colet want them to begin their study with an assumption that a command of the classics could dispel ignorance, or with an assumption that a mastery of Christian knowledge could erase the flaws and perversions of paganism? Starting a school implies some risk, especially when the school's syllabus seems to be introducing material that could be understood as competing with, or being subversive of, conventional religious opinion. The place the Latin and Greek classics occupied at St. Paul's allows for only one conclusion: Colet followed a course of caution.

In the "Statutes" Colet wrote for the school, he declared that good literature would be taught, and mention is made of the work of Latin and Greek authors. But then comes a statement that Christian authors are preferred because with them students can increase their "knowledge and wor-

shipping of god and oure lorde Crist Jesu and good Cristen lyff and manners."[12] Virgil, Cicero, Sallust, and Terence are praised, but the implication
is evident that their worth is in the purity of their Latin and not in the content of their books. Then he shies from them to recommend instead the style
of "seint Jerome and seint Ambrose and seint Austen." Genuine classical
authors are ignored too; their place is taken by Christian writers who flourished after the fourth century. He was ready to "vtterly abbanysh and Exclude oute of this scole" any literature that contained the slightest hint of
paganism or did not explicitly endorse Christian themes.

Colet's literary syllabus, setting aside for the moment the genuineness
of its classical vintage, was certainly not in step with contemporary humanist
choice, and one cannot imagine that, say, Thomas More or Erasmus would
have been ecstatic about it. Of course, Colet's school could not have everything on the reading list—no school can—so selection was imperative, but
those who so admire Colet's genuine humanism should explain why he chose
to recommend authors whose names appeared on the readings lists of Isidore
of Seville (560–636), Alcuin of York (ca. 735–804), and Vincent of Beauvais
(1190–1264)? That Isidore, Alcuin, and Vincent proposed a literary diet for
schoolboys does not illustrate that the classics were interdicted—they were
not—but it is pretty persuasive evidence that if Colet's heart was in the
present, his head was in the past. Even where his heart was can be debated,
because when Colet died his successor almost at once revised the school's
reading list and all but one of Colet's preferred authors (Baptista Mantuanus)
were removed. The record contains nothing to make us believe that St. Paul's
Christian character and scholastic resolve were eroded by this drastic revision.

In the end, then, while Erasmus's claim upon Christian humanism
remains secure, the allegation about Colet having put genuine humanism to
its first test at St. Paul's might need revision. Despite humanism's lack of
appeal to early St. Paul's, it came in time to affect the educational program
there and could have had a hand in promoting it in England as well as in
all of Europe.

A New Epistemology

To affirm Nicholas Murray Butler's appraisal ("[Comenius's] place in education is one of commanding importance. He introduces and dominates the
whole modern movement in the field of elementary and secondary education")[13] is to credit John Amos Comenius (1592–1670) with accomplishments
that equal or surpass those of Erasmus. Yet discounting Butler's assertion
as being too generous strips little luster from Comenius's reputation as an

educator whose theory began to blunt the dogmatic assumption that all knowledge worth having is buried somewhere in the books. Without the academic pedigree of a philosopher, he nevertheless perceived what educational theorists and schoolmasters of the day either never knew or had forgotten: physical reality is as important and dependable a source for knowledge as anything stored in books. We can be misled by what we see, hear, smell, taste, or feel, but books can mislead us, too, especially when they illustrate less than a full account of natural reality. If the senses are trained for discriminate observation, they can be gateways to truth.

Taking into account Comenius's geography of birth, early schooling, denominational affiliation, and language make his status as a scholastic hero all the more surprising. Born in Moravia (now the Czech Republic), Comenius was orphaned at twelve, suffered from the indifference of an aunt who neglected his education, became a priest and then a bishop of a persecuted religious sect (Unitas Fratrum), and most of his books were written in Czech, which kept them in a shallow literary tributary. *The Great Didactic*, for example, was not translated into English until 1896, although Comenius prepared a Latin version around 1632. Its complement, *The Analytical Didactic*, had to wait until 1953 for an English-language edition.

Debate about Comenius's influence upon modern education is almost never heard, yet it, one must admit, is hard to measure with precision and report with clarity. Often called the "father of modern education," a more recent assessment is even more generous: "He was not merely a reformer of method but also a pioneer in the attempt to educate a whole nation and later the whole world."[14]

Comenius's optimism is nowhere more evident than in his promotion of decent schooling as an instrument for social reform. Education, he declared time and again, must aim for the transformation of souls, bodies, and minds—an unequivocal endorsement of holistic education—but it should be commissioned, as well, to elevate persons on the social and economic ladder. A phrase like "equality of educational opportunity" was not yet part of the vocabulary of educators, but the idea is explicit throughout *The Great Didactic* and implicit in most of Comenius's writing. The conventional road to school was paved by privilege, either social position or wealth, and the opinion was common that this was in accord with natural law. Few educators spoke of an aristocracy of ability, and fewer still ever voiced the opinion that society's resources for education should be distributed equally and without discrimination. It should not be argued that Comenius took so advanced a position, except in connection with the provision of elementary schooling for women. Yet he regarded good schooling as an economic and social panacea, and some of his successors were quick to idealize it as a prescription for progress.

A popularization of the ideal of universal schooling foreshadowed and might well have been a condition allowing national school systems and democratic educational sentiments to prosper in succeeding centuries. Freeman Butts declares that "the most democratic proposals of all were stated by the Moravian leader, Comenius, who urged the establishment of a complete 'ladder' system of schools reaching from the lowest levels to the university."[15] Wherever Comenius is ranked on a hierarchy of pioneer educators, neither his theory of education nor the practice issuing therefrom, it is evident, was entirely original. An eclectic spirit prompted him to draw upon the thought of earlier philosophers and educators who were committed to a kind of reconstruction in education that would allow students to capitalize on direct experience, learn from it, and not depend solely upon a vision of reality illustrated in the classics.[16] It should be observed, however, that Comenius's friendship for the objects of sight, sound, smell, taste, and feeling did not make him an enemy of the classical inheritance and the ancient languages. It supplied a fairly sturdy foundation for an expansion of the school's curriculum and its redirection from an exclusive attachment to humanism to an openness for realistic naturalism. This stance, likely, was cultivated as a result of his conversance with the work of Juan Luis Vives (1492–1540), Francis Bacon (1561–1626), Wolfgang Ratke (1571–1635), the Irish Jesuit William Bathe (1564–1614), and Thomas Campanella (1568–1639), whose influence he was careful to acknowledge.[17] Prying open the schoolhouse door and allowing entrance to an immature but energetic physical science and an equally immature social science put Comenius in the camp of philosophical realism whose premises encouraged the development of a realist-scientific philosophy of education. As a prescient theorist and innovative schoolmaster, he was at the helm of the realist movement in education. This as much as anything else ratifies his place among the leading figures in the history of education.

In its evolution realism has often had a close kinship with naturalism. And in the past century, having become enamored of positivism, it has counted as valid only that knowledge produced by a positive method and supported by the evidence in empirical data. Whether realism and positivism are inseparable is a topic for another forum, but this much is clear: Comenius was not a positivist. He began with a proposition that is neither naturalistic nor scientific: persons are children of God and must be educated to serve God in this and the next world.[18] Subordinating knowledge to piety, Comenius kept in step with some of his humanistic predecessors when he declared that "our schools, therefore, will then at length be Christian schools when they make us as like to Christ as is possible. How wretched is the teaching that does not lead to virtue and to piety."[19]

Moral formation and Christian piety occupied first place on Comenius's list of educational objectives, but he recognized, as well, that character's best foundation rests upon a dependable body of truth. And this body of truth (knowledge) has little if any independent worth. It would be hard, then, to characterize Comenius as a genuine humanist, for he certainly repudiated any theory that valued knowledge for its own sake, but it would be equally difficult to certify him as a pragmatist: knowledge with only utilitarian worth had no place of privilege in his repertoire. In the face of an apparent jettisoning of liberal and practical education, what is left? If such a question ever occurred to Comenius, he does not advert to it, so we are left to suppose that his investment was made in supernatural virtue, infused with the spirit of a living God, an unalterable commitment to supernatural religion, and a determination to make formal education serve religious faith. Comenius's philosophy of education, it would seem, straddled the Christian humanism of Philip Melanchthon and John Colet. But what he has to say about education from this point on makes him sound more like an orthodox educational philosopher than a Christian bishop. The points he stressed were universal wisdom and universal opportunity for education. The former is always perplexing and the latter must have been especially elusive, if not illusory, in the social and political climate of the time.

In the lexicon of some scholars, universal wisdom is defined as *pansophism*, a theory so ambitious as to assign to schools the function of communicating encyclopedic knowledge to their students. It is hard to believe that Comenius or anyone else could be serious in entertaining such a proposition. So when Comenius advanced an educational program commissioned to promote pansophism, he was endorsing universal wisdom, not universal knowledge.[20] And this appears to have been his appraisal of universal wisdom:

> There is nothing in Heaven or Earth, or in the Waters, nothing in the Abyss under the earth, nothing in the Human body, nothing in the Soul, nothing in Holy Writ, nothing in the Arts, nothing in Economy, nothing in Polity, nothing in the Church of which the little candidates of Wisdom shall be wholly ignorant.[21]

This was a recipe for universal wisdom whose ingredients were supplied by humanists and scientists. Achieving it might be burdensome for some students, easier for others, and all might not see the world through eyes opened by Plato and Aristotle or other giants upon whose shoulders the intellectual legacy rests. Few might become scientists or theologians, but all would have in their possession intimations of the meaning of God's universe. The intimations of some would be superior to those of others, so much was readily acknowledged. But all, in one or another way, would be affected by their encounter with wisdom and all would in some measure be wise to the ways of men and God. If this sounds like educational inflation, Comenius did not mean it to be; it was his expectation for elementary schooling.

Comenius's prescription expressed in contemporary language was a recommendation for basic liberal education for all students, a kind of education that would have meaning and use, and supply them with the fundamental knowledge, skill, and disposition for living successful and satisfying lives. Interpreted this way, Comenius's pansophism is brought down to a level of pedagogical realism that while hard to achieve is nevertheless possible.

A goal of universal wisdom would be a vague and futile hope without schools hospitable to the attendance of children. Universal opportunity for schooling was an essential condition for the attainment of universal wisdom. Conventional educational policy, however, was in the habit of withholding schooling from many persons who could neither profit from instruction because of a presumed lack of ability nor use the dividends of instruction because of their station in life. Comenius repudiated this policy. Learning, he declared with supreme confidence, is a universal good and all persons have a capacity enabling them to reap some reward from schooling. Besides, the argument that schooling is unnecessary for the members of the lower social class, because their status does not require it, is unpersuasive. Universal schooling, moreover, could supply a foundation for social unity and contribute to spiritual integration. Comenius's expression, although patently idealistic, is nevertheless clear:

> The education I propose includes all that is proper for a man, and is one in which all men who are born into this world should share. All, therefore, as far as possible, should be educated together, that they may stimulate and urge on one another.[22]

Universal education, the instrument for promoting universal wisdom, could mold virtuous men and women and cultivate responsible citizenship. The goal of responsible citizenship should have been captivating to politicians, but during Comenius's lifetime they were blind to the benefit that could be reaped from more generous opportunity for schooling. When, later, more popular schooling was provided (although before the advent of the nine-teenth-century universal opportunity for education was only a vague hope), it was discovered to be socially useful and politically manageable. If, as some scholars allege, Comenius was the prophet for universal education, he is entitled to our admiration. There is something noble about a person who is so sensitive to human decency as to recommend universal opportunity for schooling and, one should emphasize, to repudiate the ancient custom that had kept from women the chance to develop their mental and moral capac-ity in the schools. Comenius might have doubted that many young women, or for that matter young men, would become scholars, but doubt is not the point. What matters is that he took the vanguard in pronouncing and pro-moting a principle opening educational opportunity, on equal terms, to women and men.

High hope for universal education could not disguise the fact that without schools for students to attend and teachers to conduct them, any talk about universal opportunity for education bordered on fantasy. So, be-cause he was a practical man, a school plan was an intrinsic element in Comenius's proposal for education. Schools, he said, should be public, al-though it was premature to speak of public financial support for them. A public school was a school open to children from all social classes and, ac-cording to Comenius, such schools were always superior to private, or tu-torial, instructional arrangements. Although in seventeenth-century Europe this was a social, if not an educational, heresy, it was a position from which he refused to retreat.

This heresy was compounded by another: instruction on the first scho-lastic levels should be given in the language of the people. Vernacular schools, known of course at the time, were as yet unconventional. No one should have the temerity to allege that Comenius invented the vernacular school, and even he did not maintain that vernacular languages should occupy ei-ther an exclusive or a privileged position in instruction. Besides, he recog-nized that some vernaculars were as yet too weak to bear the burden of ad-vanced instruction. Failing to employ the vernacular in early school years made instruction largely irrelevant, and this resulted in students wasting years that otherwise could have been spent with profit.

To supply unity and meaning to his educational theory, Comenius recommended a system of schools that would make possible the realization of both universal opportunity for education and universal wisdom. The Mother School designed to nurture children during their first six years of life was the first rung of the educational ladder.[23] Hardly a school in a con-ventional sense, it was nevertheless the essential foundation for all subsequent progress. It was followed by the Vernacular School, which, intended for children from six to twelve years of age, was to enroll students from all social classes and instruct them in their native tongue. Most children, Comenius believed, would terminate their scholastic career with the Vernacular School, yet a Latin School was supplied for students who wanted, or needed, the conventional classical education. The character of the Latin School course was amended only by the adoption of Comenius's natural methodology. At the end of the academic trail was the University, whose purposes were the transmission of the literary and scientific legacy and discovery. The first objective was traditional; the second, research, was novel and, it could be argued, prophetic. Every home was to have a Mother School, every village a Vernacular School, every city a Latin School, and every province a University. On this school plan, Comenius's great expectation for educational reform and pedagogical progress rested.

While it is nothing short of naive to pretend that empiricism was invented in the seventeenth century or that sense perception's role in learning was ignored before the advent of Comenian pedagogy, it is fair to maintain that neither was promoted with much zeal either in or out of the schoolhouse. Persuasive documentation for a "new epistemology" can hardly be attributed to Comenius, although his influence on schooling, despite its tardiness, turned out to be profound and extensive. His projected reform of a psychology of learning, his analogies from nature to school method, and his plea for greater opportunity for education among the people were grounded more upon a generous spirit and a great heart than upon substantial principles of philosophy. So this is about the right time to introduce a philosopher who succeeded in supplying the philosophical substance to advance the fortunes of three themes that were responsible for altering the structure of modern education: John Locke (1632–1704).

The Latin translation of *The Great Didactic* appeared when Comenius was forty years old, the year John Locke was born. Alive until Locke was thirty-eight, Comenius had spent some time in England in 1641, yet there is no evidence whatever that Locke was aware of Comenius's work or was influenced by or indebted to him. The great educational themes, alluded to by Comenius and others who preceded him, but bereft of much philosophical support until Locke came along, were empiricism, utility, and equality.

Empiricism faced two important obstacles, one psychological, the other philosophical. For as long as most scholars could remember, the question had been asked, without an entirely persuasive answer, about how a spiritual mind could have a relationship with physical reality that could lead to truth? Time and again Plato had tackled the mind-body problem and his solution, accepted by many, was that the best most persons could hope to achieve by following the elusive trail of knowledge is right opinion. Knowledge of physical reality is hidden behind a veil too dense for the mind to penetrate.

The obstacle posed in philosophy had to do with innate ideas or intuitive knowledge. It would be pointless, one could argue, for persons to spend time and energy on seeking knowledge of physical reality when all possibility of reward is lacking. If this obstacle could not be leaped, empiricism would have to be abandoned. But it would be pointless, too, to engage in empirical technique if all dependable knowledge is held in the custody of innate ideas or intuitions. Innate ideas are a mind's original possession and can be neither expanded nor shrunk, although in number and quality they might vary from one to another mind. But whatever their number or quality, they go unrealized without suitable cultivation.

Locke subscribed to dualism,[24] but it was an unconventional brand of dualism. This put him at loggerheads with a variety of scholars who leveled against him a charge of theological heterodoxy. Locke demurred from affirming human nature as a composite of spirit and matter, yet he refused to embrace either spiritual or material monism. Observation of the functioning of human beings prompted him to pose this question: Could not God create a kind of matter that possesses an ability to think? Incontrovertible evidence demonstrates that human beings are capable of thought.[25]

Had there been empirical evidence for it, Locke would have embraced traditional dualism, because he wanted to stay on friendly terms with Christians. And he did not cherish taking a position that, some alleged, put religion and morality in jeopardy and, moreover, undermined a theological doctrine asserting the soul's immortality. If human beings are merely "thinking organisms," how could anyone speak with assurance about an afterlife? And why should men and women subvert naked self-interest to an objective moral code if eternal reward is nothing but myth? Locke raised perplexing questions and in the end, failing to supply an answer to the mind-body conundrum, left his readers with a bewildering verdict: the inner nature of mind and body is forever hidden.[26]

At this point something should be added in connection with Locke's moral philosophy. Reason is capable of discerning a natural moral law and society's obligation is to make it binding. There is nothing arbitrary or subjective about a moral code produced by reason, and society should not be uncertain or equivocal in enforcing it. But authority and the power to enforce issuing from it cannot be depended upon to inculcate in persons a discipline to act morally with genuine affection for correct and responsible behavior. This is the work of education and Locke, we know, made moral formation education's primary objective.[27]

A pragmatist but not a relativist, Locke assigned to moral formation first place on a hierarchy of educational objectives because in all of life nothing is more important. Social, economic, and political behavior would be chaotic and unmanageable without an objective moral code. Ordinary moral knowledge obtained in the regular concourse of life—what might be called rules of conduct based upon convention and maintained because they work— is recognized as being useful—even necessary—but it is often uncertain, sometimes ephemeral, and frequently inexact, so ordinary moral knowledge is inadequate. Locke speaks of an eternally dependable system of morals with a scientific foundation, and he holds out the possibility of arriving at moral science.[28] Stopping there, and allowing that moral science must rest finally upon God's being,[29] he acknowledges the existence of a natural moral law and declares that it, too, must be observed.[30] Neither divine nor natural moral law is self-evident and neither can be understood and enforced without interpretation and codification. Their translation to a vocabulary for understanding and communication in and out of schools is work for reason.[31] In the end, then, despite the use of data which were jettisoned by positivistic empiricists a century later, Locke's empiricism remained intact. Reason alone, using the data available to it, is capable of defining reasonable and responsible boundaries for human behavior.

A review of Locke's empirical theory would be deficient without some attention to his rejection of the old doctrine of innate ideas. And in this rejection we detect an empiricism far less strident than anything promoted by contemporary pragmatists. His rejection of innate ideas and intuition is unequivocal, and he meant it to be, but a willingness to admit to the human ability of introspection or internal experience is evident too.

In *An Essay Concerning Human Understanding* Locke spends a great deal of time declaiming against innate ideas, and scholars have inquired against whom his rhetorical barrage was directed. The Scholastics and the Cartesians were once thought to be likely targets, although close examination might reveal that neither was guilty of clinging to a proposition that common sense appears to discredit. One should not forget, of course, that a long line of Platonic thought had made intuition respectable, but it is hard to believe that Locke had mustered the courage to mount an assault on Plato. More likely, and from Locke's perspective, pietism was the threat: woven into the fabric of Puritanism it appeared to contaminate both philosophy and religion. Ancient and in many religious circles respectable, pietism was associated with Augustine who, some interpreters declared, had suppressed reason and made it an abject handmaiden to belief. Anselm's (ca. 1033–1109) *credo ut intellegam* made the mind a beneficiary of a deposit of faith that is sufficient for persons as they make their march through life. Reason might be a useful helpmate to faith, but standing alone it is undependable and, what is worse, is potentially dangerous. Pietists and Puritans could promote an educational program that would enable persons to understand as much of their gift of faith as possible, so they were disposed to open schools and promote educational decency. But such activity, while it could organize, interpret, and disseminate truth, could never lead to its discovery, for truth's corpus is held securely within faith's original deposit.

Those sections in the *Essay* where innate ideas are discussed are written in a somewhat cumbersome style making a discernment of their meaning difficult. Locke complained of writers who used language imprecisely and he promised to redress this deficiency by resorting to a clear, simple, easily understood prose.[32] As it turned out, the promise was false, yet his flaw in composition was more a matter of inelegance than obscurity. Instinct is recognized as a subrational element affecting purely physical behavior and the senses are essential because they supply the mind with the raw material of experience.[33] Still, the mind is not a captive of sensory experience because it has the capacity for using sensory experience to construct general principles and arrive at knowledge not inherent in sensory experience. All learning, Locke maintained, is by discovery, and first principles and self-evident propositions come, if at all, from the froth and foam of experience. The principles of contradiction and identity, moreover, are learned.[34] The mind lacks any potential knowledge waiting to be actualized. Knowledge is always by discovery, not sometimes by discovery and sometimes by actualization. The origin of ideas is severely limited to sensory experience, and by ideas Locke means the immediate objects of perception and thought.

The senses convey perceptions to the mind, and how this occurs is a question that is left unanswered. It might be a physical or a psychological phenomenon, but whatever it is Locke leaves for others to decide. Yet as these perceptions enter the mind, they are what they were objectively.[35] Whether simple on complex, the mind is, nevertheless, capable of cultivating these perceptions in the fertile field of internal experience and converting them to something different from what they were upon entering the mind. The meaning of experience is generated by the mind's rational ability. This tempts us to return to a consideration of the status of Locke's empiricism. It appears to be implicit in the theory of tabula rasa, for which Locke has achieved enduring fame: the mind is originally a blank tablet whereupon nothing is written. Experience is the stylus that makes marks on the tablet, but these marks, once made can be sorted, melded, and manipulated by a power the mind only possesses. The mind can range far beyond the immediate products of sensory experience, although sensory experience shall always be the foundation for mental activity. Locke put it this way: "All those sublime thoughts which tower above the clouds, and reach as high as heaven itself, take their rise and footing here: in all the great extent wherein the mind wanders in those remote speculations it may seem to be elevated with, it stirs not one jot beyond those ideas which sense or reflections have offered for its contemplation."[36]

Putting empirical theory to work, Locke turns to a consideration of the next of the modern educational themes, one that fairly dominated educational philosophy for decades: utility. The *Essay* demonstrated Locke's supreme confidence in reason, so it is plausible to assume that somewhere he shall tell us how reason is to be cultivated. Our assumption is for the most part unrewarded, although it is impossible to find in *Some Thoughts Concerning Education*, or any of Locke's works, the slightest hint of anti-intellectualism. He begins by calling attention to the importance of physical development and good health, and then introduces moral formation. Intellectual development is clearly on his list ("I imagine you would think him a very foolish Fellow, that should not value a virtuous, or a wise Man, infinitely before a great Scholar"),[37] yet precedence goes neither to it nor to physical development but to moral formation:

> That which every Gentleman (that takes care of his education) desires for his Son, besides the estate he leaves him, is contain'd (I suppose) in these four things, *Virtue*, *Wisdom*, *Breeding*, and *Learning*. I will not trouble myself whether these Names do not some of them stand for the same Thing, or really include one another. It serves my Turn here to follow the popular Use of these Words, which, I presume, is clear enough to make me understood, and I hope there will be no Difficulty to comprehend my Meaning . . . . I place *Virtue* as the first and most necessary of these Endowments that belong to a Man or a Gentleman, as absolutely requisite to make him valued and beloved by others, acceptable or tolerable to himself. Without that, I think, he will be happy neither in this, nor in the other World.[38]

Natural virtue might, Locke supposed, be aided by maturation and abetted by reason, but virtue's genuine foundation, the place where moral formation has to begin, is with a "true notion of God." Children should be instructed in clear and simple language that God is the "independent Supreme

Being, Author and Maker of all Things, from who we receive all our Good, who loves us, and gives us all things: and, consequent to this, instil into him a Love and Reverence of this Supreme Being."[39] If Locke was a deist, one would either have to excise this statement from his repertoire or allege that he was guilty of dissemination. On the other hand, there is nothing in Locke's language to make us think that he was endorsing the doctrine of any religious denomination. Readers' attention, however, is directed to the efficacy of prayer for sustaining persons in their commitment to moral virtue.[40]

Utility might not at first seem to have a place in all of this, but Locke's position is that without virtue neither wisdom nor good breeding (civility) is likely. Both are essential if persons are to live successful, satisfying, and productive lives. Utility's dimensions are broad enough to complement the most comprehensive interpretation of use. In any case, Locke's definition of utility is never one of narrow pragmatism. Yet it is in his discussion of learning that an idealization of utility becomes most apparent.

The brand of education with which Locke was most familiar—he himself was nurtured by it—was humanistic, with attention being given mainly to study of ancient languages. Without condemning a humanistic syllabus, he, nevertheless, deplores the conventional preoccupation with it, because, in concentrating upon the study of language, it wastes valuable time and, for most persons, lacks relevance. Still, even here, his aversion to language study was far from total: persons who anticipate using ancient languages for a career in scholarship are encouraged to study them. But the preparation of scholars was low on Locke's schedule of priority. He took the education of gentlemen as his thesis, and here he finds it important to return to those studies that shall be of most use to them. Reading, writing (in English), and drawing should precede foreign-language study (most likely French). But whatever the language, although French would have precedence because of its currency among gentlemen in business, in social intercourse, and in affairs of state, it should be learned the same way native Frenchmen learned to speak it.[41] After mastering French—Locke is no more precise about its timing than this—Latin should be studied because it is essential for gentlemen, although, again, emphasis is put upon its oral use. Only a foolish schoolmaster would introduce the rules of grammar.[42] So, while Locke gives the impression that he is unfriendly to the study of language, he, nevertheless, finds room for it because he considers it useful for gentlemen, and nowhere do we find him shaping a program of study for anyone outside this social category.

A scholastic practice with roots buried deeply in a distant past prescribed age seven as the proper age for schooling to begin. The Greeks accepted this dogma without question and the Romans were eager, save for Quintilian, to follow suit. Christian and humanist educational practice found no fault with this tradition, and neither did any of Locke's contemporaries. He, however, was quick to abandon it: school instruction should begin with reading, and children are usually ready to read when they can talk.[43] What should be read? In *Some Thoughts* we are given a bibliography that need not be repeated here.[44] It contains selections, such as *Aesop's Fables*, that are easy and pleasant. Reading is followed by religious instruction: the Lord's Prayer, the Creed, and the Ten Commandments are first on the list and should be memorized.[45] Then comes the Bible. Its whole might overwhelm students, so small portions are recommended.[46] Locke's heed for prayer and Bible reading should absolve him from an indictment for apostasy.

Writing succeeds reading and religious instruction, and detail pertaining to the mechanics of good writing is abundant. Careless about what children write, he is solicitous about the process, going so far as to instruct students in the correct way to hold their pens.[47] Drawing comes next and is followed by instruction in French and Latin. The foregoing are the fundamentals, and with them in place children are ready for instruction in arithmetic, geography, astronomy, chronology, anatomy, history and, finally, something Locke calls "general knowledge."[48] The elementary- and secondary-school course of study is complete, but for some students there might be more.

Earlier in *Some Thoughts* Locke had dismissed grammar. Now he wants to return to it to clarify his thought and retrieve parts of the subject that he had appeared to jettison. Grammatical study, he says, should not be eliminated from all schools, but care should be exercised in deciding who should pursue it.[49] It should be studied only by mature men, and then usually only by scholars. Scholars have, of course, a special need for grammatical skill, but others for whom writing and speaking with precision is important are right to invest time to perfect it. For most English gentlemen, however, the study of grammar is unnecessary. They should, though, give some attention to law, because of its evident utility. The gentleman's education is capped with dancing, music, fencing, riding, and this comes as a surprise, learning a trade.[50] Locke himself was enamored of painting, but it is not prescribed, and country gentlemen are counseled to learn some of husbandry's secrets.[51] Finally, and after the tender years of youth, travel, especially on the Continent, is recommended as the best way to complete the formation of a gentleman.[52] So much is Locke's commitment to utility and, while it is short of what many of his successors wanted, it set in place a respectable philosophical stanchion for an educational program that respects only those studies whose practical application can be demonstrated.

Whether Locke's tabula rasa is an accurate description of the mind is a point whereupon sober scholars can disagree, but this much seems evident: it expressed an interpretation of human nature that was bound to cultivate a yearning for equality. One might notice, too, that such a declaration held out a prospect for a developmental psychology that without it might have been a long time in articulation. Important as tabula rasa might have been for the field of psychology, its status there was dwarfed by its implications for politics, first, and then education. Men and women begin the race of life from the same place; no one has an advantage. There are, however, and this is a side that merits special notice, differences among persons in their capacity to have experience and profit from it.

This theory, we know, affected both political philosophy and practical politics, and its impact on education, while deferred in implementation, was destined to alter the face of modern educational theory. If men and women are what their experience makes them, as tabula rasa implies, it is hardly possible for good and decent societies to ignore provision for educational opportunity, and not just for some, as old dogma recommended, but for all who could profit from it. Unsurprisingly, philosophers began to assess the meaning of social, political, and educational equality. Eventually theories were pronounced containing principles whereupon equality might stand.

Left unsettled, and still in dispute, was the issue of how indelible is the capacity to profit from experience? If capacity is fixed and unalterable by experience, the role of nurture, while important, is nevertheless limited. But if capacity can be affected for good or ill by nurture, the story has a different ending. It might be extravagant to maintain that Locke was responsible for the nature-nurture, the heredity-environment debate that has preoccupied social philosophers, psychologist, and educators for decades. But he raised the issue in such a way that it could no longer be ignored. Clearly, but without ignoring heredity, Locke elevated nurture to a position it had not formerly occupied. Yet either his disposition or his affection for convention seems to have kept him from expressing the obvious educational implications of tabula rasa. Until the end, Locke remained friendly to class privilege in education and idealized private schools while all but dismissing the need the general population has for decent schooling, supported by public resource, to advance the individual and common good. Either myopic or arrogant in connection with the practical effect of tabula rasa, Locke nevertheless made an investment in a theory of equality that was capitalized by his successors who made it pay a permanent dividend in politics and education.

In spite of Locke's stature in politics and education, his command of the field of educational philosophy was incomplete, and his audience, while large and influential, seldom marched in step. Stiff competition came sometime from other educational perspectives, and we know now that much of it was generated by Jean Jacques Rousseau (1712–1778) and, to a lesser extent, by Johann Heinrich Pestalozzi (1746–1827), both of whom distrusted reason as life's best guide and downgraded its development as an important educational objective. In their reforming, or revolutionary, creed, intellectual and moral education were made to surrender to natural education. Both began their invasion of the enigmatic field of educational theory by jettisoning conventional pedagogical practice and by abandoning the educational propositions of their predecessors. Sweeping condemnation of past instructional practice and accepted educational theory, coupled with the natural tendency of teachers to prefer the familiar, had the effect of minimizing the practical influence of their manifestos.

Rousseau and Pestalozzi were probably right when they said schooling missed its mark either, as in Rousseau's case, that it concentrated on giving upper-class children artificial accomplishments or, as in Pestalozzi's, that it either ignored children of the poor or if attending to them paid little attention to cultivating their talent.[53] It is easy to recite the flaws in seventeenth- and eighteenth-century schooling: few teachers were equipped to conduct classrooms and many were not themselves decently educated; materials of instruction were crude because textbook writers either had not heard or ignored Comenius's advice; pedagogic technique paid scant heed to learning's principle of activity or the need students have for seeing meaning in a curriculum that, despite attack upon it, still catered to instruction in Latin and conversance with the classics. It can be debated how directly either of these expositors for natural education dealt with the flaws, but it is interesting nevertheless to plumb the substance of their sometimes strident declarations.

Of the two, Rousseau is the far more provocative and, most scholars agree, the more influential in and out of educational circles. No student of politics, philosophy, or sociology finds much substance in Pestalozzi; Rousseau, on the other hand, is almost certain to come to their attention. Some of this attention, it would seem, is generated in his personality, unconventional demeanor, and revolutionary spirit. His writing illustrates, at least, a flirtation with anarchy. His purpose was either to remake or to destroy contemporary society. Besides, his aversion to conventional schooling was strong enough to prompt him to write this audacious prescription for education: "The usual education of children is such as if children leaped, at one bound, from the mother's breast to the age of reason[54] [and] . . . . Do the opposite of what is usually done and you will almost always be right."[55]

Together Rousseau and Pestalozzi gave priority to natural education. They must have meant that educational programs (both the practice and content of instruction) should accommodate to natural processes, but even the most cordial assessment of this proposition must admit to its imprecision. In almost any circumstance, it is hard to believe that educational activity can be unnatural. So we are left to decide when their statements should be read literally. It is possible, of course, that hyperbole was conscripted to solicit notice. Neither, it would seem, really meant to leave children, unattended by teachers, parents, or guardians, to fend for themselves in gardens and forests, although both were enthusiastic about the range of experience children might have when they were allowed, without intermediaries, to communicate directly with the environment. Perhaps Rousseau's "do nothing and let nothing be done"[56] should not be taken at face value. He was writing about the first years of children's development and wanted to spare them the agony of the schoolmaster's regimen before they were ready for it. Yet it is hard to ignore the fact that he was ready to give all traditional pedagogic practice a thorough housecleaning. What would replace it? If in Rousseau an answer can be found to this question, the indictment for educational anarchy might be quashed.

Students of Rousseau have often maintained that he gave all the wrong answers to all the right questions. Robert Ulich, an educational historian and philosopher with good credentials for rendering a judgment, wrote that "it would be difficult to find a man in the history of thought who with so much half-truth has made as deep an impression on mankind as Rousseau."[57] This verdict might be too harsh. If all the questions were right, an interesting but likely untenable assertion, he is being given credit for too much insight into education and its conundrums, and if all the answers were wrong, it must be that the easy solution he offered for the nurture of youth is read too literally. The place to begin is with his elaboration of the meaning of natural education. All persons have a natural capacity which can be actualized for good or ill, but this capacity cannot be expanded or shrunk.

Capacity, Rousseau declared, must be used as a map to be followed— although who draws this map and guarantees its accuracy is a loose end— and those who are responsible for the care of children must be careful not to lead them down roads they are too weak to travel. He seems to say, and has been interpreted to mean, that nothing but a laissez-faire instructional program can unearth the treasure in human capacity, but his meaning must have been more subtle than this. In any case, while he recognized that contemporary society abhorred the idea of a noble savage, he knew, too, that even with its inherent defects an educational program of some kind is essential. Conventional education is not abandoned peremptorily: "Things would be worse without this education . . . . Under existing conditions a man left to himself from birth would be more a monster than the rest."[58]

Society, moreover, is full of pitfalls that are likely to be destructive if persons are not immunized from them. Immunization from prejudice and convention, from every perverse social influence, comes, if it comes at all, when children are given the chance to follow their natural inclinations. So this natural and often negative education protects children from a society from which there is no escape. Natural education, Rousseau avers, forms habits and builds character that stand as trustworthy safeguards for everyone exposed to the hazards of life in society. Rousseau designed an educational program for Emile that was intended to equip him to live according to the "order of nature," an order, Rousseau conceded, established by divine will. Exhibiting an affinity for deism, Rousseau acknowledged the laws of nature to be immutable and seems to imply that a failure to observe them will lead inevitably to personal disaster. Throughout *Emile* (published in 1761) the conflict between the good of persons and their social environment is displayed. While this conflict cannot be eliminated entirely, it is Rousseau's best advice that it can be ameliorated by preparing persons for life in society by ostracizing them from society.[59]

Pestalozzi might have recognized the conflict which so preoccupied Rousseau, but if he did he neither mentions it nor employs it to support his educational principles. His urge to reject was less intense than Rousseau's: nothing is said about abandoning society and no praise is heaped upon the noble savage. Social institutions were spared scorn and schools were bathed in the bright light of optimism. Rousseau's exaggerated fear of schools was replaced by Pestalozzi's confidence that if their curricula and methods were sound, they could equip men and women for productive, satisfying, and happy lives. Yet, for all his confidence in schooling as a social and economic panacea, his chief assignment to education, and it was Rousseau's as well, was to undertake the formation of persons of good and decent character. Lessons taught by the old-fashioned humanists had been mastered: all together, Rousseau, Pestalozzi, Comenius, Locke, and Erasmus agreed that education's fundamental mission is the formation of character. This mission had the effect of discounting somewhat the role of teachers as schoolmistresses or -masters, hearers of lessons, and elevating them to the level of genuine educators. It was hardly possible to be satisfied with teachers and tutors who were qualified only to teach reading, writing, and Latin. Teachers themselves were expected to be persons of unimpeachable character with an ability to lead their students to moral virtue. A demanding charge, no doubt, and one, the record seems to tell us, not so commonly met. Besides, a vexing issue remained unresolved: How should teachers be prepared for this weighty responsibility and where were they to be found? Surely it is easier to recruit a hearer of lessons than to find teachers capable of directing students toward the "one science for children to learn—the duties of man."[60]

Johann Friedrich Herbart (1776–1841) was confident that he had the answer: scientific pedagogy. Herbart's position as professor of philosophy at the University of Königsberg and his ornamental intellectual accomplishments equipped him handsomely to cultivate the field of educational theory. Yet with special affinity for teaching (he had the reputation for being the university's finest lecturer), it is perhaps natural that he riveted attention upon teaching method. In the end, he offered educational advice that was filled with directions to teachers for achieving the proper goals of instruction. It would be unfair to say that Herbart ignored students, but it is nevertheless evident that his successors were left to ponder the psychological and pedagogical questions posed from the other side of the teacher's desk. His preoccupation with the work of teachers, and with teaching theory, is illustrated early in *The Science of Education*:

> The aim of all those who educate and demand education is determined by the range of thought they bring to the subject. The majority of those who teach have entirely neglected in the first instance to construct for themselves their own range of thought in view of this work; it opens out gradually as the work progresses, and is formed partly by their own characteristics, partly by the individuality and the environment of the pupil.[61]

If we understand Herbart, teachers are accused of paying scant heed to the fundamental dimensions of their role as agents in the learning process before they begin to teach. Only while they are engaged in what must under any circumstance be critically important to students, do they begin to assess the principles that should guide them. Shaping and reshaping theory as one goes along is not good enough to satisfy the exigent Herbart. He is not, it is evident, presuming that educational theory has lacked cultivation under the husbandry of good scholars. He often recites the names of Locke, Rousseau, and Pestalozzi, near contemporaries, and of the giants in educational philosophy who preceded them. So the point of his assertion is not that theory is or has been ignored; it is that theory exists in a vacuum and neither affects the minds of teachers nor the methods they employ. Antiseptic theory would not do, Herbart declared, because education is a practical, not a speculative, enterprise. Teachers need to command dependable knowledge about instructional goals and methods before they enter their classrooms. Time, of course, but, and more important, human talent wastes away while teachers engage in trial and error.

To redress a major flaw in the process of instruction—that is, indifference to the philosophy of teaching—Herbart established a school for teachers at Königsberg and conducted it while pursuing the regular duties of his professorship. His assertion that "education cannot merely be taught; it must be demonstrated and practiced" should be recognized as a principal plank in his theory. The school, or seminar, for the preparation of teachers began modestly, with Herbart recruiting a few promising students from his lecture class on educational theory and taking them to a *Gymnasium* (a secondary school) where he gave demonstration lessons and confirmed his position that theory and practice should be complementary. After students had mastered Herbart's instructional theory and technique, they were assigned classes of their own, with Herbart at hand to supervise their work. Step by step these student-teachers were prepared by a combination of pedagogical principle and active experience in the classroom. The art and science essential to their success as teachers were perfected by mutual observation and exchange of experience. This teachers' seminar enjoyed enough success to become a college for the preparation of teachers, and teachers prepared in it became the ornaments of a German secondary-school teaching corps. Yet when Herbart left Königsberg for Göttingen the school for teachers closed, and for reasons now unclear he demurred from starting one at Göttingen.[62]

To attribute genuine novelty to Herbart's assertion—"The one and the whole work of education may be summed up in the concept—Morality"[63]—we should have to ignore much in educational philosophy's history. Locke and Comenius before him left little doubt about the location of education's genuine treasure. And this is to say nothing about Socrates who, after several false starts, took the position that knowledge either is or leads to virtue, and Quintilian's definition of education's goal as "a good man skilled in speaking." It neglects Erasmus and all other humanists as well, who never tired of setting good character at the pinnacle of educational accomplishment. Herbart, then, was the beneficiary of a cultural and educational doctrine that put moral virtue on the top rung of the educational ladder.

Embracing tradition could not make Herbart's commitment to reshaping educational policy easy: to have settled for the acquisition of knowledge as the proper end for education would have been much simpler, for it is unquestionably more difficult to structure an instructional plan capable of bearing the weight of character formation than of informing the mind. But Herbart found little satisfaction in proposing an educational theory that assigned pride of place to mental cultivation. Along with many illustrious predecessors he acknowledged that intellectual acumen without the stabilizing influence of moral conviction might be dangerous. Yet the trained intelligence was heralded as a dependable rudder for morality, although Herbart stopped short of declaring that right knowledge leads to correct behavior. Sound instruction was, nevertheless, imperative. The instructional role of the school occupied a middle ground between pupils' self-activity and the moral molding that comes from mastering the content of a curriculum. His assertion is both clear and ringing: "man's worth does not, it is true, lie in his knowing, but in his willing." And then he adds: "There is no such thing as an independent faculty of will. Volition has its roots in thought; not, indeed, in the details one knows, but certainly in the combinations and the total effect of the acquired ideas."[64] His intention evidently was to impress upon his readers the fault in formulas for educational practice that neglects a theory of teaching where incitement to mental activity rather than a command of all things worth knowing is the legitimate goal.

Herbart wants educators to know from the outset the kinds of mental activity that should be promoted, and he wants them, too, to be capable of making prudent choices from various types of generative instruction. Such knowledge is clearly philosophical, and if it is to be coherent and consistent, it must have as its starting point a mature conception of the nature of persons and end with an ethical and psychological code explaining what they are capable of becoming. Without such knowledge at their disposal, educators are almost certain to fail in designing and conducting a program of education.[65] In *The Science of Education* he asks this question and then answers it: "Can we know beforehand the aims of the future man, a knowledge for which he will one day thank us, instead of having to find and follow them by himself alone?"[66] We can, he wrote, otherwise it would be futile to spend time trying to mount and maintain schools.

Yet, it should not be thought a simple matter to state educational purpose with clarity. And, moreover, one would be guilty of wishful thinking to suppose that once these aims are stated, they will command universal assent. Children have a variety of interests, all distilled mysteriously from their early nurture, and these interests are multiplied by their experience in and out of school. With an unshakeable conviction that morality is education's ultimate goal, Herbart concedes that subordinate goals stand as conditions for moral formation: "I therefore believe that the mode of consideration which places morality at the head is certainly the most important, but not the only and comprehensive, standpoint of education."[67]

Proof for this assertion, although possible to muster, would require, Herbart admitted, more space than *The Science of Education* could afford. In any case he thought the proof had been supplied earlier in "A B C of Observation."[68] Still, although he thought the proof sufficient, Herbart implied that universal adherence to any one system of philosophy was too much to hope for and declared that "education has no time to make holiday now, till philosophical questions are once and for all cleared up. Rather it is to be desired that pedagogy shall be kept as free as possible from philosophical doubts."[69] So, if common ground in philosophy (he meant ethics) is unlikely, and if education is to be spared from marking time while philosophical wrinkles are smoothed, a substitute shall have to be found to supply the bedrock whereupon educational practice can stand. Herbart turned to psychology for the light it could shed on the way children think and act to unearth the major ideas or values which constitute moral life. He then made it instruction's responsibility to integrate them with the whole of schooling so that in the end they could become trustworthy guides to life. Ethical standard, Herbart averred, begins with basic feelings about harmony and pleasure, discord and displeasure. But in their original state these feelings are often unclear and confused, and they will remain so unless the work of instruction is able to refine them. They need translation to educational objectives that in the hands of good schoolmasters can be converted from an antiseptic objective set of moral principles to a subjectively compatible moral code which persons will embrace and according to which they will live. Herbart is ready to introduce the major ideas. There are five.

A hierarchy is neither stated nor implied, so there is no way of knowing if Herbart intended one. In any case, he begins with the idea of inner freedom. "Inner freedom," he wrote, "is a relation between insight and volition." It is the teacher's duty to make "actual each of these factors separately, in order that later a permanent relationship may result."[70] This is a somewhat roundabout expression of two points: one, that persons come to recognize freedom on the basis of internal experience; and two, that they have the experience of choosing. Yet it is apparent that without knowledge, without an ability to assess the worth of alternative courses of action, one choice could hardly be credited with more worth than another. How can a person know when choice is praiseworthy or base? A code of right conduct, a dependable moral philosophy must be taught, otherwise there is little point in talking about, or hoping for, any moral standard in society. Sound instruction is the only way to ensure immunity from moral nihilism.

The idea of perfection or efficiency is next, and is followed by the idea of benevolence. Perfection (or efficiency) is a matter of strength of will and is characterized by intensity, concentration, and extension. Intensity and concentration are natural endowments, largely unaffected by instruction. But extension, shaped by information, is a determination to do always what ought to be done. However resolute the will might be, it cannot engage meritorious choice without dependable ethical knowledge. Still, there remains the possibility of a strong but bad will, a possibility of which Herbart is entirely aware.[71] Benevolence is mainly an outcome of instruction in ethics and of understanding different levels of the good, especially in connection with discriminating between the individual and the common good. The outcome of this kind of instruction is a disposition to choose habitually the good that, while serving the interest of the individual, does not impair the good of others. Herbart knows that direct moral instruction—the communication of a positive moral code—will not ensure ethical behavior. Nevertheless, he is at pains to underline his conviction that in the last analysis the will is a blind faculty, like a locomotive without an engineer.

Justice and equity complete the list of the major moral ideas. The foundation of justice is absolute, built apparently upon natural law, but the meaning of justice, or better, its application, depends upon an anthropology of time and place. Herbart rejects relativism. His conception of justice is analogous to the administration of civil law: law's principles are firmly fixed in the nature of persons and society, but an application of the principles that might have satisfied, say fifth-century Rome, would have been pointless and futile for eighteenth-century Germany.

Instruction need not tackle a definition of justice or engage in interpretations of it. Yet the general idea of justice and the social necessity of recognizing, protecting, and preserving it must constitute an essential part of schooling. Equity is an idea that confirms the worth of just behavior, makes virtue practical, and displays the benefit that accrues from moral rectitude and intellectual honesty. Equity contains assurance that virtue shall be rewarded and vice punished.

These five moral ideas are, Herbart assures us, fundamental. Moreover, they are essential elements in the business of instruction. Attending to them, educators can be confident of their compliance with Herbart's declaration that morality is the chief object of education.

When Herbart's work on educational theory was over, it had graduated from a codification of expressions by philosophers and scholars, and from the recommendations of social and religious reformers, to a body of ethical and psychological knowledge confident of its doctrines with respect to educational policy and practice. Pedagogy had come of age and a theory or philosophy of education matured with it. Herbart's disciples helped educational doctrine cross the Atlantic and energetic Americans began to till the soil wherefrom educational philosophy could spring.

These pioneers in the vineyard of theory were too wise to miss the groundbreakers who preceded them. They paid attention mainly to a theoretical tradition consisting of the literary and Christian humanism of Erasmus and the social realism and rationalism of John Locke. There were others, of course, and we have observed them at work: all together they tried to design of program of education that, inspired by morality, piety, reason, and a vigorous religious legacy, would contribute to the general welfare of the citizens of this good land. The story forms the substance of the following chapter and begins almost with the founding of the Republic.

NOTES

1. Petrarch's opinion of the work of teachers was especially low and this, one must say, is surprising, because he put such high value on the outcome of learning. Paul F. Grendler, *Schooling in Renaissance Italy: Literacy and Learning, 1300–1600* (Baltimore and London: Johns Hopkins University Press, 1989), 3, supplies an example.

2. Desiderius Erasmus, *On the Method of Study (De ratione studii ac legendi interpretandique auctores)* in *Literary and Educational Writings*, edited by Craig R. Thompson, translated and annotated by Brian McGregor (Toronto: University of Toronto Press, 1978), 24: 662–91.

3. Among the most prominent were: Guarino of Verona, Giacopo di Scarparia, Roberto Rossi, Niccolo Niccoli, Leonardo Bruni, Carlo Marsuppini, Ambrogio Traversari, Vergerio, Uberto Decembrio, and Poggio (R.R. Bolgar, *The Classical Heritage and Its Beneficiaries* (Cambridge, Eng.: University Press, 1954), 403).

4. What follows is based on Bolgar's summary in *The Classical Heritage* of Guarino's letter, pp. 87–88, in Remiggio Sabbadini, *Epistolario di Guarino Veronese* (Venice, 1916), 2: 269ff.

5. Erasmus, *De Ratione Studii*, in William H. Woodward, *Desiderius Erasmus Concerning the Aim and Method of Education* (Cambridge: Cambridge University Press, 1904; New York: Teachers College Press, 1964), 164.

6. John B. Gleason, *John Colet* (Berkeley and Los Angeles: University of California Press, 1989), 229.

7. Erasmus, *Copia: Foundation of the Abundant Style (De duplici copia verborum ac rerum commentarii duo)* in *Literary and Educational Writings*, edited by Craig R. Thompson, translated and annotated by Betty I. Knott (Toronto: University of Toronto Press, 1978), 24: 280–659.

8. The title of the 1887 reprint of Seebohm's book is *The Oxford Reformers John Colet, Erasmus, and Thomas More: Being a History of Their Fellow-Work* (London, 1887).

9. London: Methuen, 1916; New York: Barnes & Noble, 1969.

10. Kingston, Ont.: McGill-Queen's University Press, 1989.

11. Gleason, *John Colet*, 230.

12. Joseph H. Lupton, *The Influence of Dean Colet upon the Reformation of the English Church* (London and Cambridge, 1893), and quoted in Gleason, *John Colet*, 226.

13. Nicholas Murray Butler, *The Place of Comenius in the History of Educa-*

tion (Syracuse, N.Y.: C.W. Bardeen, 1892), 4.

14. John Amos Comenius, *The Analytical Didactic*, translated from the Latin with introduction and notes by Vladimir Jelinek (Chicago: University of Chicago Press, 1953), 6.

15. R. Freeman Butts, *A Cultural History of Education* (New York: McGraw-Hill, 1947), 257.

16. John W. Adamson, *Pioneers of Modern Education: 1600–1700* (Cambridge: Cambridge University Press, 1905; New York: Teachers College Press, 1972), 64.

17. Will S. Monroe, *Comenius and the Beginning of Educational Reform* (New York: Charles Scribner's Sons, 1900), 28–37; and John E. Sadler, *J. A. Comenius and the Concept of Universal Education* (New York: Barnes & Noble, 1966), 54.

18. John Amos Comenius, *Comenius*, translated by M. W. Keatinge (New York: McGraw-Hill, 1931), 23. This book is a reprint in shortened form of Comenius's *The Great Didactic*, translated by M.W. Keatinge (London: Adam and Charles Black, 1896).

19. Comenius, *The Great Didactic*, 166.

20. Monroe, *Comenius*, 64–69; Sadler, *J.A. Comenius*, 229–33.

21. Quoted in S. S. Laurie, *John Amos Comenius, Bishop of the Moravians: His Life and Educational Works* (Cambridge: At the University Press, 1884), 201.

22. Comenius, *The Great Didactic*, 418.

23. Comenius, *The School of Infancy*, edited by Ernest M. Eller (Chapel Hill: University of North Carolina Press, 1956), 70–75.

24. John Locke, *An Essay Concerning Human Understanding*, edited with a foreword by Peter H. Nidditch (Oxford: Clarendon Press, 1979), II, xxiii, 15.

25. Ibid., IV, iii, 6.

26. Ibid.

27. John Locke, *Some Thoughts Concerning Education*, edited with introduction, notes, and critical apparatus by John W. Yolton and Jean S. Yolton (New York: Oxford University Press, 1989), pars. 18–23, 135, 195.

28. Locke, *Essay*, IV, iii, 18.

29. Ibid., I, iii, 12.

30. Ibid., I, iii, 13.

31. Ibid., II, xxi, 49.

32. Ibid., "Epistle to the Reader," xii.

33. Ibid., II, I, 3–4.

34. Ibid., I, ii, 4; I, iv, 4.

35. Ibid., II, vii–x.

36. Ibid., II, i, 24.

37. Locke, *Some Thoughts*, par. 147.

38. Ibid., pars. 134 and 135.

39. Ibid., par. 136.

40. Ibid., par. 139.

41. Ibid., par. 162.

42. Ibid., pars. 163–65.

43. Ibid., par. 148.

44. Ibid., pars. 148–59.

45. Ibid., par. 157.

46. Ibid., par. 158.

47. Ibid., par. 160.

48. Ibid., pars. 179–94.

49. Ibid., par. 168, 1–3.

50. Ibid., par. 201.

51. Ibid., par. 204.

52. Ibid., par. 212.

53. Jean Jacques Rousseau, *Emile*, translated by Barbara Foxley (New York: E.P. Dutton, 1911, 1938), 43–45; and J.H. Pestalozzi, *Leonard and Gertrude*, "Preface to the Second Edition," in Henry Barnard, *Pestalozzi and Pestalozzianism*, edited by Henry Barnard (Syracuse, N.Y.: C.W. Bardeen, 1874), 523.

54. Rousseau, *Emile*, 133.

55. Ibid., 57.

56. Ibid., 58.

57. Robert Ulich, *History of Educational Thought* (New York: American Book Company, 1945, 1950, 1968), 211.

58. Rousseau, *Emile*, 5.

59. Ibid., 9.

60. Ibid., 19.

61. J.F. Herbart, *The Science of Education: Its General Principles Deduced from Its Aim*, translated by H.M. Felkin and E. Felkin (London: Swan Sonnenshein, 1892; Washington, D.C.: University Publications of America, 1977), 78.

62. H.B. Dunkel, "Herbart's Pedagogical Seminar," *History of Education Quarterly* 7 (Spring 1967), 93–101, speculates about Herbart's decision not to continue it at Göttingen.

63. J.F. Herbart, *On the Aesthetic Revelation of the World as the Chief Work of Education*, translated by H.M. Felkin and E. Felkin (London: Swan Sonnenshein, 1892), 57.

64. J.F. Herbart, *Outlines of Educational Doctrine*, translated by A.F. Lange (New York: Macmillan, 1901; Folcroft, Penn.: Folcroft Library Editions, 1977), par. 58.

65. Herbart, *Aesthetic Revelation of the World*, 59.

66. Herbart, *The Science of Education*, 106–7.

67. Ibid., 108.

68. In J.F. Herbart, *A B C of Sense Perception and Minor Pedagogical Works*, translated by W.J. Echoff (New York: D. Appleton, 1903).

69. Herbart, *The Science of Education*, 108.

70. Herbart, *Outlines of Educational Doctrine*, par. 8.

71. Herbart, *The Science of Education*, 110–11.

CHAPTER 4

PHILOSOPHY AND EDUCATION IN EARLY AMERICA

In the preceding chapters many antecedents to American educational philosophy have been illustrated. How this inheritance was used when our ancestors undertook to articulate an educational philosophy for shaping the character of schooling in this good land is a matter for attention now.

As a preliminary it should be noted that in popular parlance the word *education* is usually taken to mean school instruction. Our colonial forebears, though, paying heed to classical connotation, supposed education to be a process for introducing children to life's realities: first and foremost its dimension was moral and religious, to which might be added literary elements and vocational or professional skill. Much like the Romans of antiquity, who associated education with the whole of life and used the word *erudition* to designate literary instruction and cultural formation, colonial educational writers never narrowed education's meaning to school instruction. Thus, the scope of an educational philosophy that appears on the first pages of American educational history is almost too broad to fit between the covers of a standard twentieth-century discourse on educational philosophy. Such treatises that belong to educational philosophy were more theories about life and personal formation than manuals on how to mount and maintain programs of school instruction. They would not have contained much technical pedagogical information beneficial to anyone disposed to consult them. That most pronouncements on education were so broadly gauged might explain why their readers who wanted something more practical liked Francis Bacon's (1561–1626) book, *The Advancement of Learning*.

From the years of colonization until nearly the end of the eighteenth century, speculative philosophy, the kind of inquiry perfected by Plato and Aristotle, and cultivated by their successors, was never a preoccupation with American intellectuals. The curricula of early colleges illustrate the common belief that moral formation needs help from a substantial intellectual foundation, so courses in moral philosophy, almost always taught by a clerical college president, were offered. Yet these courses evidenced theological and religious perspective more than commitment to strictly reasoned philosophical inquiry, and in all this natural philosophy was severely neglected until after the first quarter of the nineteenth century. With genuine philosophy undernourished, it is hardly surprising that its special branches, so much tilled later, should have been given little or no attention. Logic, rhetoric, and some form of literary and linguistic criticism were staples in the curriculum, and might have contained a philosophical component. At rare times and in special places, metaphysics and natural theology were taught, usually because the college president or a professor had an interest in them.

About two decades into the nineteenth century American scholars began to redefine the dimensions of the college course of study and, due likely to influence from Europe, to alter their assessment of philosophy. Instead of clinging to the old paradigm that classified philosophical study and inquiry into natural and moral, they abandoned natural philosophy, or better, allowed it to secede to the husbandry of the fledgling natural sciences, and proposed a new philosophical pattern that was called mental philosophy. Mental philosophy had two parts, intellectual and moral. Although usually approached independently, unavoidably they shared much common ground and proceeded from the same basic assumptions. Almost at once, and to supply textual material for the courses this revision generated, "a flood of American texts appeared."[1]

Before this occurred, however, our colonial ancestors had time and again demonstrated their interest in a decent education for their children. When not distracted by practical questions of providing schoolhouses, teachers, textual, and other materials of instruction, they looked for substantial theoretical bases to support the enterprise of learning. Francis Bacon seems to have captivated them and they paid special heed to his book, *On the Dignity and Advancement of Learning* (styled in later editions as simply *The Advancement of Learning*), which had appeared in 1605 along with *Novum Organum* as part of *The Great Instauration*.

Bacon expected his work to lead a crusade revolutionizing epistemology by demonstrating that what is represented as knowledge is hardly more than a digest of ancient supposition, with little or no relationship to reality. Science is especially victimized, he declared, because ideas whose validity is dogmatically assumed block the employment of methods of inquiry capable of ensuring the advancement of knowledge.[2] Aristotle was indicted for obscurantism in science, because, as a firm friend of deductive reasoning, his syllogisms had paralyzed curiosity and intimidated discovery.[3] Surrounded by error and inundated by worthless belief, men and women ignored the world of nature, from which by employing the right method of investigation they might garner knowledge of solid substance that could free them from false worship and liberate them from a vast accumulation of worthless and dangerous habit, or idols.

Had colonists understood Bacon's explicit purpose, they might have demurred from much, if not all, in his assertion. Safe to say, the voice of nature seldom excited them, for the cosmology they had adopted regarded physical reality as God's clockwork. Nature's light might illuminate something of the mechanical character of God's providence, but in investing in a search for truth they were certain that divine light rather than nature's light would reveal God's plan and purpose. It is by no means clear that they were ready to ride Bacon's empirical and naturalistic bandwagon or even that they understood the subtle quality of its cosmological and epistemological load.

Heeding this reservation, the inquiry is nevertheless pertinent: What did they learn from perusing *The Advancement of Learning*? Before opening the book, they knew that Bacon was a man of superior intelligence and sharp wit with a solid reputation in law, politics, science, and philosophy. They could not have been entirely confident about his religious deportment— he was neither a Puritan nor a papist—but there is plenty of evidence in the book to show he put a high premium upon the lessons of scripture and the promise of empirical method. Line after line of this famous book attests to his knowledge of holy writ. Yet what likely caught their attention most was his ability to demonstrate that neither a quest for erudition nor erudition itself was an impediment to civility and piety. Our colonial ancestors, especially those from the codfish colonies, were tormented by the same dilemma of knowledge vis-à-vis piety (education and faith) that had troubled so many early Christians. Church fathers and others were sometimes successful in resolving the dilemma, or at least finding a manageable compromise, but doubt lingered on and the question of whether learning was a dangerous thing, capable of warping faith, awaited still a final answer.

Bacon warned his readers that certain kinds of knowledge could be dangerous and would have to be shunned, but prudent, religiously dependable scholars could sift through the corpus of learning and winnow the bad from the good. They could discern and discard the shackle of past mistake that had for so long interdicted the wisdom contained in the books of ancient authorities. The indispensable instrument for accomplishing what turned out to be a monumental task was a new method of interpretation, a new brand of logic, and with this new method at their disposal scholars could redress the undependability of traditional science and philosophy. If knowledge were put in direct competition with religious piety, the former was sure to lose. Yet, colonial religious writers came close to making a career out of proving that religion and learning were not necessarily hostile and that a profession of faith was not an affirmation of ignorance. What Bacon wrote ratified their thesis when he undertook to demonstrate how the errors of the past could be corrected and how learning could be advanced without sacrificing faith, piety, and civility. With this warrant, little wonder that the colonists who wanted assurance, who wanted to have a sound foundation for educational policy, were captivated by Lord Bacon.

The general introduction to *The Great Instauration* contained assertions that colonial readers might have endorsed, although here and there Bacon must have disappointed them. The foundations of grammar and logic with which they were familiar and which they were tempted to embrace came from Aristotle. Still, they harbored suspicion that Aristotelian philosophy was unfriendly to their brand of religious orthodoxy. They counted Bacon's warning sound: "And as to the point of usefulness, the philosophy we principally received from the Greeks must be acknowledged puerile, or rather talkative than generative—as being fruitful in controversies, but barren in effects."[4] Yet Bacon stopped short of discrediting the whole of the literary and philosophical legacy and went out of his way to compliment the best of the antique authors while rejecting the worth of commentary on them: "The intellectual sciences . . . sometimes appear most perfect in the original author, and afterward degenerate." So, starting by deploring the degeneration of knowledge and the paralysis of learning, he supplied a formula for redressing both.

After the introduction, Bacon deployed a reasonable and perceptive, though a not entirely comprehensive philosophy of education. It appealed to colonial readers whose attitude toward learning ranged well beyond what schools were capable of doing, for Bacon's educational theses, although heeding schooling, were never limited to it. The family, the church, all of society for that matter, had huge parts to play in the education of youth. This position appealed to colonists and elicited their support because it complemented their experience, so Bacon's discourse did little more than confirm what they themselves believed. In the long run, Bacon might have attained prominence in the colonies because he articulated truths already firmly fixed in the minds of his readers.

Besides, the author of *The Advancement of Learning*, although deploring excessive dependence on ancient authority, on knowledge stored in stately libraries, and on deductive logic, displayed a ready conversance with classical authors, scripture, and philosophical method. Hardly a page in the book neglects classical reference, scriptural allusion, or philosophical erudition, and this was not missed by readers who were eager to acclaim scholarly talent: any author who commanded sources and used them effortlessly, and who seemed to rely so heavily on the authority of the Bible, was worth reading. At the same time, readers adopted, perhaps without realizing it, Bacon's paradoxical stance: the testimony of ancient authority was used to discredit the old storehouses of knowledge that ancient authority itself had filled.

There is no indication anywhere in *The Advancement of Learning* that Bacon was in sympathy with Puritans or their colonial enterprise; yet he succeeded in attracting their attention by telling them what they wanted to hear. And most of all they wanted to hear that education was good for faith; that they could almost with impunity undertake to improve their minds and the minds of their children without at the same time putting faith and piety in jeopardy. On this point, Bacon was accommodating: philosophy and learning, he declared, were useful to faith and religion when used for illustration, ornamentation, and persuasion, but this was somewhat beside the point. What counted more than rhetorical flourish and eloquent expression was a kind of philosophy "effectually exciting to the exaltation of God's glory," and human learning "affording a singular preservation against error and unbelief."[5] Scriptural authority, he said, sustained this statement, and he went on to assure readers that there is an abundance of divine testimony affirming the merit and dignity of learning.

Religiously sensitive colonists could find in Bacon a basis for resolving a lingering doubt about faith being damaged by learning, and this was not an inconsequential resolution when one takes into account the pietistic disposition to discredit intellectual accomplishment. In many a colonial settlement, learning's status was precarious; in the absence of sensible and prudent counsel it might have been completely abandoned. By any standard, what Bacon wrote was prudent and sensible.

His colonial readers could follow easily a distinction between sacred and profane knowledge. Although their religious creed declared that inspiration and faith could lead them to the truth in divine revelation, they were often unsure about how to tackle secular subjects, how to use methods of selection and analysis, and how to organize the profane legacy so that it would be useful and yet not conflict with any article of faith. This was by no means a novel conundrum; for the past five hundred years or more, Christian scholarship had tried to solve it. But the solutions proposed in the past contained some troublesome points which, when introduced by religiously heterodox persons, could be contaminating. The old paradigms were better discarded in favor of something new. Bacon's formula had the appearance of novelty, was handy, erudite, analytical, and, best of all, illustrated an independence of prescriptions from the past. Bacon's declaration that he had found a new approach was believed by a colonial audience.

A proper organization of secular knowledge, he said, has its genesis in the nature of the soul, where three faculties are lodged, each corresponding to one kind of knowledge: the faculty of memory deals with history, imagination with poetry, and reason with philosophy. History is an account of human behavior over the ages; poetry uses fictional themes and fanciful characters to reveal the human condition; but philosophy transcends "individuals, fixes upon notions abstracted from them, and is employed in compounding and separating these notions according to the laws of nature and the evidence of things themselves."[6] While Bacon's proposition does not seem to realign the epistemological compass—it harbored many traditional elements—the temptation to attribute novelty to it was strong.

In consequence, a mixture of Bacon's declarations and conventional opinion about what knowledge has worth was adopted in colonial schools and colleges. Besides, Bacon was persuasive in recommending the worth of colleges, a point that must have been comforting to colonial Americans who were proud of having set the foundations for higher learning before doing much of anything about lower schools. He encouraged an investment in the cultivation of letters, and told his readers that "this excellent liquor of knowledge, whether it descend from Divine inspiration or spring from human sense, would soon hide in oblivion, unless collected in books, traditions, academies and schools."[7] He added, as well, that schools and colleges needed buildings, endowments, privileges, and charters, and that learning would thrive best in an environment of quiet and seclusion where professors and students could work without impediment from care and anxiety. Colleges with good libraries, he wrote, "are as the shrines where the bones of old saints full of virtue lie buried." And libraries should contain modern authors whose books represent "correcter impressions, more faultless versions, more useful commentaries, and more learned annotations" than their predecessors.[8]

The colleges, he continued, should pool their resources to feature advancement of learning in the arts and sciences. They should eschew competition, independence, and institutional isolation. They should not, as he declared European universities were doing, concentrate upon professional study at the expense of cultivating the arts and sciences. He exudes optimism in connection with a study of science and admonishes the colleges to make a greater investment in science by increasing the number of its professorships.

Then there is an urgent appeal to the schools and colleges, to all of society for that matter, to reward the accomplishments of scholars:

> Since the founders of colleges plant, and those who endow them water, we are naturally led to speak in this place of the mean salaries apportioned to public lectureships, whether in the sciences or the arts. Such offices being instituted not for any ephemeral purpose, but for the constant transmission and extension of learning, it is of the utmost importance that the men selected to fill them be learned and gifted. But it is idle to expect that the ablest scholars will employ their whole energy and time in such functions unless the reward be answerable to that competency which may be expected from the practice of a profession.[9]

Colonists exhibited an unusual fondness for colleges, as the record of institutional founding attests, but it is probably wrong to conclude that Bacon was their adviser. Certainly they ignored his counsel both with respect to supporting these infant institutions and providing attractive emoluments for professors. Yet they put a high premium upon useful knowledge, and their reading habits, even in perusing the classics, show a penchant for useful and edifying reading. Bacon must have impressed them with his assertion that the great appendix to natural philosophy should be realized in practical mathematics and applied science. Astrology, medicine, physiognomy, and the interpretation of dreams (none much influenced then either by mathematics or science) were singled out for special praise because, he said, they were most likely to contribute to an improvement of the human condition. But most of all medicine and mechanics were promoted.[10]

Bacon acknowledged a hierarchy of knowledge, one giving pure science high rank, and he was eager to rescue applied science from what he said was a deplorable dormancy. Throughout this hierarchy the power and utility of knowledge were unequivocally endorsed. Now Bacon was either teaching the colonists a lesson or kindling in them a disposition toward pragmatism that could, without abandoning allegiance to the higher things of life, stress the importance of using their energy for the accomplishment of useful, profitable, and temporal reward.

The chain linking colonial and European intellectual life was intact, and its strongest link, logic, allowed many colonists to think and act like educated Europeans. It was in connection with logic that Bacon's reputation gained special luster, for he promised to blaze a trail through a scientific wilderness to new ground which could be cultivated to produce a harvest of intelligence for making the natural world heel to human need. The relationship between religion and natural philosophy (science) was frigid, due mainly to the erratic journey Aristotelian science took during its long interlude in the custody of Arabic translators and commentators. The natural philosophy of the medieval and early modern era needed a great deal of interpretation and correction to suit the prescripts of Christian belief, and the scholars who tried to do this work, depending upon the resources available to them in deductive logic, were unsuccessful.

No more successful were the followers of Peter Ramus (1515–1574), who had remodeled Aristotelian logic from an instrument capable of leading to discovery to a tool for organization and classification. The logic the colonists, especially the Calvinists among them, knew and used belonged to the Ramian camp. They had heard, and for the most part believed, those tales about the danger lurking in deductive logic and were terrified at the possibility of treachery in the syllogism. So when Bacon said that "this part of human philosophy which regards logic, is disagreeable to the taste of many, as appearing to them no other than a net, and a snare of thorny subtlety,"[11] he had an attentive and sympathetic audience.

Neither Bacon nor the colonists dismissed the importance of logic as an essential corollary to philosophy and science; under no circumstance could it be neglected. It needed, however, a more precisely defined purpose and its ability to lead scholars astray should be defused. Logic's fault, Bacon averred, was not its preoccupation with analysis: "We find no deficiency in analytics; for it is rather loaded with superficialities than deficient."[12] A majority of colonial scholars and ministers concurred, for they wanted a logic that would separate truth from error. Their abandonment of deductive logic, and the syllogism, was total; Bacon was their authority. Referring to various kinds of demonstration, but centering on the syllogism, he wrote that "each of these demonstrations (common consent, congruity, induction, and syllogistic) has its peculiar subjects, and parts of the sciences, wherein they are of force, and others again from which they are excluded; for insisting upon too strict proofs in some cases, and still more the facility and remissness of resting upon slight proofs in others, is what has greatly prejudiced and obstructed the sciences."[13] Fragmented by the sharp file of subtle genius, the syllogism was, Bacon declared confidently, nothing more than reducing propositions to principles by means of middle terms, and middle terms (minor premises) were undependable and could lead the unwary into thickets of confusion.[14]

Despite Bacon's promise that *The Advancement of Learning* amended logic by substituting inductive for deductive methods, thus rendering

Aristotle obsolete, the temptation is strong to believe that he was hoeing a well-tilled garden. The parts of the discourse dealing with logic rely heavily upon a traditional formal logic whose indebtedness both to Aristotle and the Scholastics is evident, although going beyond them in asserting and justifying an essential requirement of empirical verification. So, without opening any genuine frontier on logic's horizon that colonists could occupy, he, nevertheless, left intact their infatuation with Peter Ramus's logic of classification and allowed them to sort out religious and philosophical truth without any help from the authorities they had come to despise.

They could depend upon Bacon's support when they made logic a staple in the college curriculum, but there were other subjects that needed attention too. Their affection for books, one not explained simply by the poverty of their libraries, is almost legendary. Once read, a book might not again be available, so it was important to retain the treasures it contained. The worth of retention could not be gainsaid: How should memory be trained?

Throughout pedagogy's long history, this question had been pondered by good minds, and answers—some bordering on the fantastic and others, such as mnemonic technique, remarkably clever—had been framed. But the practical colonial mind was disposed to inquire whether time and effort spent mastering tricks to aid memory might be better used. So Bacon's assertion that "all the things of this kind [are] no more than rope-dancing, antic postures, and feasts of activity,"[15] must have been reassuring. Rather than trying to enforce memory by abusing the intellect, Bacon declared for writing: "We must observe, that the memory, without this assistance [of writing], is unequal to things of length and accuracy, and ought not otherwise to be trusted."[16] A dependable and accurate memory was a reward from sound learning, so colonial schoolmasters who sent boys to the books and required exercises in memory were embracing a pedagogy that had Bacon's complete support.

In company with logic were grammar and rhetoric. Together they formed the spine of colonial (especially higher) education. Grammar had a claim on all scholastic levels, and was sometimes thought to be the heart of secondary education, but rhetoric, a more demanding subject, was usually reserved for the college course. None of these subjects needed an explicit theory to sustain it, for the colonists, themselves the beneficiaries of classical study, were disposed to follow practices that had been tested in their own experience. *The Advancement of Learning* confirmed their disposition. Bacon's handling of literature—conventionally a part of grammar—lacked novelty. He preferred to give attention mainly to grammar's linguistic dimension and essayed to make language a more effective medium for scientific communication. He said:

> Grammar holds the place of a conductor in respect of the other sciences; and though the office be not noble, it is extremely necessary, especially as the sciences in our times are chiefly derived from the learned languages. Nor should this art be thought of small dignity, since it acts as an antidote against the curse of Babel, the confusion of tongues.[17]

Serious students who might someday engage in scholarly enterprise should, of course, spend effort to master grammar, although Bacon was quick to concede that grammar had "little use in any maternal language." Here, Bacon was only recognizing the scholastic status of Latin and acknowledging the low state of development among the several European vernaculars that had yet to gain enough strength to carry the weight of decent learning, to say nothing of scholarship. English, we have learned, was specially victimized by slow development; its critics and promoters alike had to admit to an impoverishment of both rules and standards.

Quite apart from the status of English, about which there could have been little dispute, colonial readers were delighted with Bacon's downgrading of grammar's literary side. Caution was recommended in connection with literature, for colonists knew, or had been told, that all kinds of religious infection and moral contamination were buried away in the lurid tales and graphic stories told by antique authors. If this genre of literature had to be read, it should by all means be selected with a care to ensure that any elements of indecency and immorality were pruned.

Rhetoric might be thought less of a problem for, although it had dangerous sides, it was not so susceptible to blight as literature. Bacon said the "end of rhetoric is to fill the imagination with such observations and images as may assist reason, and not overthrow it."[18] To use rhetoric for ornamenting discourse and making clear and persuasive argument was a universal ambition among colonial writers and preachers, so it was easy to solicit support for it if, at the same time, rhetoric's purpose could be left unsoiled. Eloquence could adorn virtue, but it could idealize vice; coupled with its capacity for good, rhetoric could be an instrument of deceit. Bacon wanted to rehabilitate rhetoric and his commentary on it, one should think, was a giant stride in that direction. Plato, he said, had treated rhetoric unfairly, although he had "proceeded from a just contempt of the rhetoricians of his time, to place rhetoric among the voluptuary arts, and resemble it to cookery, which corrupted wholesome meats and, by a variety of sauces, made unwholesome ones more palatable."[19] Bacon counseled his readers to make rhetoric obedient to reason and he tried to show them how this could be done. Colonists paid close attention to what he had to say.

The Advancement of Learning, preoccupied with a philosophy of knowledge and an art of learning, gives day-to-day pedagogic technique a wide birth. This was usual for educational tracts of the day. So it might be said that Bacon was only following convention, but there was another, more important, reason: Bacon was sensible enough to know that he lacked the experience to make specific recommendations relative to pedagogy. Yet, if his book were to have standing among scholars, it could not afford total silence about scholastic method. Moreover, Bacon realized that the subject was important and should not be neglected. What he had to say, while it might have given comfort to some, would surely have disappointed any colonial audience.

In Book Four, he directs readers' attention to "the doctrine of school-learning," declaring that "it were the shortest way to refer it to the Jesuits who, in point of usefulness, have herein excelled."[20] It stretches imagination to the limit to suppose that our colonial ancestors would have owned, much less read, the Jesuit classic on the conduct of schools, *Ratio Studiorum*. But when they read on they saw that Bacon preferred schools to tutorial arrangements, and that he recommended a scholastic program where able students would have the freedom to conclude their lessons and then "steal time for other things whereto [they are] more inclined."[21] They would have seen, as well, that his interest was mainly in gifted students and how best to provide for them by instituting an instructional regimen to exercise the powers of the mind and to communicate knowledge quickly and pleasantly. It is one method, he wrote, "to begin swimming with bladders, and another to begin dancing with loaded shoes."[22] Study should be suited to student capacity, and substantial scholarship must be demanded, yet teachers are admonished to remember that their students, whatever their talent, live in a society where social skill and practical knowledge are indispensable.

Study of mathematics is recommended for students of quick mind and ready wit who, after mastering their lesson in other subjects, waste their time. "Inattention and volatility of genius may be remedied by mathematics, wherein, if the mind wander ever so little, the whole demonstration must begin anew."[23] The commentary on the art of teaching concludes with a plea for discipline in learning, a discipline sturdy enough to withstand the stress in life and remain intact long after school days are over. Again, he refers to Jesuit practice with approval: "We mean the action of the theatre, which strengthens the memory, regulates the tone of the voice and the efficacy of pronunciation; gracefully composes the countenance and the gesture; procures a becoming degree of assurance; and lastly, accustoms youth to the eye of men."[24]

Extant record is silent on the reception this recommendation received among colonial preachers and pedagogues, but it would be hard to believe that it was cordial. Often, especially in New England, drama was outlaw and everywhere in the colonies, except for a time in Maryland, anything having to do with Jesuits was rejected. Still, colonists of substance and sagacity could be selective; they had both the skill and prudence to embrace what they thought good and abandon the rest. On the whole, they counted Bacon's *The Advancement of Learning* an instructive book and, more than any other educational document of the time, were guided by it.

Despite Bacon's popularity in the colonies, the ideas he advanced never succeeded in monopolizing educational thought. This might have been a blessing in disguise, because had Bacon's theses carried the day, they would likely have undermined the compact our ancestors crafted between the sacred and the profane, the natural and the supernatural. In any case, with little more than curiosity about the physical world surrounding and nourishing them, colonists who probed the purpose and practice of education did what most of their forebears had always done: they conducted the educational enterprise along familiar avenues and justified its direction with the vocabulary of convention. In the end, though, despite this cautious course, some room to maneuver was left for educational theory and instructional practice.

Except in the most remote corners of a colony, most early Americans wanted their children to be literate. It was not until after the vigor of transplanted attitudes toward learning had been sapped, probably close to the advent of the nineteenth century, that much talk was heard about the burden of school attendance and the impediments book learning erect before personal freedom. No one in colonial America would have thought, much less said, that reading and writing deprive persons of any natural right, although they might have debated their utility for some persons. And, though the debate was far from over, few would have dismissed as inconsequential opinions about educational responsibility: Is it a collective or an individual obligation?

These were policy issues to be thrashed out in the future, but in the first colonial century we can imagine that a reader who sampled parts of *The Advancement of Learning* might have pondered the place and purpose of a plan for instruction that would stand upon a foundation of elementary literacy. Doubtless, all persons neither needed nor could profit from instruction in secondary schools and colleges. The question was important: If advanced instruction were to be made available, who should seek its advantages and what should be studied?

During the half-century following the publication of Bacon's book, a controversy that was raging in England about the efficacy of liberal (classical) learning, the kind of study promoted by the educational writers of the Great Renaissance and one that had been embraced in British secondary schools and universities, began to echo in the colonies. Some extremist sectarians, bitten no doubt by the bug of evangelicalism, repudiated liberal learning, which they said was needless, and with it all divine study as well. Christ's message, they declared with supreme confidence, is communicated to the faithful by ministers whose words are inspired by the Holy Spirit. Lawyers, physicians, poets, and teachers might profit from humane learning, although even this is uncertain, but surely Christian ministers are absolved from need for it. When religious anti-intellectualism threatened to become virulent in the colonies, Charles Chauncy (1592–1672), Harvard's second president, campaigned to disinfect it.

Keeping faith with Harvard's original commission, Chauncy delivered a sermon in 1655, "God's Mercy, Shewed to His People, In Giving Them a Faithfull Ministry and Schooles of Learning, for the Continued Supplyes Thereof," to repudiate the declaration that since Christ and the apostles had found the inspiration of the Holy Spirit good enough for them, why should ordinary ministers pretend to more than their master possessed? To follow this line of reasoning, Chauncy argued persuasively, was analogous to maintaining that "no man need to be an apprentice to learning any Mechanical trade, seeing the teaching of the Spirit is sufficient for any cunning work, [and] who is there who would not account this reasoning ridiculous?"[25] Seldom straying far from this theme, Chauncy nailed the twin banners of a learned clergy and the Congregationalist version of liberal learning to the schoolhouse mast.

Yet for all his wit, Chauncy's definition of a proper education for ministers and liberal learning's place in it was not entirely satisfactory to New England Calvinists. This was work better done by such keepers of the Christian conscience as Cotton Mather (1663–1728) and Benjamin Wadsworth (1670–1737). Neither spent much time considering the conduct of schools, although Mather, who had benefited from Ezekiel Cheever's (1615–1708) instruction in the Boston Latin School and called Cheever the "American Corderius"—after Mathurin Cordier (1479–1564)—demonstrated a decent respect for sound learning.[26] Six years earlier, in a sermon to parents, *Cares*

About the Nurseries, Mather set the dimension and tone for a proper Christian upbringing of children. Saying little about conventional literary instruction, he concentrated upon catechetical techniques for communicating religious truth. He ended the first part of the discourse with an appeal to parents to supervise the behavior of children at church services. In an epilogue of sorts, he counseled children on how to behave when they were older.[27]

Both Mather and Wadsworth concentrated upon the family's obligation to attend to the piety, conduct, and manners of children as they travel though life to eternity. Strictly orthodox in insisting that boys and girls be properly instructed in religious duty, together they enjoined parents and masters to either conduct or provide for such instruction under pain of divine retribution. Then Wadsworth stepped ahead of Mather to remind parents and masters that life is practical as well as spiritual: charged with the education of saints, they were responsible, as well, for ensuring to children the means to succeed in secular society.[28]

So matters stood when John Clarke (1687–1734), in 1730, introduced John Locke's theory of education to colonial America.[29] The first edition of Clarke's book, published in London in 1720, was virtually unknown in the colonies, but its second edition commanded a large American readership. In the early years of the eighteenth century familiarity with Locke's writings on education was slight on this side of the ocean, although, likely, well-educated persons were conversant with his politics and might have sampled something of his philosophy and psychology, so Wilson Smith is right to call Clarke Locke's missionary to America.[30]

Later Locke's theory of education had prominent and eloquent heralds—Franklin and Jefferson come to mind—but for now it was expressed fairly faithfully in Clarke's expository style and, from all accounts, the *Essay* had a considerable audience. Clarke undertook little more than a transmission of Locke's theory, although here and there, it should be conceded, some of Locke's declarations were amended or excised, but none of his principal themes was abandoned or discredited. Expectation for students and their rate of achievement should be commensurate with their ability. Goals, while high, should not be unrealistic. Instructional technique should capitalize on what Locke called the principle of proceeding from the simple to the complex. Rules of grammar were not to be introduced apart from students' experience with linguistic expression, and sometimes, as in the case of teaching Latin, not at all. Locke was critical of the way Latin was taught, even to those who might have use for it, and Clarke followed suit in disparaging what he called the *vulgar method* of teaching Latin, although he was considerably more friendly than Locke to Latin's staple place in the curriculum. In an age when severe punishment might be visited upon students, without any attempt by teachers to distinguished between a student's inability or unwillingness to learn, Clarke followed Locke in calling for sensible school discipline and prudent use of corporal punishment. This long discourse, clothed in a style that today seems clumsy and inartistic, kept Locke's educational views alive for the next half-century.

Americans were unready to make much of an investment in educational theory, but busy British disciples of John Locke made his voice heard in the land across the Atlantic. Few were busier than Isaac Watts (1674–1748), whose *Improvement of the Mind, To Which Is Added, A Discourse on the Education of Children and Youth*, published in London in 1751, popularized Locke's erudite and cumbersome *Essay on Human Understanding*. It is puzzling why a treatise on rational psychology that emphasized the mental faculties of reason and understanding should have made such headway in America. Probing the human psyche, searching for the genesis of motivation and interest, and plumbing the operation of mental faculties might have been thought too private or too spiritual to be laid bare by psychological speculation. These were things better left to the intercession of theologians than philosophers.

Despite this, however, and despite, too, Watts's unfriendliness to English and American Puritans, *Improvement of the Mind* was published in twelve American editions in the fifty years after 1793. An explanation for Watts's popularity in America, although mainly conjecture, is that readers skipped over the first part of the book, ignored Watts's heterodoxy, and paid special heed to the *Discourse on the Education of Children and Youth*, a patient and practical treatment of pedagogic technique, vocational development, and moral formation. These topics, always fresh, were worth considering.

If Locke and his interpreters were emancipating education from religion, which seems to have been the case, although they stayed close to objectives of moral formation and were careful not to be too brazen in idealizing profane education, Henry Home, Lord Kames (1696–1782), was not so cautious. In his *Loose Hints Upon Education, Chiefly Concerning the Culture of the Heart*, published in Edinburgh in 1781, Home bravely declared the purpose of education to be social improvement and human happiness and not, as had been stated so often before in the Puritan educational credo, eternal salvation. It would take a great deal of temerity to allege for Home a loyal followership in American educational and religious circles. Certainly he was wading in a shallow tributary, but if his audience was small it was also important and influential: Benjamin Franklin and Thomas

Jefferson paid him heed.

Before Franklin and Jefferson appeared on the educational scene, however, the pot of controversy was simmering in connection with the control of colonial colleges. Everyone knew that the first colleges, and for a long time those following in their wake, were founded and controlled by communicants of religious sects. Was this desirable? William Livingston (1723–1790), editor of the *Independent Reflector*, an Anglican, and later the governor of New Jersey, led a cadre of journalists and lawyers who opposed sectarian control of higher education, and to bring their case to a point argued against Anglican control of New York's King's College (now Columbia). Reasonable and temperate in expression, they were able to mobilize sentiment for a nonsectarian approach to education.

Without by any means commanding a majority opinion, their views seemed threatening enough for Thomas Clap (1703–1767), president of Yale College, to make a sharp rejoinder. In *The Religious Constitution of Colleges*, written in 1754, Clap undertook to defend the status quo and to maintain with a considerable degree of eloquence that colleges without sectarian affiliation would be dangerous educational institutions: they would lack principles to guide them. Over the long run, Clap's argument fell on deaf ears, but in the short run his brief was adopted in America. Few of his generation were ready for a divorce of religion and higher education. But this was before Benjamin Franklin and Thomas Jefferson turned mind and pen to the education of Americans.

Benjamin Franklin (1706–1790), the founder of the famous Philadelphia Academy, a school where the classics and Latin were supposed to take a back seat to study in English and where ornamental knowledge was to be superseded by practical subjects, should not be teamed with Thomas Jefferson (1743–1826) as a proponent for a nineteenth-century version of democratic opportunity for education. Franklin's educational vision was broad, and when coupled with a nationalistic aspiration for America unquestionably promoted the construction of a social order capable of offering persons opportunity for self-improvement. Yet as a child of an aristocratic social order, sympathy and affection for it almost certainly shaped his outlook. Often unconventional when convention ill-suited him, neither intellect nor temperament tempted him to jettison it. He mastered the lessons John Locke and John Milton (1608–1674) taught and did his best to plant their educational theory in this new land. In the end, because they, especially Locke, expressed so much educational common sense, Franklin diagrammed a prudent, and in the amendments to pedagogy it proposed, a dependable plan for his educational heirs to follow.

Less a progressive than Jefferson, Franklin nevertheless spoke an educational language that prescribed a repair in the way schools and colleges were conducted, what was taught, and how they were supported. Their first commitment, he declared, should be to the common good and an indispensable condition to fulfilling this commitment was a government assumption of greater responsibility for education. Hardly an avant-garde proposition—a government role in provision for education must have had its American genesis as early as 1647 in Massachusetts Bay—Franklin's superior credentials gave it greater weight. The balance in the debate over individual versus collective responsibility for education began to tip in favor of the latter. But before going too far in attributing to Franklin pure altruism on this point, one should remember that antipathy to religious control and domination of education might have led him to look for an alternative: the handiest one was civil authority. On the other hand Franklin's motive might be irrelevant, for in the long run his prudent counsel gave respectability to the principle of state responsibility for education that before it had lacked. Still, despite Franklin's encouragement of public cooperation in the educational enterprise, there is not a line in any of his writing on education that retracts his solid conviction that irrespective of opportunity's source, personal success depends upon diligence and persistence. Educational opportunity is but an ally in the formation of "self-made men."

Having set the compass in the direction of public and private cooperation for improving the prospect for educational opportunity, Franklin turned to the next page of educational theory where the worth and source of knowledge were appraised. In connection with the first, he was eager to disregard declamations from the past, take his place beside Locke, and embrace the doctrine of utility. Such a position came close to dismissing an immense reservoir of knowledge contained in the classics to pay attention instead to a treasury of useful knowledge that might be mined from the social and physical worlds.

Perhaps always an empiricist, Franklin, after reading Locke, gained confidence in empiricism and in a trained reason's ability to guide judgment along a dependable route. Persuaded from the first that experience is the best, maybe the only, teacher, under Locke's tutorship his compact with scientific knowledge and the utility guaranteed by it became unbreakable. Despite an undiminished admiration for Locke, Franklin was never a blind disciple: Locke seldom spoke of educational opportunity, and never to liberalize it, but Franklin was more generous. While this generosity lacked precision of definition and application, safe to say Franklin was on the side of greater opportunity for education than then extant.

Almost certainly Franklin distinguished education from school instruction, although he was never explicit, but evidence is abundant in the *Idea of the English School*[31] that Franklin followed Locke, along with hundreds of others, in affirming character as education's ultimate purpose. One is left to speculate how this squared with his declaration about the utility of knowledge, although good sense is exhibited in the assertion that good and decent character has supreme utility. When Franklin spoke of character as an educational objective, it was likely in a civic context and he meant good citizenship. Doubtless he wanted to strip from educational purpose its conventional association with religious orthodoxy.

And at this point, Franklin and Jefferson are in league. But when we look at the curriculum for the English school, the matter becomes complex. For as long as anyone could remember, classical education promoted character formation and the curriculum of the schools used classical literature, confident in its contribution to moral development. Franklin, it appears, followed suit, and modified conventional practice only to require that the classics be taught in English. Even when the classics were taught in English, his confidence in them as moral teachers is hard to assess, for lingering in the background is the epigram that good character is shaped mainly by a personal determination to be always honorable, upright, and honest. The genesis of personal determination is a gigantic loose end.

Franklin's exploitation of personal effort and his affection for "self-made men" were rooted in the experience of a lifetime. As a youth in Boston, his parents wanted him to be a clergyman and tried to steer him in that direction.[32] But Franklin must have lacked a religious vocation. Besides, his formal schooling, amounting to about two years equally divided between Boston Latin School and a private master, George Brownell, and his evident aversion to such instruction was an impediment to a career as a preacher. Lack of schooling, however, was only a temporary obstacle that Franklin hurdled by personal effort. He was quick to adopt the attitude, common among "self-made men": what worked for him was unquestionably good for everyone.[33] Even so, perceiving the possibility of self-education, he knew it to be enormously difficult and turned to the books available and commissioned them as his teachers. In maturity he spoke of the good that could come from an expenditure of public effort and state investment in the cause of education and was tireless in organizing private groups for the promotion of all manner of humanistic causes. Franklin's Philadelphia Academy, itself a creation of mutual venture, was succeeded by philosophical and library associations, all illustrative of a belief that properly motivated men and women can be masters of their fate.

Picking a way through a thicket of accomplishment, from Franklin's humble start and his abbreviated schooling to nearly the end of his life when he was called the most civilized man in America, and seeking illustrations of a full and coherent educational philosophy might be a disappointing adventure. Yet, without fullness or coherence, there is abundant expression of educational conviction and ample illustration of educational recommendation. Likely the most rewarding of his works on education is *Proposals Relating to the Education of Youth in Pennsylvania*, a work that took about six years to produce. It appeared in 1749.[34]

The discourse acknowledges indebtedness to John Milton's *Of Education* (1644), Locke's *Some Thoughts Concerning Education* (1693), David Fordyce's *Dialogues Concerning Education* (1745), Obadiah Walker's *Of Education* (1673), Charles Rollin's, *The Method of Teaching and Studying the Belles-Lettres* (1726–1728), and George Turnbull's *Observations Upon Liberal Education in All Its Branches* (1742). There is no pretense whatever that the ideas expressed in *Proposals* are solely the property of Franklin's fertile mind, so one should be careful about exaggerating their originality. In any case, the immediate effect of *Proposals* was that it became the charter for the Academy in Philadelphia, but one should be quick to declare that the Academy did not follow its charter to the letter.

For decades readers of the *Proposals* seemed unable to see beyond two of its striking assertions: the imperative need for the teaching of English in American schools, and the admonition that a balance be maintained between "the most useful and the most ornamental" knowledge in order to avoid overburdening the curriculum with everything useful and ornamental. Interpreting these assertions, it would seem unfairly and incorrectly, Franklin was made to appear as an enemy of the classics, on the one hand, and a strident utilitarian, on the other. The *Proposals* contained a school plan considerably more liberal and humane than this.

Franklin began by outlining a fairly conventional scholastic program for students who would live at school and be instructed by a master whose reputation for broad and humanistic scholarship was sound. The curriculum was designed to contain the well-established cultural staples, although it was not driven by any dogmatic assumption that everything worth knowing can be found in the classics. Yet there is nothing in the plan or in Franklin's explanation of it that comes close to suggesting that utility alone is to be served. What is emphasized is the right students have to be supplied with a curriculum capable of meeting their cultural and vocational need. Their principal need, Franklin supposed, was a command of the English language, so, and almost for the first time, we see a school ready to elevate the study of English to a level that few vernaculars enjoyed. Neither ancient nor modern languages were excluded from the curriculum, but Franklin welcomed them only for those students who wanted them.

Safe to say, the *Proposals* reserved special praise for useful knowledge and the study of English, but these emphases are not the whole story. "The great aim and end of all learning," Franklin declared, is to lay a foundation for good breeding and a spirit of service to family, community, and country. The hard crust of utility is softened by the balm of altruism, and Franklin's reputation for indifference to religion is redressed when he endorses "a Publick Religion" that can contribute to the stability of personal and social moral standards. Unaffected by the doctrine of piety—or, more likely, repudiating it—and steering clear of sectarianism, Franklin, nevertheless, testified to the "Excellency of the Christian Religion above all others ancient or modern."

The advice in the *Proposals*, silent on the point of public support and control for secondary education, was heeded mainly by private schools, although there is plenty of encouragement for extending opportunity for schooling to the country's youth. Universal opportunity for education is not even hinted at, and nothing is said about elementary schools. The plan was for secondary education where schoolboys for so long sentenced to live out their school days in the company of the classics were given commutation: now, with the exception of English study, they could choose their scholastic direction according to personal disposition and need. Under, we suppose, the care of their masters, they could choose from a range of subjects: arithmetic, handwriting, bookkeeping, and drawing are on the menu, as are geometry, astronomy, rhetoric, geography, moral philosophy, and history. And, illustrative of Franklin's affection for useful knowledge, natural history, natural philosophy, mechanics, and gardening have a place in the curriculum. With an eye to Locke's praise for health and exercise, a place is reserved for recreation and sport as well. At the end of their school course young men were expected to be ready to step into society as good citizens with the credentials of public men.

Nothing in the *Proposals* makes us think we have read a revolutionary manifesto, but there are clear signs that Franklin was trying to reconstruct the conventional school course to accommodate the novel features of American life. Such an assessment can neither shrink Franklin's stature in the annals of American education nor blunt his Academy's bold assault on scholastic habit.

Thomas Jefferson's political and social philosophy stood on a foundation of natural right reinforced by a confidence that human intelligence equips free people to manage their affairs so to ensure life and liberty, and allow for the pursuit of happiness. Surely Jefferson had read the classical utopias and, likely, had learned from them, but his optimism for America was expressed in a vocabulary of realism, of what could be achieved when a principle of equality is put to work as social policy. There is no utopian myth in the declaration that all men are created equal or any flight of fancy in claiming for the people control of their government.

Persuaded from the first of the people's sovereignty, Jefferson knew at once the difference between capacity and ability, and recognized as well that a translation from capacity to ability must rest ultimately upon education. Whatever their capacity, without its translation to realized ability men and women are helpless. And without means for obtaining educational decency, the possibility of effective self-government is a forlorn hope. Ignorance and illiteracy are prescriptions for anarchy or despotism.

With a profound faith in a policy of separating church and state, Jefferson was filled with misgivings about education's long compact with religion. His appraisal of American educational history led him to conclude that so long as schools were subject to sectarian control, educational standard for a democratic society and a republican political system were in jeopardy. His petition for broad and generous distribution of educational opportunity divorced from organized religion was uncompromising.

Commitment to schools and learning, evident in almost all of Jefferson's public utterances and actions, is certified in "A Bill for the More General Diffusion of Knowledge" filed with the Virginia legislature in 1779, shortly after he became governor.[35] The bill's most progressive feature was provision for three years of publicly supported schooling for all free children. Although unrecognized at the time, Jefferson's proposal was prophetic and put him in the vanguard of a cadre of nineteenth-century educational reformers who could see the promise of democratic education. One should not miss the point that the public schools projected in the bill would have excluded many children, so it failed the test of genuine universal opportunity; yet to assess the judgment of our ancestors by using the yardstick of contemporary social policy is unfair. As it stood, Jefferson's bill was unsuited to the appetite of his confreres, was rejected by the legislature in 1779 and again in 1817, but could not have had any hearing at all had its provision for educational opportunity been more generous.

At the same time, it would be a mistake to claim for Jefferson's social policy any anticipation of the Fourteenth Amendment, or even that the thought of supplying public education for all the children of all the people ever entered Jefferson's fertile mind. Accepting all this, simple justice is served in citing him as the expositor of an idea too revolutionary to be embraced, but one that in the long run became an operative policy governing American education: equality of educational opportunity.

Dedicated to a revision of the legal code to make it comply with conditions of life in Virginia and to strip away elements of British law incompatible with republicanism, Jefferson made his school plan an essential plank in public policy. The plan sought to achieve two objectives: to establish a foundation for active, intelligent citizenship, and to expand citizens' prospects for personal and economic success.

The plan's novelty alone is enough to attract our attention, but when we recognize that many of its provisions were destined to become conventional American educational policy, it takes on a special luster. Virginia was organized into districts, then called hundreds, five or six miles square and, according to the plan, each district was to have "a school for teaching reading, writing, and arithmetic." Districts paid teachers' salaries and free children attended these schools without paying tuition or rates. Should they want or require more than three years of schooling, they had to pay for it. The practice of collective responsibility for the support of elementary instruction had, of course, been experimented with about a century earlier in New England, and Jefferson might have been impressed by it, but lacking general appeal it had to lie dormant until revived by Jefferson to have a substantial place in his bold plan.

With provision made for three-year district schools, the bill went on to create twenty grammar schools where talented students from district schools, "whose parents are too poor to give them further education," could go if scholarships at the disposition of school supervisors were awarded to them. The curriculum of the grammar schools was Greek, Latin, geography, and "the higher branches of numerical arithmetic." After a one- or two-year interlude in a grammar school, "the best genius" of the class was awarded a scholarship for the full six-year course. In this way, Jefferson wrote, "twenty of the best geniuses will be raked from the rubbish annually, and be instructed, at the public expence, so far as the grammar schools go."[36] From each grammar-school graduating class ten students were to be awarded public scholarships to the College of William and Mary (the University of Virginia, one of Jefferson's fondest hopes, was yet to be founded), where a study of science was recommended. Students who had benefited from public support, but who were not awarded scholarships, might attend college at their own expense, and students forgoing college could, Jefferson supposed, become teachers in district and grammar schools.

The school plan supplied educational opportunity to talented children from poor families, as well as to children from families who could afford the cost of schooling. It, Jefferson declared, provided "an education adapted to the years, to the capacity, and the condition of every one, and [is] directed to their freedom and happiness." Its first level, where all free children could be instructed at public expense for three years, set the main foundation for social solidarity. And the curriculum of these schools, after the elements, combined a study of history with principles of practical ethics preparing students to form judgments on moral and political issues almost certainly to face them. Such instruction, Jefferson was confident, would be more effective in forming good citizens than conventional indoctrination in morals based on the Bible and sectarian doctrine.

Elementary schools were commissioned to educate for citizenship, but grammar schools concentrated upon language study. During grammar-school years, Jefferson said, students are ready for instruction where memory plays a central role and, although he did "not pretend that language is science . . . it is an instrument for the attainment of science." He rejected the advice of Locke, and others, who were urging European schools to discount study of Latin and Greek. "I know not what their manner and occupations may call for: but it would be very ill-judged in us to follow their example in this instance."[37] The university, always available to the wealthy, was open now to talented youth from poor families. Society, Jefferson urged, should eagerly capitalize upon "those talents which nature has sown as liberally among the poor as the rich, but which perish without use, if not sought for and cultivated."

Jefferson's plan, an illustration of educational theory at work, allowed for the development of talent and somewhat tentatively embraced liberal learning, but its principal purpose, one is right to allege, was "that of rendering the people the safe, as they are the ultimate, guardians of their own liberty." And this commission weighed most heavily upon the first rung of the educational ladder where elementary schools open to all free children paid attention first to the rudiments to ensure basic literacy and then turned to history. Schooled in history, citizens would be in a position to "judge the actions and designs of men," and recognize ambition in any disguise to keep it from destroying their liberty. Ambition, if vested solely in the private aspirations of leaders, infects government; so steps must be taken to block inordinate ambition: "The influence over government must be shared among all the people . . . because the corrupting the whole mass will exceed any private resources of wealth: and public ones cannot be provided but by levies on the people."[38]

Jefferson's intense affection for schooling is amply illustrated in his educational theory and was as genuine for the first as for the highest levels, but schools alone cannot account for the whole of education. His bill, therefore, asked for public libraries, where citizens could sample the wisdom contained in books, and for museums whose painting and statuary might embellish rational truth with beauty. Still, one should not stray too far from its central theme: universal education as a safeguard of liberty and a foundation for civic virtue. We see now the adumbration in Jefferson's definition of universal education, but we should see as well that his educational theory contained seeds for opportunity that germinated in the richer soil of the later years of the nineteenth and the early years of the twentieth centuries.

With Franklin and Jefferson as principal spokesmen, although others, for example, Benjamin Rush (1745–1813) played a part, the importance of education to the realization of effective citizenship became one of the burning questions of the early nineteenth century. They would have not called themselves educational philosophers, and most of their contemporaries might have doubted their declarations had kinship to philosophy of any kind, but what they had to say contained a bedrock whereupon their successors were able to construct what we have come to regard as conventional educational philosophy. In the second and third quarters of the nineteenth century, educational philosophy, hammered out in a forum of politics and controversy, seldom found many vocal exponents in school and college halls.

We are ready now to see how educational philosophy began to climb the educational ladder and bargain for an influential place in an infant discipline of education. Its hope (not always realized) was to shine as a beacon to guide and guard educational practice, to become a respectable academic field worth scholars' time and energy, and to enter the college curriculum as a course intended to link theoretical perspective with pedagogic technique and equip prospective teachers to function as cooperative artists in the American educational enterprise.

NOTES

1. Herbert W. Schneider, *A History of American Philosophy*, 2d edition (New York: Columbia University Press, 1963), 209.
2. Francis Bacon, *The Novum Organum*, translated and edited by Peter Urbach and John Gibson (Chicago: Open Court, 1994), Book I, Aphorism 8.
3. Ibid., Aphorism 63.
4. Francis Bacon, *The Advancement of Learning*, edited by Joseph Devey (New York: American Home Library, 1902), 11.
5. Ibid., 71.
6. Ibid., 93.
7. Ibid., 87.
8. Ibid.

9. Ibid., 88–89.

10. Ibid., 171–99.

11. Ibid., 211.

12. Ibid., 237.

13. Ibid., 243.

14. Ibid., 236.

15. Ibid., 245.

16. Ibid., 244.

17. Ibid., 250.

18. Ibid., 269.

19. Ibid.

20. Ibid., 302.

21. Ibid.

22. Ibid.

23. Ibid., 303.

24. Ibid.

25. Charles Chauncy, "God's Mercy," quoted in Wilson Smith, ed., *Theories of Education in Early America 1655–1819* (Indianapolis and New York: Bobbs-Merrill, 1973), 7.

26. Cotton Mather, *Corderius Americanus. An Essay Upon the Good Education of Children. And What May Hopefully Be Attempted, for the Hope of the Flock. In a Funeral Sermon upon Mr. Ezekiel Cheever. The Ancient and Honorable Master of the Free-School in Boston. Who Left Off, But When Mortality Took Him Off, in August, 1708, the Ninety-Fourth Year of His Age. With an Elegy and an Epitaph Upon Him. By one that was a Scholar to him* (Boston, 1708).

27. Cotton Mather, *Cares About the Nurseries. Two Brief Discourses. The One, Offering Methods and Motives for Parents to Catechise their Children While Yet Under the Tuition of Their Parents. The Other, Offering Some Instructions for Children, How They May Do Well, When They Come to Years of Doing for Themselves* (Boston, 1702).

28. Benjamin Wadsworth, *The Well-Ordered Family: or, Relative Duties. Being the Substance of Several Sermons, About Family Prayer, Duties of Husbands & Wives, Duties of Parents & Children, Duties of Masters and Servants* (Boston, 1712).

29. John Clarke, *An Essay Upon the Education of Youth in Grammar-Schools. In Which the Vulgar Method of Teaching, and a New One Proposed, for the More Easy and Speedy Training Up of Youth to the Knowledge of the Learned Languages; Together with History, Chronology, Geography, etc.,* 2d. ed., with very large additions (London, 1730).

30. Wilson Smith, *Theories of Education,* 62.

31. *Benjamin Franklin on Education,* edited by John Hardin Best (New York: Teachers College Press, 1962), 165–71.

32. The most recent biography of Franklin is Esmond Wright's, *Franklin of Philadelphia* (Cambridge: Belknap Press of Harvard University Press, 1986).

33. Carl Van Doren, *Benjamin Franklin* (New York: Viking Press, 1938), 260–68.

34. In *The Papers of Benjamin Franklin,* edited by Leonard W. Labaree and Whitfield J. Bell, Jr. (New Haven: Yale University Press, 1959), 3: 397–421.

35. Thomas Jefferson, in *The Papers of Thomas Jefferson,* edited by Julian P. Boyd et al. (Princeton: Princeton University Press, 1950 et. seq.), 2: 526–33.

36. Thomas Jefferson, *Notes on the State of Virginia, with an Appendix,* 26 vols. (Boston: David Carlisle, 1801; New York: Harper & Row, 1964), 14: 216–17.

37. Ibid.

38. Ibid.

CHAPTER 5
THE DEVELOPMENT OF PHILOSOPHIES OF EDUCATION

Until about the middle of the nineteenth century most genuine educational philosophy was domiciled in Europe, and the contributions of its principal expositors have been rehearsed. In the United States, an educational awakening that began in the 1840s had the effect of riveting attention on principles and policies vis-à-vis the purpose, the content, and the process of education. Accompanying this awakening, the first normal schools were established as places for the preparation of teachers. And for three or more decades thereafter most persons (mainly young women) who wanted pedagogic training attended normal schools. Education seldom achieved the standing of a college subject or was regarded as a fully credentialed member of the academic family until the last quarter of the nineteenth century. Attempts on the part of the colleges to introduce educational studies were stiffly resisted by normal schools, which considered teacher education their special preserve.[1]

William Payne (1836–1907), appointed professor of the science and art of teaching at the University of Michigan in 1879, seems to have been a pathfinder. A decade or so later, according to Bruce Kimball, 114 American colleges and universities were offering courses in pedagogy and thirty-one had established professorships in the subject.[2] In 1906 John Dewey is said to have declared that education had attained "standing as a university subject."[3] College philosophy professors were tempted to dismiss as unphilosophical what some of their colleagues in normal schools and, later, in teachers colleges and departments of education were saying about educational ends and means. In spite of indifference to their discourse, or in some instances, perhaps, hostility to it, educators tried to be philosophical in the tone if not the substance of their commentary on education.

Although both had predecessors, neither John Dewey (1859–1952) nor Herman H. Horne (1874–1946) was superseded during these years as an architect of American educational philosophy. Their main accomplishments, however, came at the beginning of the twentieth century after others had labored for more than fifty years trying to apply a precise philosophical vocabulary and a grammatical structure to the enterprise of education.

The mood of aspiring educational philosophers who only sometimes found academic platforms from which to speak fluctuated between what J. J. Chambliss has called inductive and naturalistic empiricism.[4] Joseph Neef (1770–1854), a disciple of Pestalozzi and the importer to America of object-lesson methodology is credited with having been the spokesman for inductive empiricism.[5] His plan for pedagogy depended, as had Pestalozzi's, upon instruction through the senses (one wonders what the alternative might be) and it invested so heavily in pedagogic technique that its credentials as genuine philosophy are suspect.[6] Belonging to the same ideological camp as Neef, but with surer philosophical instinct, was George Jardine (1770?–1849?)whose views on education, although promoted by Albert (1771–1850) and John Picket in America,[7] had little influence upon educators here. Likely the best recommendation for Jardine's brand of educational philosophy was its theoretical kinship to Francis Bacon's *Advancement of Learning*.

Showing the same fondness for Bacon, and likely knowing the implications of his philosophy more thoroughly than Jardine or the Pickets, was James G. Carter (1795–1849). Most accounts of American educational history couple Carter with Horace Mann, and accurately characterize him as an advocate for common schools for children and normal schools for aspiring teachers. What they miss is his philosophical predilection, Baconian in origin, which prescribed a philosophical foundation for any respectable science of pedagogy, and his rendering of it in "Letters to the Hon. William Prescott, L.L.D., on the Free Schools of New England, with Remarks on the Principles of Instruction"[8] and articles in the *American Journal of Education* in 1829. Another follower of Bacon, and a pioneer in the field of educational philosophy, was Thomas Tate (1807–1888). His *Philosophy of Education; or, The Principles and Practice of Teaching*[9] illustrated inductive empiricism and showed signs of philosophical sophistication, but one must be cautious about inflating its influence in the United States.[10]

The extent of inductive empiricism's influence on educational philosophy in America is a matter of conjecture. Whether it was virile enough to be a school of thought can be debated. It might have done nothing more than keep alive the inductive tradition in logic promoted by Bacon and applied to pedagogy by Pestalozzi. At the same time, one should note, its theological implications were benign. Nothing in inductive empiricism threatened to capsize the conventional compact philosophy had with religion. The story in connection with naturalistic empiricism is strikingly different: its codifier, Herbert Spencer (1820–1903), tilled the fields of science, philosophy and education to achieve distinction as an important nineteenth-century philosopher who, according to James Kaminsky, was the intellectual linchpin between Britain and America. His influence in American philosophical circles was enormous.[11] The concession that he did not produce a comprehensive philosophy of education should not imply that his articles on education (later reproduced in a book, *Education: Intellectual, Moral, Physical*) lacked genuine philosophical substance and character. One of the articles, and the book's first chapter, "What Knowledge Is of Most Worth?" belongs to a special category of educational discourse, for it made explicit a question whose implications had piqued the curiosity of educators for centuries. It is, moreover, a question that in any age demands an answer before the curricula of schools can be shaped.

Naturalistic in his theory regarding the nature of man and scientific (empirical) in connection with the acquisition of dependable and useful knowledge, Spencer supplied one species of naturalism with credibility and introduced to education an epistemological pragmatism that before his time had been scorned by most serious thinkers. Friendship for the evolutionary hypothesis put naturalism at loggerheads with religion and made its reception among nineteenth-century educators all the more frigid.

Despite the awkward relationship between naturalistic empiricism and religion, there was just enough cordiality to allow naturalism to thrive and form a foundation whereupon the educational philosophies of idealism and realism could build. Yet as it made inroads on the educational thought in this country, Spencer's naturalism, in answering the question posed in the essay "What Knowledge Is of Most Worth" stressed the unassailable significance of science. This emphasis was daring when one takes into account the immaturity of science, and also optimistic, for science's promise was by no means evident. In any case, Spencer declared, science offers the only intelligent way of obtaining a kind of knowledge that, while generally dependable, is by no means absolute or ultimate. Besides, and this might be equally important, depending upon science is a way of acting intelligently, and all naturalists want to act intelligently.

What has this to do with education or, more exactly, in what sense is it a bedrock for a philosophy of education? If Spencer's program represents naturalistic empiricism fairly, it means that children are neither more nor less than animals, and highly dependent ones at that.[12] Spencer knew at once what others took a long time to learn: the unavoidable preamble to any philosophy of education is the nature of persons. Compared to many other animals, children grow and mature slowly and deliberately. A long process of growth, maturation, and instruction is required to bring a child to a level of independence and responsibility. So, with scientific knowledge nailed to his educational mast, it is right to inquire where the process of education, in which naturalists place a great deal of confidence, is to lead. Complete living is the general answer, which, likely, can be translated into such a phrase as "the good life."[13] Of what does *complete living* consist? The first objective, which if missed stops the entire process, is self-preservation. And in realizing the first objective instinct plays a large role, aided and abetted by knowledge of the laws of health and the skills to sustain life. The skills are those for securing food and shelter, and as time passes they must be honed to enable persons to provide for the necessities of life.

Two objectives in Spencer's litany are in place, to which a third, family life, is added. One of the most serious flaws in the educational system familiar to Spencer was its indifference, or worse, its total neglect, of preparation for family life and the care and upbringing of children. European educational models seemed to thrive on the notion that caring for families and rearing children belonged to the area of instinct and that preparation is unnecessary, for the curriculum of the schools gave the impression that the whole society is celibate or that children never need nurture. Next on the list is a kind of education preparing persons for effective citizenship in politics and in society generally. Individualism and avarice are no more likely than an urge to community and an attitude of altruism, but neither are they less likely. It is incumbent on an educational program, therefore, to cultivate a kind of citizenship that will contribute to the common good. Finally, although in his own life Herbert Spencer never seemed to have time for fun, there is the provision for a side to education that will enable persons to use leisure profitably and enjoyably.[14]

Unsurprisingly, and in keeping with a long line of naturalists as far back as Rousseau, Spencer emphasized the point that learning is natural. He demurred from following Rousseau and his disciples who were eager to exclude teachers and teaching from the educational process. Spencer's common sense refused to repudiate the role parents and teachers must play in the education of youth. Still, there is nothing in Spencer's view with respect to the role of teachers that allows for an educational practice indifferent to a natural process of learning. In addition, education, while it might not always be fun, should at least be pleasant.

Taking seriously into account the dogmatic assumption that children are material organisms subject mainly to the laws of mechanics, naturalists, and Spencer chief among them, celebrated the centrality of the principle of activity in learning. No one can declare them wrong, for activity is essential to learning, but does the activity need to be, as they asserted, physical? Besides, there is a preference for spontaneity, although it is always subordinate to activity. Somehow, naturalists maintained, activity is always better, or more likely to produce good results, if it is spontaneous rather than being induced by parents, guardians, or teachers.

Some early naturalists—Rousseau is a leading example—paid the acquisition of knowledge scant heed, because they distrusted both the process that led to knowledge and knowledge itself. Spencer's theory of knowledge was less restrictive. Using dependable methods of investigation and scrutinizing the results with care, useful and generally reliable knowledge can be acquired. No naturalist would go so far as to call such acquisitions truth, but those who followed Spencer's lead never discounted them. Knowledge is essential and naturalistic empiricists were confident that it could be obtained. So, while the educational process could not be accounted for in declarations concerning acquiring knowledge, for Spencer and his followers it was chiefly a matter of acquiring knowledge.

Spencer's educational perspective provided for a program of instruction that cultivated both mental and physical faculties. In keeping with a long tradition that had its origin with genuine classical culture, education was for the body as well as the mind.[15] And now we come to a novel point of naturalistic method: honoring the timing of nature. Nature takes its own good time, neither braking nor accelerating development. Education, Spencer and his naturalistic friends said, should follow nature's example and prudently practice the art of delay. At any rate, delay or not, instruction should not be forced upon students before they are ready and able to learn.[16] The entire process of instruction, whether in or out of school, should of course be inductive.

Finally, we come to an item that despite our fondest hope will disappear neither from formal education nor from life generally in the care and upbringing of children: discipline. Naturalists never went so far as to declare discipline essential to any degree of excellence, but they believed that individual and social deportment needs standards of guidance. Being neither moral theologians nor philosophers, they depended upon experience for setting these standards, for saying, and giving the statements the status of convention, what behavior is or is not acceptable. Generally, naturalists preferred to allow the natural consequences of unacceptable behavior to define the nature and extent of punishment, but when natural consequences are ineffective sterner measures might be appropriate. In any case, unacceptable behavior should be punished; punishment should be prompt and certain but, naturalists added, tempered with sympathy. And punishment, whatever its form, should be considered part of an instructional process and not an act of vengeance. Human beings are the superior products of the evolutionary process and they act morally when their behavior is in harmony with nature. Being either agnostics or atheists, for naturalistic empiricists recognize neither God nor a supreme being, they are nevertheless tempted to acknowledge a supreme force in nature.

In step with Spencer, but with a shorter stride, was William H. Payne, who in *Contributions to the Science of Education*[17] praised without adopting outright the naturalistic, revolutionary, and, in some respects, the irresponsible educational recommendations of Jean Jacques Rousseau. The place Payne occupies in the history of American educational philosophy, though, is uncertain. That he was America's first education professor is likely; that he was well-known and respected is undebatable; that he was influential is a matter for speculation. The same kind of naturalism, without, it is true, allegiance to Rousseau, is evidenced by George E. Partridge (1870–1953), who had high praise for G. Stanley Hall (1844–1924) as an educational philosopher, although he characterized philosophy of education as a "'point of view' from which educational problems are seen in perspective."[18] Clearly, Hall made a mark on American education, but almost certainly it issued from his psychology rather than from his philosophy.

While the empiricists were tilling the field of educational philosophy, hoping to produce a harvest that would supply all the educational insight necessary, transcendentalists, idealists, and realists were becoming more outspoken about education's theoretical basis and were making some difference in the direction educational thought began to take. Ralph Waldo Emerson (1803–1882) wrote essays on education, as did Bronson Alcott (1799–1888).[19] Both claimed for human beings a spiritual power that transcends both nature and reason. Transcendentalism heralded a renewal of interest in philosophy, especially idealism, in the early years of the nineteenth century, so an interpolation reflecting its formative years is worth our time, although its influence on education, if any, is far from clear.

Our colonial ancestors thought themselves prudent and wise, and so they were, but they were not philosophers and they chose to disregard philosophy except when, as in the case of logic, it could be a useful instrument. And they could afford to be unphilosophical because they had, they thought, an inexhaustible reservoir of truth in theology. In later years, however, the theological citadel was weakened by dispute and defection. So almost by accident philosophy was invested with dignity and trust, and accorded a new and cordial reception. Philosophical quickening began in the early years of the nineteenth century and responsibility for its nurture was assumed by a cadre of Americans with philosophical interests who called themselves transcendentalists.[20]

Inspired by the philosophical idealism of German scholars (Kant, Schelling, Fichte, and Schleiermacher) and the romanticism of British poets (Samuel Taylor Coleridge [1772–1834], for example), American transcendentalism undertook to lead a new intellectual movement, one especially compatible with this country's taste and temper, which, on the one hand, would halt recruitment to rationalism and naturalism, both philosophical products of the Enlightenment and, on the other, soften the harsh rhetoric of sectarian doctrine. They hoped to replace the emphasis traditional philosophy gave to reason, scientific method, and positive laws of nature with a theory positioning human nature as the source and motive for behavior. Their vision of human nature was essentially spiritual and always in harmony with the universal spirit, sometimes called God. Personal spiritual nature, they declared, transcends the human body and all material reality, thus the name, transcendentalism.

This definition contained elements of paradox when transcendentalists were disposed to ignore nature, and nature's laws, as objects of study. Indifferent to the scientific method, they nevertheless idealized nature as testimony to God's providence and, moreover, evidenced an obsession with nature as the custodian of human spirit. Their cordiality to theism and their outright rejection of naturalistic materialism made their views congenial with those of orthodox sectarians, but this good will atrophied when they said God was "oversoul," a divine immanence, not the personal God recognized and worshiped by Christians. And to make matters worse, they rejected revelation and dismissed the authority of the Bible.

Some critics called transcendentalism a strange mixture, more a liberal religion (like Unitarianism and Universalism) than a philosophy, and they were at least partly right. Yet, its proponents were philosophical enough to steer clear of absolute idealism and set a course toward individualism, self-reliance, and personal responsibility. Transforming individualism into a cult, they talked about universal perfection among persons, and some sounded like they had just finished reading Rousseau. The doctrine of original sin, taken seriously and explicitly by orthodox Christians, was jettisoned: freedom from creedal restraint, institutions, and conventions was the transcendental recipe for personal and social progress. Sincere in their conviction about freedom, transcendentalists perceived plenty of limitations. Devoted to the proposition of human perfection, they were frequently bruised by the evils of materialism, industrialism, commercialism, and capitalism.

Assuming the posture of social protest, this philosophy could make common cause with humanitarianism, the ground-breaking theory of the preceding generation, which discovered the key to social progress in a more equitable management and distribution of economic resources. But this fellowship was fractured from the outset, for transcendentalism found progress in an elevation of the human spirit and in opportunity for self-realization and not in material reward and creature comfort.

The cities, the factories, even the farms, were poor places to cultivate an inner spiritual vigor promoting self-realization. It was better to forsake civilization and return to a more pristine society where persons left to themselves could contemplate the mystery of existence in splendid isolation. The cry "back to nature" was heard often but seldom heeded, and some brave, dedicated souls went to the country where, far enough from cities, they could have a genuine adventure with nature and speculate about the human condition. This flight from social reality, from concrete conditions in American life, to conduct such utopian experiments as Brook Farm, could hardly enhance the credentials of transcendentalism. It made the men and women who were its advocates appear disingenuous in trying to solve society's problems by escaping from them.

The other side to transcendentalism, however, was only partly obscured by rural isolation. It evidenced a confidence in the ability of men and women to use reason. Essential to social amelioration, reason needed enlightenment from intuition. Intuition would come, so transcendentalists promised, either from religious piety or moral value generated in the experience of daily life. Truth and goodness could be grasped when men and women went beyond sense experience to discover the good and the true in a spiritual reality impenetrable by the methods of science.

Looking back, we can see that transcendentalism's prospects for being either a prominent or dominant American philosophy were slim. Its good and capable leaders had admirable and praiseworthy instincts and aspirations. Its theories were tolerantly nonsectarian without being antireligious. It could appeal to the American intellect without being a secular philosophy or a kind of theological rationalism. But if these were its strengths, they were never quite sufficient to outweigh a stubborn neglect of scientific method and knowledge, and a tendency to let philosophy speak for itself. Failure to promote the doctrine, while clearly a serious flaw to greater visibility and currency, kept transcendentalism as a cult among an initiated few. But more importantly, commitment to this theory (or doctrine) demanded a kind of spiritual fervor and zeal so characteristic of evangelical religious sects. In an age where the trend was away from sentimental spirituality and vague introvertive trances, converts to transcendentalism were hard to find. So, if in the end transcendentalism must be counted a failure, it did nevertheless cultivate ground whereupon other philosophies could grow. In the wake of its decline we see an American temper disposed toward things of the mind and in a maturing intellectual climate philosophy was accorded a warm welcome. One is almost certainly right to maintain that idealism was the principal beneficiary of our brief flirtation with transcendentalism.

Returning now to the central theme of the story, James P. Wickersham (1825–1893) reintroduced realism to educational discourse by maintaining that the principles of reason are as important to science and education as are the data of experience.[21] And this brand of conservative rationalism was advanced in the work of William T. Harris (1835–1909) and later in the idealism of Herman H. Horne. Typical of idealism, Harris declared that the nature of mind determines the goals of education and went on to say that such goals are achieved only through the process of self-activity.[22]

In addition to the contributions to the literature on educational philosophy already cited, contributions that hastened the discipline's maturity, a word might be added concerning other work on education that had either a direct or an indirect impact on the formation of educational philosophy as a legitimate field of scholarly inquiry. Chauncey Wright (1830–1875), often mentioned as a precursor of the educational perspective of John Dewey, wrote a number of articles on philosophy that affected education and are said to have influenced Dewey.[23] One might add, as well, some of John Dewey's early articles on education that are reproduced in Paul Monroe's *The Cyclopedia of Education*.

Illustrative of pioneer effort is John Angus MacVannel's *Outline of a Course in the Philosophy of Education*.[24] Neither the book's title nor content is arresting, but it was intended as a textbook for a course in educational philosophy. This sustains the belief that early in the twentieth century educational philosophy began to find a comfortable and conventional place in a college curriculum that was designed to prepare teachers. Because of its native authorship, MacVannel's book was likely more enthusiastically received than Rosenkranz's (1805–1879) earlier *Philosophy of Education* that in its second edition benefited from William T. Harris's translating and editing.

Other authors who took the vanguard in producing books either on or bordering on educational philosophy were: Emerson E. White, *The Elements of Pedagogy*;[25] Francis B. Palmer, *The Science of Education, Designed as a Textbook for Teachers*;[26] Thomas J. Morgan, *Studies in Pedagogy*;[27] Arnold Tompkins, *The Philosophy of Teaching*;[28] George E. Vincent, *Social*

Mind and Education;[29] Nicholas Murray Butler, *The Meaning of Education*;[30] C. Hanford Henderson, *Education and the Larger Life*;[31] M.V. O'Shea, *Education as Adjustment: Educational Theory Viewed in the Light of Contemporary Thought*;[32] Herman H. Horne, *The Philosophy of Education, Being Foundations of Education in the Related Natural and Mental Sciences*;[33] William E. Chancellor, *A Theory of Motives, Ideals and Values in Education*;[34] and Ernest N. Henderson, *A Text-Book in the Principles of Education*.[35]

SYSTEMATIC PHILOSOPHIES OF EDUCATION

Much of the philosophizing about education that occurred in the United States before the last years of the nineteenth century was inspired by religion, on the one hand, and political philosophy, on the other: salvation and citizenship. Only now and then, as in the case of the "Report of the Yale Faculty," was theoretical discourse intended to represent the educational ideas of a group or in any sense suggest a school of thought.[36] Philosophical-sounding statements about education were personal, solitary expressions without any semblance of corporate status. But toward the end of the nineteenth century philosophical individualism began to wane, although it is not easy to say why. Likely the maturity of national consciousness and the loosening of the grip that religion had for so long held on the national mind were contributing factors.

In any case, educational theory began to cooperate with philosophy and to form a sort of compact replacing the earlier competition or hostility between the two that in the end produced systematic philosophies of education. These philosophies of education—idealism, realism (along with its humanistic tributaries), and pragmatism—dominated the field for the first fifty years of the twentieth century, and were then superseded by either linguistic analysis or logical positivism as branches of analytic philosophy. Without ever asserting a clear claim to being a philosophy of education, much less a systematic one, existentialism operated on the fringe of philosophical respectability for some part of the twentieth century.

Idealism

Likely because of the close relationship philosophical idealism had with religion and the fact that idealism had been planted in the intellectual soil of America by pastors and pedagogues, idealism was the first of the academic-historic philosophies to make overtures to education. And without undertaking to define educational philosophy as an independent discipline, or even to identify it as a separate category in philosophical thought, idealism had made room for education from the first. Plato's *Republic*, often, though mistakenly, classified as a discourse in educational philosophy, belongs properly to political philosophy. After Plato and the *Republic*, the standard editions on philosophy's history record the idealistic predisposition of Augustine (350–430) and his penetrating influence upon early Christian thought.[37]

Without calling the roll for every idealist or every philosopher who demonstrated idealist disposition and who put planks in the platform that eventually became modern educational idealism, the principal actors should be named. Among Continental European philosophers one recognizes René Descartes (1596–1650), Baruch Spinoza (1632–1677), Gottfried Wilhelm von Leibniz (1646–1716), George Berkeley (1685–1753), Immanuel Kant (1724–1804), Johann Gottlieb Fichte (1762–1814), Georg Wilhelm Friedrich Hegel (1770–1831), Arthur Schopenhauer (1788–1860), Henri Bergson (1859–1941), Benedetto Croce (1866–1952), and Giovanni Gentile (1875–1944).

In British literary circles Samuel Taylor Coleridge, James Hutchinson Stirling (1820–1909), John Caird (1820–1898), Edward Caird (1835–1908), Thomas Hill Green (1836–1882), and Bernard Bosanquet (1848–1923) formed an idealist cadre. In America the idealistic cause was aided by Ralph Waldo Emerson (1803–1882), William T. Harris (1835–1909), Josiah Royce (1855–1916), Herman Harrell Horne (1874–1946), Michael Demiashkevitch (1891–1938), Boris Basil Bogoslovsky (1890–1966), Robert Ulich (1890–1977), and J. Donald Butler (b. 1908). In defining the dimensions and setting the direction of idealism as a philosophy of education in the United States, pride of place belongs to Horne.

During the years educational philosophy was being separated into systems, two interpretations of educational purpose and practice began to capture the attention of Americans. Without ever being genuine philosophies of education, progressive education and essentialism began to compete as drivers of the American educational enterprise.[38] Each spoke about method and curriculum and what they had to say might have kindled some interest in fundamental issues of educational theory without, at the same time, trying to elucidate them. Progressives (who sought to reform schooling by introducing methods and materials of instruction to serve student need and interest) and essentialists (who declared for a scholastic program that recognizes a common core to basic culture) represented hostile educational camps and neither was ever tempted to seek for compromise. Both claimed to ensure the promise of education and its contribution to American society, but the roads each chose to follow to achieve that ideal were strikingly different.

We have seen enough of American education to know of its relationship to philosophy: sometimes the relationship was warm and affectionate, but sometimes it was cool and distant. Yet long before progressives and essentialists appeared on the scene, education and philosophy had formed a sort of alliance that honored the perennial bond between them, but this bond kept educational philosophy in the unenviable position of stepchild of general philosophy. It was a paragraph or a footnote in philosophical discourse. Promoted in part by the controversial relationship between progressives and essentialists, but probably more by internal vigor, educational philosophy began to emerge as an independent discipline with genuine academic credentials.

Sensing that the rhetoric of educational controversy spelled trouble for American education, the American public began to worry about the need education had for a foundation in theory strong enough to protect society's investment in republican government. Although this was too ambitious a commission for any kind of philosophy, it had the effect of placing educational philosophy at the center of the fledgling discipline of education. A further indication of renewed interest in educational philosophy, especially as a subject for collegiate study, was the formation of the Philosophy of Education Society by professors of the subject at meetings in Philadelphia in late 1940 and early 1941.[39]

Throughout most of its history, American education had been affected by idealist thought, although such thought was more religious than philosophical. It has been argued, and there is substance to the argument, that progressive education was mainly a revolt against the idealist dispositions that were infecting the educational process. On the other side of the coin, there is the tendency to believe that essentialism was simply an expression of the idealist educational creed artfully camouflaged to conceal its identity. Idealists might have infiltrated the essentialist camp, but it would be hard to demonstrate where essentialism was indebted to idealism. One of the most prominent of modern idealists, Herman Horne, whose book, *The Democratic Philosophy of Education*, used almost every page to contradict John Dewey's *Democracy and Education*, rehearsed essentialistic themes, yet Horne maintained an arm's length association with essentialism. Despite his extraordinary scholarship, along with the clarity and cogency of his writing, Horne could neither revive idealism nor restore it to a position of commanding influence in American educational philosophy.[40]

Idealism's decline was due, likely, neither to a lack of eloquent expositors nor to its internal logic, but to the changing temper of Americans. Once zealously religious, Americans, while still maintaining decent respect for religion, allowed other allegiances to replace it. And idealism, even without explicit denominational affiliation, was intensely spiritual and traditionally regarded men and women as extensions of an absolute or divine spirit. In an age that was becoming increasingly materialistic in its attitudes, such spiritual tendencies were greeted with skepticism and sometimes with scorn. Besides, for those who probed more deeply the philosophical issues, idealists were clearly rejecting common-sense explanations of reality: they made reality substantially spiritual without denying its material side. But a theory of reality was not the only hurdle. Idealist epistemology raised doubt about the possibility of valid knowledge being secured through the employment of the discursive process. It declared instead for the place of intuition and cultural conditioning in producing knowledge. Immunizing knowledge from a heavy dependence upon the senses and questioning the validity of the discursive process made idealism seem eccentric and undependable.

Added to these metaphysical and epistemological issues, the idealist statement of educational objectives and its characterization of the educational process as a mental exercise made American school patrons wary. Toward the end of the nineteenth century materialism and its stalking horse, evolution, had made persons keenly aware of their physical nature, and a new brand of psychological literature reminded teachers and students of mind-body relationships. Meanwhile idealists concentrated upon mental development and seemed indifferent to the fact that students came to school with bodies as well as minds. Refinement of the intellect counted most; attention to an environment conducive to learning was slight, a point entirely consistent with idealist ideology. Rigor and discipline should be stressed in schools at the expense of any pedagogic technique endorsed by a psychology and a physiology of learning. The content of the curriculum should be drawn from the accumulated wisdom of the ages without reference to practical considerations of daily life in late nineteenth- and early twentieth-century America.

This was the kind of schooling most educated Americans knew well, for they had been nurtured upon it, and for the most part they had few fond memories for it. Their children should have something more humane and, at the same time, more practical. Since idealism promoted a kind of education many educated Americans despised, it was not difficult for them to turn away from it with disdain. What could justify turning back the calendar? Idealism's place in the history of philosophy recommended its retention in the library, but as an effective philosophy containing principles upon which policy and practice could be based, it was jettisoned.[41]

Realism

The roots of realism are as deep in the history of thought as those of idealism, but for centuries the hostility of theologians to what was perceived as materialism and their cordiality toward idealism because of its alleged friendship for Christianity kept realism as an undernourished school of thought. Yet the common-sense view that a real and knowable material reality exists independently of any knowing mind made an embrace of realism almost irresistible. But common sense does not translate directly to the popularity of philosophical doctrine. So the philosophical dispute between Plato and Aristotle while Aristotle was a student and then a master in the Academy turned out to be perennial. Although history's final verdict went to Aristotle and realism, idealism superseded realism until well into the eighteenth century. Besides, many philosophers who eventually cast their lot with realism had from time to time been infatuated with idealism.

Calling the roll of realism's founding fathers is fairly easy, but one must be cautious and not ascribe to all of them an allegiance to realism that repudiated any connection with some elements in other schools of philosophical thought. Aristotle, of course, heads the list of realists and it would seem that his theory of matter and form, and the principle of the self-evident made idealist theses untenable. From about the fourth century B.C. until around the middle of the thirteenth century, realism, with the exception of some Arabic commentators and interpreters, had Aristotle as its sole proponent.[42] Then St. Thomas Aquinas (1255–1274) joined the ranks of the realists and elaborated its Christian version. Thereafter come Descartes, Spinoza, and Kant, all with some sympathy for idealism, John Locke, who despite an idealization of reason could never be teamed with idealists, Herbart, and, in America, William James (1842–1910).

A tributary feeding American realism and always keeping it close to common sense was its Scottish blend. In addition to an affinity for a common-sense view of reality—that is, accepting the validity of sense experience—Scottish realism was preoccupied with ethics. If a philosophy of education had been elaborated, it would have given primacy of place to moral rather than intellectual education, although by no means was the latter sold at discount. Besides, and a point making this brand of realism attractive to both Jefferson and Franklin, its basic moral propositions issued from reason, not religion. While ethical principles might be supported by theological faith, they did not originate with it. The theology was a theology of deism, where God was understood to be the architect of reality, who having completed the work of creation was disposed to stand aside. The watch was wound; men and women were left to read its movement. These interpretations of theology, of creation, and of education were inconsistent with a vigorous residue of Puritan perceptions that remained to affect, if not dominate, so much of American social philosophy. The elaboration of the themes of Scottish realism were likely as much American as Scottish, although their genesis is attributed to the Scot, Henry Home, Lord Kames (1696–1782).[43]

Quite likely the man most responsible for supplying ingredients for the American version of Scottish common-sense realism was James McCosh (1811–1894), president of Princeton. The outcome of his work was a melding of religion and science, with an attempt, by relying on what he called common sense, to prevent philosophy from indulging in speculative extremes. McCosh, some say, was wrong in believing his philosophy was a common-sense brand of realism when, in fact, it was based upon Platonism.[44] In any case, McCosh and others who called themselves Scottish realists, were engaged in using "philosophical reason as a moral sedative, which was administered in our colleges in excessive doses by the clergy in the hope that it would be an antidote to the powerful stimulants of the experimental sciences."[45] It is probably fair to say that by the time philosophy's development reached the versatile and eloquent William James, Scottish realism had undergone considerable dilution.

After James interest in realism was cultivated mainly in America, where it split into two camps: neo- and critical realism. The leading neorealists, Ralph Barton Perry (1876–1957), Edwin B. Holt (1873–1946), Walter T. Marvin (1872–1944), Edward Gleason Spaulding (1873–1940), Walter B. Pitkin (1878–1953), and William Pepperell Montague (1873–1953), seldom applied their theory to education. These new realists, as they called themselves, were committed mainly to refuting the idealist doctrine that knowledge of a thing makes changes in it, and in promoting the idea that the process of knowing is a simple relation between the knower and the object known, where the object is presented through the senses to a conscious mind.

Critical realists, who counted Durant Drake (1878–1933), Arthur O. Lovejoy (1873–1962), James B. Pratt (1875–1944), George Santayana (1863–1952), Roy Wood Sellars (1880–1973), Arthur K. Rogers (1868–1936), and C. A. Strong (1862–1940) as their leading spokesmen, found the theses of the neorealists too rustic for their philosophical taste. Likely subscribing to the same metaphysical propositions as the new realists, critical realists rejected their epistemology. Instead of objects being presented to the mind through the senses, they are represented to the mind, otherwise, said the critical realists, error in perception could not be explained.[46]

Yet, writing in the forty-first yearbook of the National Society for the

Study of Education, Part I, *Philosophies of Education*, Frederick S. Breed (1876–1952), himself a realist, discounts this schism. He "is much more interested in the resemblances than in the differences" among realists. The strongest resemblance of all, the one thing that "unifies the realists is known in brief as the *principle of independence*."[47]

Nineteenth-century American education, we know, to the extent that it was on speaking terms with a genuine educational philosophy, was affected by idealism, but with the advent of the twentieth-century pragmatism, as it turned out, wore the mantle of philosophical progress. And, safe to say, had pragmatism been compatible with basic principles of realism—for example, the principle of independence—realism likely would have been nothing more than a tributary to the mainstream of educational philosophy. But pragmatism introduced propositions relative to knowledge and reality unacceptable to idealists and realists. When any chance of compromise between idealism and realism was foreclosed, realism parted company also with a contemporary pragmatism that was being crafted by John Dewey and his disciples. The new realists rejected idealism with propositions that in turn were refuted by critical realists. But critical realism proved to be fertile soil wherein logical positivism and linguistic analysis could germinate and both, in time, affected the fortunes of educational philosophy. It was critical realism, however, that developed a philosophy of education capable of competing for a role in defining the purpose and process for education in the United States. One might add, though essentialism as we have seen eschewed precise philosophical links, that the expressions of educational philosophy issuing from critical realism gave an immense amount of comfort to essentialists.

Realist educational philosophers were eager to demonstrate how realism affected schooling. Henry C. Morrison (1871–1945), Frederick S. Breed, William C. Bagley (1874–1946), Ross L. Finney (1875–1934), and Harry S. Broudy in their writing and teaching succeeded in making realist educational philosophy known and respected throughout the country. As spokesmen for realism they meant to reject the theoretical positions of pragmatism and to denounce what they called its assignation with soft pedagogy. Beginning with a decent respect for stubborn physical phenomena recognized and verified by proper method, they asserted the validity and stability of knowledge. Order rather than change or chaos characterizes the universe. It is possible for men and women to understand how the various parts of the universe function and accommodate to them. It is unlikely that we can alter the world's order, but its structure can be fathomed. So there are natural laws governing both physical and social reality. One of the principal functions of education is to see to it that these laws are discovered and taught.

Some of nature's laws are immutable; others are relative; none is in a constant state of flux. Knowing the world and our relationship to it and how we can adjust and accommodate to the order it dictates is education's chief responsibility. When education fulfills its purpose it offers men and women the chance to lead full, happy, and decent lives.

Beginning as all educational philosophy must with an understanding of the nature of persons, and defining them as physical organisms capable of rational behavior and of thought and expression, realism avoided flagrant materialism by acknowledging the existence of material and spiritual substance while rejecting supernaturalism. Men and women are defined by what they are capable of doing and what they are capable of doing must be discovered and tested empirically. An abundance of empirical evidence demonstrates conclusively that men and women are capable of thought and expression. A determination to refine these capacities must be first on the list of educational objectives.

In the final analysis, realist educational philosophy expressed a conservative principle: it conceded the possibility of truth as the result of the use of scientific methods and commissioned schools to engage in the communication of intellectual and moral truth.[48] Moral truth has its basis in natural law and in connection with moral truth, realists seldom speak in concert about the freedom of persons to make choices. Of course, if freedom is a myth, any talk about moral education or character formation is futile. While many realists affirm free will, others adopt some degree of determinism, so care must be exercised in attributing to realist philosophy one position between the extremes of freedom and determinism.

Following the advice of prominent realist philosophers who only occasionally attended to realism's implications for education—for example, Alfred North Whitehead (1861–1947) and Bertrand Russell (1872–1970)—realist educational philosophers stressed the importance of making educational objectives cohere with life's realities. It is possible, they declared, to discover what men and women need to know if they are to live decent and productive lives by conducting a scientific inquiry into physical and social reality. Schools should admit that the knowledge obtained from such inquiry is the basic culture of learning, and use it both to form the content of the curriculum and design techniques of communication to assure that such knowledge is taught and learned. Teachers, therefore, must be masters of knowledge and skillful in communicating it; moreover, as cooperative artists they must testify to the worth of their work as teachers and be constant in their commitment to what is true and honorable.

What and how knowledge is to be taught, realists aver, does not depend upon what children think they want to learn or how they want to learn it, but upon the stark necessities of life itself. Schools should embrace an educational program that encourages training, instruction, and discipline. It is pointless and profitless to mount and maintain a system of schools unless there is both zeal and devotion for teaching students what they need to know in order to live well. Life, realists declare, is too short to allow, or worse, to encourage, students to follow uncertain and unmarked routes of unaided discovery.

A tributary to realism, often but erroneously allied with idealism, is humanism. In the course of philosophy's history, all kinds of humanism appear. The educational humanism referred to here can be classified further as literary, rational, and Christian. In the great debate between progressive and essentialistic educators, a debate, we know, that occurred during the first half of the twentieth century, humanists associated themselves with essentialists who, they supposed, were promoting an educational program that would contribute most to the cultivation of the distinctive human abilities: thought and expression. As it turned out humanists could agree upon a common core to basic culture and concede that it should be taught with zeal and devotion, yet be sharply divided about the nature of human nature, the nature of physical and spiritual reality, the nature and possibility of knowledge, and the fundamentals of morality.

Nicholas Murray Butler (1862–1947), Mark Van Doren (1894–1972), and Norman Foerster (1887–1972) blazed the twentieth-century trail for literary humanism. Susceptible to a charge of elitism, because of their preoccupation with the conventional literary tradition, these scholars maintained that literature is the most likely vehicle for perpetuating those ideals that make for excellence and civility in life and society. Rational humanists, led by Robert Maynard Hutchins (1899–1977) and Mortimer Adler (b. 1902), promoted a philosophy of education that paid special heed to intellectual formation and a trained reason. Christian humanists in the United States were legion, but principal spokesmen, safe to say, were Thomas E. Shields (1862–1921), William F. Cunningham (1885–1953), William J. McGucken (b. 1889), and Jacques Maritain (1882–1973). Together they endorsed education for culture and reason and, three being Roman Catholic priests, emphasized a deposit of religious revelation that declared for supernaturalism and explained a person's relationship to God.

Opposition to materialism and naturalism and to all kinds of monism has the effect of attracting strange bedfellows, and humanism was no exception. Yet, humanists, although seldom able to circle the same tree of philosophical outlook, found it possible to speak almost with one voice about education's purpose and means. They differed in their philosophy of the person and this always caused trouble, because neither literary nor rational humanists were able to acknowledge the validity of revealed knowledge about human origin, nature, and destiny. They could, however, find agreement on a wide range of metaphysical propositions and there was hardly anything in a theory of knowledge to separate them. Metaphysically and epistemologically, humanists were dualists—matter and spirit were real and distinct as were the knower and the things known—and in the end were philosophical realists.

Education (schooling is probably a better word here) is a means for cultivating the human abilities of thought and expression. While humanists sometimes differed in their answer to the question—What knowledge is of most worth in performing this duty?—they quite readily subscribed to the goal itself. Besides, they refused to treat children in schools as persons incapable of reasoning and abstracting. In a word, they were distressed when pedagogic technique was regarded as nothing more than a physiology of learning.

Asserting the existence of truth, on the one hand, and the possibility of achieving it, humanists put in place one sturdy plank to a platform of schooling. On the other hand, they were eager to promote moral standards to make the educational experience one wherein morality and decency are inculcated. They understood the desire men and women have to live well and were prepared to campaign for an orderly society. But they were prepared, as well, to speak about the life of the mind and the virtue to be found in intellectual culture. Humanists of all persuasions aligned themselves with educational objectives attuned to civilizing men and women.

Literary, rational, and Christian humanists marched in cadence through the natural and human virtues, but when literary and rational humanists halted, Christian humanists went on to embrace revelation as a source of dependable knowledge and a spiritual character to men and women endowing them with supernatural dignity. Christian humanists made supernaturalism an essential plank in their philosophy of education. While humanists in other camps might, as individuals, have subscribed to supernatural religion and displayed a private religious disposition, they did not allow it to affect—or more exactly, to infect—their philosophy. However important this point was in connection with philosophy and religion, its educational consequences were lodged mainly in the curriculum. Christian humanists, acknowledging revelation as a source for truth, were persuaded of the need to introduce religious teaching to the schools and to regard such teaching as a necessary foundation for moral formation and character education. The curriculum of Christian humanist schools should both explicitly and implicitly communicate the religious inheritance and seek to introduce a genuine religious perspective to students.

Educational humanists had their priorities and sought to impose them upon educational objectives and curricula. These priorities illustrated a fundamental conviction that the main business of education is to form the intellect and shape the will. Yet attention was not visited solely upon liberal studies in humanist educational philosophy. It would be wrong to think of the humanists as archaic schoolmasters conspiring to reverse the scholastic calendar. They, as much as progressive educators, were eager to educate men and women in a way enabling them to live well in contemporary society, but such an education, they declared, should stand on a bedrock of truth and moral value.

Besides, they thought of society as being demanding and rigorous rather than permissive and fluid, so they wanted the educational program to make a commitment to mental discipline. They were ready to abandon harsh scholastic regimens and replace them with pleasant and happy schools, but these schools, nevertheless, were to be places where excellence in the realization of human talent is prized, for discipline, they said, is essential to any degree of excellence, and it matters not whether excellence is sought in the liberal, the fine, or the practical arts. Educational decency was the motto nailed to the humanists' educational mast, because it offered men and women the best chance to realize their full potentiality.

Pragmatism

If America has produced a systematic philosophy of its own, it must be pragmatism,[49] for in this country pragmatism was rescued from an obscure existence on the fringe of philosophical thought and plunged into the mainstream of the science of reason. Centuries before Charles Sanders Peirce (1839–1914), William James,[50] and John Dewey wrote new chapters in the book on philosophy's history, pragmatism had been hardly more than a tributary to philosophy, and a shallow one at that. Beginning with the issue of knowledge's dependability, pre-Socratic philosophers expressed doubt that truth could ever be grasped in a world whose most obvious characteristic is change. Ancient Sophists whose crude promise to teach everything and anything embraced a fundamental skepticism that enabled them to deliver on their arrogant claim to be masters of all knowledge. Their point was: if truth is unattainable, opinion alone is possible, and on the level of opinion one is as good as another. This stance allowed the Sophists to inflate the significance of rhetoric, easily accomplished if truth is unattainable, because without truth the opinion adopted must be the one supported by the best argument.

In addition to being seduced by skepticism, ancient pragmatists refused to rely upon any principle or practice simply because it had reason's support. Their test was consequence. So, almost from the outset, pragmatism infected philosophical thought, and we should not be surprised to learn that it was durable enough to enter the modern world.

As philosophy moved forward and was subjected to Christian and medieval influence, it came to depend more and more upon the deductive logic of Aristotle as a way of arriving at knowledge. The deductive method, it should be conceded, was influential in shaping some of the great ornaments to philosophy, but in the seventeenth century deduction was challenged by Francis Bacon's *Novum Organum* and thereafter had to share a methodological platform with induction. Few philosophers had the temerity to dissolve all their compacts with deduction and invest entirely in inductive method. So, for the most part, deduction and induction were partners in the quest for dependable knowledge. But this turned out to be an uneasy partnership and pragmatism was able to gain a more secure grip on philosophy when August Comte's (1789–1857) *Positive Philosophy* made the scientific method the sole avenue to a knowledge of reality and Charles Darwin's (1809–1882) *On the Origin of Species* raised serious doubt about conventional theistic doctrines concerning the origin of men and women.

American pragmatism stood on foundations supplied by energetic architects: Charles Sanders Peirce, William James, and John Dewey. Whether Peirce was a genuine pragmatist who could fulfill the expectations of later pragmatists is a subject for debate. Many contemporary pragmatists appear ready to disown Peirce, but in any case his contribution was to propose a formula for redressing the epistemological subjectivism in modern philosophy and the empirical arrogance of modern science. To his satisfaction and to the satisfaction of most pragmatists as well, Peirce succeeded by affirming a perennial pragmatic criterion: the meaning of an idea is revealed in the consequences of its application. Yet, Butler, whose credentials for making a judgment about Peirce's pragmatism are impeccable, declares that "Peirce was a realist, not a pragmatist, much more to be compared to Bertrand Russell or A.N. Whitehead than to either James or Dewey."[51]

It is likely impossible to declare James's philosophical affinity. Although embracing only part of pragmatism's creed, he nevertheless played a huge role in popularizing it both in this country and in Europe. His book, *Pragmatism*, tilled the philosophical soil wherefrom the systematic work of John Dewey sprang.

John Dewey found his way through the thicket of philosophical dispute by starting out as a realist and engaging in a brief flirtation with idealism before committing himself to pragmatism where he matured to become its principal builder and most authoritative spokesman. Exaggeration is absent in crediting Dewey with having articulated pragmatism's philosophical creed, wherein the evolutionary hypothesis is taken seriously, and the principles of educational philosophy, the final product of philosophical thought, are tested in the schools.[52] An embrace of evolution put pragmatism outside conventional boundaries of philosophy and theology, but this was not all: any proposition making men and women the products of an evolutionary process was explicitly antagonistic to the dogmas of Western religion concerning their origin, nature, and destiny. Pragmatism took men and women as it found them, and it found them as highly complex material organisms, but organisms nevertheless. They were neither above nor below other forms of matter: they were one with nature, different in degree but not in kind.

Neither creatures of God nor distinct species composed of mind and matter, women and men are subject to all the forces of nature, and these forces combine to make them what they are. Men and women proceed through three evolutionary stages beginning with a biological stage, then moving to a psychological level, and finally reaching the highest, the sociological stage. The genius of education, Dewey was quick to declare as his disciples sounded a refrain, is to make men and women active agents in the world by elevating them from a private, subjective experience to sensitive social relations and to school them for useful and responsible membership in the community.

Besides expressing a purely naturalistic philosophy of human nature, Dewey's pragmatic code adopted the dogmatic assumption that change alone is real, thus making a general theory of reality (metaphysics) both impossible and unnecessary. The principle of change that appears to have had its origin with Heraclitus—"into the same river we step and do not step; we are and we are not"—declared the principle of permanence redundant. In a world described by pragmatists, it is pointless to look for what is ultimate, essential, and substantial. The possibility of arriving at truth, moreover, is foreclosed. Yet pragmatists did not counsel despair: they counted on tested hypotheses which are more or less dependable. Dependable or not, there is nothing else. But this, the optimistic pragmatist could declare, is better than it sounds: tested hypotheses are hammered out on the anvil of scientific method and, while the explanation might offend all traditional conceptions of truth, it allows persons to deal directly with daily reality. Behavior is not hobbled by myth masquerading as truth. Finally Dewey embraced the criterion proposed by Peirce: to determine the meaning of an idea, apply it; the consequences of application constitute its meaning.

One might inquire whether these pragmatic expressions were meant to have anything to do with education. Dewey essayed to make pragmatism illustrate his pedagogic creed. Besides, pragmatism described men and women, knowledge, reality, and ethical behavior. Schools were expected to make their programs of instruction accommodate to these descriptions. Schools should meet social and physical reality face to face, and teach their students how to adjust to it without depending upon antiquated, even mystical, appeals to an illusory truth. It should be clear that faithful pragmatists find it hard, if not impossible, to state precise educational objectives or to construct a conventional curriculum.

Knowledge cannot be a scholastic goal, because at best it is relative.[53] Educational objectives must be phrased as effective experience for the person who is experiencing or, put another way, the goal of education is to provide experience in effective experiencing. Good schools concentrate upon the process of experience, not its product. This makes sense to the confirmed pragmatist because the world students face upon leaving school is indeterminate: it is itself in a process of becoming something different from what it now is. Only in the most general way can schools be commissioned to prepare their students for life, and most pragmatist educators prefer to speak of schools as being the custodians of life itself rather than institutions preparing persons for it. When the principle of change is taken seriously, who can predict the future or say what the needs of life shall be? This kind of flexibility, Dewey supposed, allowed education and educators to set their sights on social efficiency and to affirm social efficiency as education's finest objective.

When one moves from the level of theory to the level of scholastic practice—that is, when one leaves the library and enters the classroom—it is evident that pragmatism and progressive education had something in common. Many of the pedagogic techniques developed in progressive schools were compatible with the methodological intimations of pragmatism. Dewey never tired of praising the experimental method as the method of learning equally useful in all avenues of intellectual and moral behavior. And personal interest based upon intimate and probably unique experience must be utilized if scholastic excellence is to be realized. Interest stimulates a reorganization of experience and this reorganization of experience is genuinely educational.

Together with progressive schoolmasters, most pragmatists embraced the child-centered school to allow the interest (critics said the whim) of children to infiltrate the curriculum and dilute or, sometimes, suppress respectable subject matter. They demonstrated disdain for the content of the learning experience. But Dewey, as it turned out, parted company with them on this point. He admitted to lack of inherent worth in many of the data that appeared from somewhere in the school's curriculum, but declared, nevertheless, that experience cannot be had in a vacuum. Experience must be of something. Some kinds of experience are more formative than others—a discovery that comes not from edict but from experience itself—and these are the experiences that should be put into the curriculum. Progressives appeared to put trust in what students wanted to do; Dewey and his most loyal pragmatic disciplines demurred: students should be nourished by experience that is socially most useful.

The educational process, if it is to be most effective, should be dominated by problem-solving technique. Dewey wanted schools to produce persons skilled in the art of thinking, and thinking, he declared, is mainly a matter of solving problems. In the last analysis there is the implication, and now Dewey comes closer to the progressives, that schools are responsible for offering their students experience with a life that is genuine and good, for when all is said and done, education is life itself.

EDUCATIONAL PURPOSE AND STANDARD

A decade or so after World War II, American society began to show signs of change for which the war itself was partly responsible. As old and often divisive social issues were raised, almost inevitably the conduct of the nation's schools was scrutinized. This scrutiny proceeded at a steady pace and seemed to produce testimony that the conventional philosophies of education lacked answers to fundamental questions or, what was worse, were incoherent in guiding an inquiry that the public craved. So as idealism, realism (with its various humanisms as friendly satellites), and pragmatism declined in significance and the influence of systematic philosophy waned, analytical philosophy—by no means a novelty of the last half of the twentieth century—began to assert itself as a method of inquiry for unraveling difficult educational riddles rather than a code of answers to questions that might be asked about education. Analytic philosophy represented most prominently by linguistic analysis promised nothing more than a search for meaning in educational discourse and practice. Standing in the shadow of analytic philosophy and representing, too, a departure from systematic educational philosophy, existentialism began to make occasional overtures to education.

A conventional view of philosophy, one represented prominently in the various philosophies so far reviewed, is that of unifier and interpreter.

Philosophy essays to distill meaning from a broad range of human experience and to speculate about the nature of things. But when we meet analytic philosophy, although some commentators have been disposed to call it a method more than a philosophy, we come face to face with a way of thinking that is ready to abandon the traditional purposes of philosophy in favor of a search for meaning in what has been said about reality, knowledge, and virtue or, as with logical positivism, of establishing an epistemology based on the premise that only those statements capable of being verified by empirical data have meaning. Analytic philosophy wants to clarify language and thought rather than advance propositions about the nature of reality. Language and logic are the tools used by linguistic analysts as they look for meaning in what has been said or done or, as with logical positivists, in a direct sensory contact with the data of experience. So, although the approach of linguistic analysis and logical positivism is different, both employ logical and linguistic techniques in a search for meaning.

The British gave analytic philosophy its contemporary thrust, and as the fortunes of systematic philosophy waned, it spread throughout the world and achieved a status in the United States second only to the one it enjoyed in Great Britain. Its reputation for intellectual responsibility was helped over the years by such scholars as George Edward Moore (1873–1958), Bertrand Russell (1872–1970), Ludwig Wittgenstein (1889–1951), Gilbert Ryle (1900–1976), and Alfred J. Ayer (b. 1910). Moore and Russell were intent upon refuting idealism and returning to realism, and this refutation involved them in linguistic analysis when they undertook to clarify a theory of knowledge. Adopting a posture of indifference to reality, their neglect of metaphysics was almost total. It was Wittgenstein, however, who can be credited with having articulated the foundation of analysis:

> Most of the propositions and questions to be found in philosophical works are not false but nonsensical. Consequently we cannot give any answer to questions of this kind but can only establish that they are nonsensical. Most of the propositions and questions of philosophers arise from our failure to understand the logic of our language.[54]

Wittgenstein's prospectus for philosophy withheld from it any commission to establish truth. Truth is the business of science. Philosophy has the burden of clarifying the results of scientific investigation.

Despite its prominence, we should be careful not to concede to analytic philosophy a monopoly over the exercise of critical technique. Philosophers of all loyalties do their best to use rational, logical means to find meaning in the world around them. Every philosophy claims to employ a severely critical perspective as it weighs propositions to assay their meaning. Acknowledging this, we should at the same time agree that there are some general educational principles that linguistic analysts salute. The purpose of education, they aver, is to equip persons with the technical ability to appraise reservoirs of knowledge and value that are available to them and upon which, at least to some extent, they must depend. Most of this technical ability for criticizing, analyzing, and interpreting is honed in studies of language and logic.

Logical positivists refer to themselves as scientific humanists, a phrase not easily understood, although it appears to imply a rejection of absolute value in deference to dependence upon the outcome of experience. Moreover, they acknowledge the existence of critical human ability and the possibility of intelligence without involving themselves in debates about their origin and nature. These may or may not be issues of significance, but they are surely beyond the ken of positive method, and in the absence of positive method dependable knowledge is impossible.

Analytic philosophers begin by abandoning any commission for educational philosophy to give direction to educational practice, but there is nearly universal agreement among them to adopt prescriptive methodologies for conducting an inquiry into the educational process. They sometimes wrestle with the same educational questions only to give different answers, but at the same time they employ common linguistic and logical techniques. When variety is evident in answers to educational questions, it is meant to open a field of inquiry and to demonstrate that easy prescriptions cannot be written for complex issues in education or anything else. This tendency to refuse to supply solutions has led critics of analytic philosophy to indict it for educational fault-finding and for engaging in hypercriticism. This, the same critics say, is nothing more than a surrender of philosophy and a confession that philosophy is either impractical or useless.

If complaint is registered that analytical philosophy is swamped in method, commentators on existentialism must stand in awe of a philosophy almost totally indifferent to method. At the same time they are left to investigate a philosophy whose principal proponents choose to use literature rather than conventional philosophical discourse to express their view of life. Still, we should probably begin by acknowledging that all of us subscribe to a basic element of existentialism: we begin with an immediate experience of our existence and this raw empirical interlude is neither fully explained nor understood. Yet, unless we commit to existentialism, we do not stop here. We search for meaning and purpose in the world we occupy while the existentialist depends upon introspection. Meaning is buried somewhere within an individual's personality or person.

To assert that everyone is tinged by existentialism should not be disquieting even for the most dedicated extrovert, anymore than it is disquieting to say that everyone is to some extent a pragmatist and that if pragmatism could be rejected totally, life would be hard and ineffective. After saying so much in connection with a native existential disposition, we should refuse to concede that existentialism is a common philosophical point of view. As a philosophy it is relatively young. As a systematic philosophy it is not only young but probably incoherent as well. And as a philosophy of education it operates on the outer fringe of educational purpose and practice.

Modern philosophy has intellectual roots in the past, as has existentialism, but for all this, and either from lack of cultivation or an absence of intrinsic vitality, existentialism's roots were unproductive until after World War I. Thereafter, evidence of existential thought began to appear in France and Germany. Yet, when existentialism achieved sufficient maturity to be called a philosophy is uncertain, for its principal expositors seldom said or wrote much that could be regarded as conventional philosophical expression. The names of Sören Kierkegaard (1813–1855), Martin Heidegger (1889–1976), Gabriel Marcel (1889–1973), and Albert Camus (1913–1960) are regularly associated with existentialism. But they did not think of themselves as professional philosophers and some, Camus for example, did not admit to being existentialists. Jean-Paul Sartre (1905–1980), however, promoted existentialism and the popularity it enjoys is due largely to him.

Passion for life appears to be existentialism's dominant theme, but when it is plumbed further it might be a cry of despair. Life is filled with conflict and contradiction, and no one is immune, so when one philosophizes about it, all the scars and blemishes must be revealed. It is not the role of philosophy to interpret reality in a way that makes it neat, orderly, and livable; philosophy must reject fraud and represent reality as it is with all its failures and fallacies.

Human beings are finite. This is a point no existentialist disputes, but it does not keep them from dwelling on the absurd. Their preoccupation with the past is intense, although they are tempted to confess—at least Sartre does—that "it is the future which decides whether the past is living or dead."[55] Men and women are at the summit of reality, yet the world with all power and substance of a being that just *is* stands ready to overwhelm them. And how can they protect themselves from the inevitable cruelty of nature? They have intelligence to determine and freedom to guide their destiny. There is nothing else. Moreover, existentialists are not disposed to identify or argue about the source of intelligence and freedom.

When persons are first exposed to the world surrounding them, they are in danger of being overwhelmed by its magnitude and by the fact of experiencing itself. The force of experience is great and commanding. But when men and women grow, mature, and learn, they come to understand their experiences. And the more they understand them, the better chance they have of controlling the vagaries of nature and for putting themselves in positions where they can resist the threat of the universe. Their great friend is freedom; their demonic foe is determinism. But in the last analysis freedom and determinism might be nothing more than states of mind. Still, belief in freedom is essential to any kind of decent life, and to succumb to determinism is both dangerous and dehumanizing. Yet, freedom itself raises a problem, for only free persons are capable of recognizing that other persons have freedom too. This could be troublesome when freedoms conflict. The only sensible way to prepare for conflict and decide whose freedom has precedence is to cultivate responsibility. Had Sartre, and other existentialists, elaborated a doctrine of freedom and responsibility, we should be in a better position to understand existentialism's direction to education. As it is, the threshold over which any existential philosophy of education must pass is freedom and responsibility. It rests with existentialists themselves to define and explain this threshold for us.[56]

Existentialism and Marxism make strange bedfellows. Although they need not be juxtaposed here, it can be said that where the former has a spiritual texture, the latter is starkly materialistic. What the two have in common as they tackle education, and maybe everything else on a philosophical spectrum, is a tentative and tangential approach to educational philosophy, while at the same time illustrating a confidence in the ability of education to sponsor intellectual and moral progress. Lacking a disposition to quarrel with characterizing either as a philosophy of education, one might vigorously demur from calling either systematic. There are almost as many avenues to educational thought as there are existentialists and Marxists. Even more troublesome in the case of Marxism is the absence of a clear line of demarcation between it and critical theory, which is regularly, and possibly accurately, called Western Marxism.

The background to Marxist educational philosophy is further complicated by the fact that Karl Marx (1818–1883) only implied an educational point of view, and by the various contributions made by socialists and social activists to what has come to be recognized as Marxist educational philosophy. Whether or to what extent Henri Saint-Simon (1760–1825) was Marx's ideological ancestor might be debated, but Saint-Simon clearly mounted a crusade to spread an industrial doctrine communicating the proposition that society should be directed by active and productive men and women rather than by idle aristocrats. One need not probe Marxist economic theory very deeply to discover an identical thesis. And in much the same vein the social doctrine of Charles Fourier (1772–1837) asserted the primacy of a community of interest as the fulcrum for progress. Men and women will work in concert for perfection if first they can find and prosecute their common interests.

All this emphasis upon progress depended upon an embrace of the idea that human beings are motivated by the chance for material gain; all else is secondary on a motivational scale. These pronouncements were heeded by Robert Owen (1771–1858) when he led a march to improve the lot of child laborers in Manchester, England, and New Lanark, Scotland. When the crusade crossed the Atlantic to the United States, Owen campaigned for child-labor laws, for schools for working children, for increasing the activity of infant school societies that were offering instruction to children between ages four and six, and for a cooperative social system.

Community of interest was tested in Owen's New Harmony, Indiana, experiment and found wanting. So he, Frances Wright, Orestes Brownson, and others determined to institute social reform by infiltrating the Workingmen's Party in New York State. Among the many reforms proposed for society, and ones to which the party could make a contribution, most were economic, but a radical educational plan stands out. Beginning with the adoption of a system of universal education, Owen urged the party to accept his definition of public education as a plank in its platform. By public education Owen meant an educational system where children would be wards of the state until they attained their majority. Conventional educational control was abandoned and parents were shunted to the sidelines. This reform, Owen declared, would ensure equality of educational opportunity and guarantee the establishment of an educational program worthy of the American republic.[57]

A full recitation of Marx's economic, social, and philosophical theory is too ambitious for these pages, as is the complication of meaning indigenous to dialectical materialism. Besides, Marx wrote sparingly about education, so it was left to others to decipher his educational ideas and reconstruct them as Marxist educational philosophy. Yet, if Marx had never uttered a word about educational philosophy, extant representations of Marxist educational philosophy are genuine and can be studied. With or without Marx's authorship, an educational philosophy issues from his general theory.

The aim of Marxist education is comprehensive and in some respects humanistic, for it respects and undertakes to preserve the cultural monuments of the past. But it has no intention of being swamped in the past, which amid some signs of brilliance testifies as well to the savage inequities in a class society. So, the fundamental aim of Marxist education is to produce a socialist society. Translated to educational practice, this is social reconstruction with a vengeance, but its implementation is dependent upon a successful nurturing of social conscience among a nation's youth.

Forming social conscience is achieved by suppressing alienation among persons by eliminating acquisitive habits that have their origin in private property, on the one hand, and by removing control of the factors of production from a paternalistic elite, on the other, and giving control to the working class. The working class, in turn, should be able as well as free to exercise control. Freedom is awarded to the workers in a reconstituted political system that eliminates a ruling class, and ability is shaped by the instructional programs of good schools. On this level education becomes especially prominent. Most of all it must be of a kind and character capable of creating socialist men and women by erasing paternalistic policies instituted by the ruling class and intended to shape docile and obedient citizens. In this context the following questions are highlighted in Marxist theory, although answers are frequently indirect and imprecise: Who shall be taught? What shall be taught? How shall it be taught? Who will be the teachers? Who will teach the teachers?

With supreme confidence Marxist educational philosophy answers the first two questions. Universal education is taken for granted and scholastic instruction is commissioned to equip all citizens for full participation in shaping public policy and mastering self-government. So in addition to an obvious commitment to civic education, a commitment of the highest order, citizens are readied to make a living and at the same time make a genuine contribution to economic life and value. Technical and industrial curricula are given more than ordinary attention. These emphases barely conceal a hostility to liberal education, although most Marxists are eager to discount them. In any case, promotion of liberal learning is far from evident. Marx himself seems to have worried about the construction of a curriculum that would insulate the process of education from the infection of a class-structured society. How shall political and technical education be taught, by whom, and how will teachers themselves be educated? Can the system be trusted to do what ought to be done? Here Marxists should be given high marks for candor: all education begins with indoctrination, but if handled correctly, does not end there.

The rules of grammar, the fundamentals of mathematics, and the laws of physical science are subject neither to interpretation nor class distinction, so they, along with other basic disciplines, should be taught directly, with zeal and devotion, and without any implication that their content is open to discussion or amendment. When this instructional foundation is secure, the next step is to introduce curricular materials that are considered preferable and, in addition, can be defended. Materials, ideas, interpretations that fail the test of preference are given a hearing but are not embraced. Partiality has its use, but is not good enough for the final instructional step, one reached by only the most talented students: everything in the schools curriculum must be open to scrutiny and, verified by the canons of logic, be authentically scientific.

Marxist educational policy is on the side of public, compulsory education, and in this context should be taken to mean compulsory school attendance. But there is a caveat: if this kind of education is controlled by an unreconstructed (bourgeois) state, such control must be restricted to an enforcement of general school law. Broader control would inevitably mean an imposition of the doctrines of a capitalistic, parasitical society. On the other side of the coin, where the state is reconstructed, it should be authorized to control the curriculum, the education and selection of teachers, and everything that pertains to the substance of public education. Free public education for all children is a recommendation found in the *Communist Manifesto*. So one is on solid ground in asserting it as the main plank in Marxist educational philosophy.[58] Yet in those lands where Marxism enjoyed political domination, few of its progressive educational theories were translated to scholastic practice.

If in past decades Americans were mesmerized by the dignity of philosophy, their new outlook was less philosophical and more programmatic. Instead of seeking explanations rooted in philosophical wisdom, they sought solutions to educational problems that were daily becoming more troublesome. One problem wore the face of threat: in 1957 the Soviet Union invaded outer space by launching the famous Sputnik. Such an achievement by a cold war antagonist was perceived as a bad omen: America's global power and influence were in jeopardy. Perceived elements of failure in an American society that allowed a foreign power to wrestle from it military, economic, and scientific supremacy worried Americans and prompted them to conduct an intensive examination of their schools. Had American education betrayed the nation by allowing schooling to be swamped in ineptitude? Had the schools, despite all the talk the philosophers could generate, lost their way? In failing to emphasize achievement and to promote mathematical and scientific culture, had educators undermined America's stature in the world community?

At least temporarily the sting of being outrun by the Soviet scientific community was enough to rivet attention on the schools and to encourage the appropriation of resources to support educational programs that were in full retreat from progressive ideologies. Schools began to promote mathematical and scientific study. Schools and students who excelled in these subjects were singled out for praise. Humanists and social scientists sometimes complained about the lack of attention given to their disciplines, but for the most part were paid scant heed as the superior claims of science and technology were honored. But this was a temporary interlude. While science and mathematics were respected and studied, the apex of interest in science was reached and decline was almost inevitable.

Traditional education, although often caricatured by progressive tormentors, was based on an easily understood premise that schools are intended to instruct children in skill and knowledge enabling them to function effectively and productively in society. Whatever else educational programs might be, they are first and foremost academically centered and geared to a preparation for life. Schools are places where learning is prized and the kinds of learning that are given pride of place are literary and linguistic. For a while after 1957 it appeared that traditional attitudes about education had been restored and that the schools would concentrate upon academic achievement, but appearances can be deceiving. By about 1960 echoes of the old progressive education could be heard by avant-garde educators who rejected the notion that schools should be centers for academic excellence. They said schools were ineffective, uneconomical, and what was worse, were ruining American youth by refusing to allow them to set their own goals and create the educational means to achieve them. These were the romantic humanists.[59]

Sharing the conclusion of romantic humanists that schools were ineffective and uneconomical, but parting company with them on the point of personal achievement, modern behaviorists talked about how good citizens could be produced if behaviorist methods of instruction were adopted and if environmental determinism were taken seriously. So humanism and behaviorism competed for prominence in directing the course of American education. To the extent that they received attention, the fortunes of systematic philosophy of education continued to decline.

Capitalizing on the indecision of American educators in connection with the purpose of education, and not knowing whether schools were to be in the vanguard of social change or merely instruments in explaining it, humanists issued their indictment of education. The first charge was that schools were indifferent to individualization. They, the allegation went, were committed to the proposition that education should strive for social solidarity, always at the expense of individual development. Moreover, whatever schools were doing, they were doing it poorly, inartistically, and impersonally. The academic lock step had dehumanized schooling and stolen the soul of education. And if this were not enough, humanists went on to write and speak about petty and oppressive rules, about fear of failure as a chief motivator, and about the distrust of society and disrespect for persons that were bred in the schools' environment. Learning and life were so far separated in the schools that students either ended up with an abundance of irrelevant information or, equally disturbing, learned nothing at all in their years spent in school. Now humanists had their rallying cry: relevance. Students should not be held to account for anything that for them was irrelevant. But who was to define what was or was not relevant? Add to this the humanist affection for affective learning, which they said was neglected in a majority of the nation's schools. The report card was sad: American schools were hardly more than custodial agencies where the promise of youth was crushed by indifference. Radical reform was essential and urgent.

Humanists wrote their prescription for reform. It began with the assumption that human nature is good (a point reminding us of Rousseau) and that scholastic standards are artificial and meaningless. More than anything else save relevance, the model of the child-centered school was praised, and the model most often used was Summerhill, a British school started by A.S. Neill (1883–1973) in the 1920s. Student freedom characterized school life at Summerhill. Academic requirements were abandoned as students mapped out their educational program. Educational materials, instructional facilities, skillful and scholarly teachers were available should students be disposed to use them. Examinations were absent, as were standards of achievement. In connection with moral education, although it was encouraged, no set of objective moral standards was recommended. Despite its notoriety and, as well, the affection displayed for it in the United States, the Summerhill model was rarely adopted here. Other plans, faint copies of Summerhill, were instituted instead.

So, absent the credentials of philosophy and lacking genuine novelty, romantic humanism nevertheless took philosophy's place by idealizing discovery as being central to relevant learning. Of learning's laws humanists were captivated by the law of effect. And in addition to mastering what is satisfying and avoiding the unpleasant and immediately unrewarding, students under the direction of humanists were motivated by the social environment. Their disposition to learn was intrinsic; external influence supplied by skillful teachers or ingenious methods was rejected. Students alone are capable of making decisions about their education. Anything less than this is arbitrary, authoritarian, and undemocratic.

Humanists stood mute about standards of achievement. It was, they declared, pointless to speak about essential curricular content. Students should have the freedom to discover their personalities and to be themselves by having the latitude to capitalize, to the extent they desire, whatever talent they possess. Talents vary, and no humanist thought of denying this stark fact, so curricular opportunity for the development of talent must vary enormously. One learns what one wants to know, and here there should be plenty of opportunity for students to become introspective, to discover knowledge of self, and to cultivate mental health. After all, according to the humanist creed, education's goal is to create conditions that will lead to personal happiness and satisfaction. A judgment on these points is to be made personally: what is good and praiseworthy for one, might be disdained by another. Still, even humanists recognize that there are elements of preparation in all of schooling: students leave school and are faced with the need to earn a living in a society which is always complex and often demanding. The marketplace sets standards of achievement, has its system of reward, penalizes failure, and enforces rules. How can humanist schools ignore this reality? Humanists answer that they cannot and do not. Their environment provides students with the best preparation to face the vicissitudes of life by giving them the opportunity while in school to arrive at their own standards of achievement and conduct. Nothing is forced or fed; the rules of life in society are learned best in the setting of a good humanistic school.

One tributary to romantic humanism that was seldom sailed except by the most hardy is noteworthy because it jettisoned schools. The faults of schools are indelible and ineradicable. Rather than engaging in a vain attempt to erase fault, the best solution is to abandon schools entirely and to allow the youth of the nation to learn what they need to know in a society which is free and open. In the last analysis, this tributary might have been the logical outcome of romantic humanism, but it was one that could not be followed because American society in the 1960s and 1970s simply refused so drastic an educational prescription.[60]

One side of the coin promoting a rehabilitation of American education displayed an image of freedom and a diminution of control. The other side exhibited an abundance of control while issuing an ominous challenge to the notion of human freedom. The first side we recognize at once as romantic humanism; the second is behaviorism. If, as humanists are tempted to say, schooling too often misses the mark, behaviorists recommend schooling, when properly managed, as the sole solution to the lack of order and discipline in society. The deschooling and anti-instructional assertions of humanists are summarily rejected. Neither good people nor good societies just happen, behaviorists declare; they are produced. And it is the responsibility of schools to produce them.

As a theory in psychology, behaviorism dates from the nineteenth century. But over the years, except as it affected the work of Edward L. Thorndike (1874–1949), its relationship to education was distant. The bold declarations of behaviorists that a controlled environment can mold persons without regard to will, talent, and disposition had a mechanistic ring too shrill for rank and file educators. They preferred to follow a more conventional route that took into account talent, motivation, and free will as determining factors in intellectual and moral formation. Most would concede that environment could play a part, but only a part, in shaping the character of persons. This educational conclusion, represented as quaint, was turned on its head in B.F. Skinner's *Beyond Freedom and Dignity* in 1971.[61]

Skinner (1904–1991) built a persuasive argument upon a foundation of research he had been conducting for years that persons are the products of environmental conditioning. They are what their environment makes them: nothing more or less. Due partly to Skinner's influence, but perhaps more to the dissatisfaction the American public began to voice with contemporary schooling, behaviorism fastened itself to education with the fanfare of a new savior. It might have been thought a savior, but it was hardly new: behavioral engineering had been invented almost a century earlier.[62] Yet in new dress and with empirical support, earlier lacking, it gained a respectability among educators mesmerized by empiricism. Armed with various kinds of empirical data, the behaviorists who made the schools their home said that romantic humanism was too vague and left too much to the vagaries of chance. Moreover, humanists simply ignored the reality of life when they allowed children to follow their own bent when, in fact, they were not captaining their fate but merely drifting in a direction dictated by an unplanned, chaotic environment.

When humanists preached a policy of nonintervention, believing that freedom from outside interference would allow students to realize their genius, behaviorists maintained that intervention, more than being desirable, is essential if good and decent citizens are to be produced by the schools. If intervention is to be faulted, it is for being of the wrong kind. Behaviorists took for granted that the job of teachers is teaching in a way to induce good behavior. Behavior, they went on, can be modified. So schools must, first, determine what standards of behavior are desirable and then create an instructional climate to assure their realization. Learning by conditioning is behaviorism's fundamental premise. Its proud boast is that persons can be shaped by any environmental mold. The road to good and decent education is to find the right mold.

When schools are clear about the goals of education and when teachers realize that learning is neither more nor less than a conditioned response, then and only then can schools be effective. They must be precise and careful about what is taught and the way it is taught. Teachers must reduce the complexities of the curriculum to specific competencies and use their skill and command of technique to see to it that students master them.

Earlier in the twentieth century, we know, progressive educators had praised the student-centered school. In the 1960s and 1970s romantic humanists idealized individuality and gave progressivism a contemporary sound. Behaviorists were scornful of such pandering. While they refused to endorse harsh and cruel discipline in the schools, they nevertheless regarded the business of education to be a serious matter, too important to be left to the direction, or whim, of students. Schools are places where behavioral skill is to be mastered and where teachers have the responsibility to occupy the center of the instructional stage and to see to it that what is taught is mastered. Students and teachers are accountable: students for learning the knowledge and skill taught, and teachers for seeing to it that the competence goals for their scholastic level are met.

While behaviorism was prominent (if not exactly popular), educators listed toward defining behavioral objectives and teachers were recruited to identify them in the curriculum. Besides, attention to specific competencies produced what is called competency-based education. This had the effect of promoting various kinds of programmed instruction where the conditioned response is most obvious. But this, the critics of behaviorism allege, turns schools into factories where all association with human and cultural qualities is lost. The behaviorist rejoinder, predictably, is that human and cultural features to learning, rather than being discounted, are attended to by this kind of educational engineering much better than by haphazard and chaotic humanistic and traditional methods. Behavioral approaches to schools are, moreover, more likely to provide for the individualization of instruction, because what a student lacks in skill can be identified and the deficiency can be corrected. Students can learn what they need to know and the extent of their achievement (and the skill of teachers) can be assessed with precision.

By declaring learning to be conditioning and nothing more, behaviorism struck at the core of traditional education without changing its image. There is the conventional attachment to classroom management, all signs of soft pedagogy are stripped away, and when punishment is employed it is used with specific purpose as part of the conditioning process: pleasant responses are reinforced; dissatisfying responses are avoided. Affective education is handled, too, say the most eloquent of behaviorists, and the prize of all schooling—thinking—is cultivated in ways impossible in the absence of behaviorist method. Behaviorists promised to remake the schools to fit the image of educational respectability and effectiveness.

So as American education worked its way into the eighth decade of the century, the issues of purpose and process remained unsettled. Earlier the debate centered on educational philosophy, school support and control, and religious teaching in the schools. But the 1980s introduced a decade where attention was paid to method, for the differences between humanism and behaviorism were pronounced more on the level of pedagogic practice than on the level of philosophy. One is entitled to wonder at about the time the eightieth yearbook of the National Society for the Study of Education was published (1981) whether educational philosophy was any longer relevant.[63]

Philosophy's relevance is defended in the yearbook's chapters, as one would expect, but most striking is the drastic metamorphosis between its content and the content of the two yearbooks preceding it. This shift goes a long way toward illustrating how with the eighth decade of the twentieth century educational philosophy was wearing a new face. With its "professional" status secured by a pilgrimage that had transported it from the ancient to the contemporary world, educational philosophy claimed disciplinary standing and asserted independence because it could draw upon the resources of education, from a respectable body of literature in educational philosophy that is almost as long as philosophy's legacy itself, and from the methods and techniques of general philosophy. Put quickly, and possibly too simply, educational philosophers began to invest their time and talent in philosophizing about education rather than constructing, elaborating, and applying a philosophy of education. And the topics the philosophers analyzed, interpreted, and explained, produced, as Jonas Soltis correctly noted, "a useful mix of philosophy and education" that had its genesis in the problems contemporary educational policy and practice were facing.[64]

Reciting the chapter titles of the yearbook, without any attempt to summarize their content, should show quickly and vividly the shift in emphasis as educational philosophers in the late twentieth century began, as they liked to say, to "do philosophy of education." The second chapter, by Harry Broudy, is a perceptive reflection surveying the field of educational philosophy from the yearbooks of 1942 and 1955 to 1980, and an effective introduction to the succeeding chapters. Jane Martin and Donna Kerr, in chapters three and four, deal with the theory of curriculum and the theory of teaching, respectively. Jonas Soltis undertakes to expand our conception of epistemology by introducing "sociocentric" perspective in chapter five. Aesthetic education is promoted by Maxine Greene in the next chapter. Robert Ennis writes about the importance of logic in all rational discourse about education in chapter seven. Clive Beck takes ethics and values education as his subject in chapter eight. In chapter nine Kenneth Strike writes of social philosophy and certain Supreme Court decisions and their relation to education and justice. In chapter ten, Denis Phillips is intent upon relating recent developments in the philosophy of science to research, knowledge, and theory in education. Finally, in chapter eleven, James McClellan introduced metaphysical considerations to such things as knowledge, belief, truth, reality, and value.

Educational philosophy's shift (or drift) in direction over the thirty-nine years between the first and the last National Society for the Study of Education yearbooks on the discipline is so clearly demonstrated by comparison that to dwell further on the issue is waste. Moreover, the shift might be taken as a warning that the philosophical systems which good scholars had spent so much time and intelligence refining and explaining were anachronisms. Their remnants could be preserved in books on educational philosophy. They might be grieved over by traditionalists who believed them to be essential foundations for a study of educational philosophy. But their day, the new breed of educational philosophers said, was past.

Logical sophistication, prudent skepticism, specialization in particular problems, and doctrinal and political neutrality replaced the systems and were rewarded with philosophical respectability. Still, intelligent outsiders who were nevertheless deeply concerned about education in the United States continued, perhaps habitually, to look to educational philosophy for guidance. Their definition of education rejected neutrality and they tired quickly of erudite distinction. They wanted an educational enterprise capable of supplying them and their children with the essentials for life in society. They wanted a kind of education that understood something and stood for something.

So after all this time disciplinary identity appeared to be an elusive dream. We should turn back the pages of the calendar and try to discover how educational philosophy's search for identity was conducted.

1. Bruce A. Kimball, *The "True Professional Ideal" in America: A History* (Cambridge, Mass.: B. Blackwell, 1992), 225.

2. Ibid., 225–26.

3. Ibid., 251.

4. J.J. Chambliss, *The Origins of American Philosophy of Education: Its Development as a Distinct Discipline, 1808–1913* (The Hague: Martinus Nijhoff, 1968), 6–8.

5. Joseph Neef, *Sketch of a Plan and Method of Education Founded on an Analysis of the Human Faculties, and Natural Reason, Suitable for the Offspring of a Free People, and for Rational Beings* (Philadelphia, 1808); and Joseph Neef, *The Method of Instructing Children Rationally in the Arts of Writing and Reading* (Philadelphia, 1813).

6. Chambliss, *Origins*, 8.

7. Albert Picket and John W. Picket, *The Academician: Containing the Elements of Scholastic Science, and the Outlines of Philosophic Education, Predicted on the Analysis of the Human Mind, and Exhibiting the Improved Methods of Instruction* (New York: Printed by C.N. Baldwin, 1820).

8. Carter's work, published in 1824, appears now under the title *Letters on the Free Schools in New England* (New York: Arno Press, 1969).

9. Syracuse, N.Y.: Bardeen, 1884.

10. Chambliss, *Origins*, 21–25.

11. James S. Kaminsky, *A New History of Educational Philosophy* (Westport, Conn.: Greenwood Press, 1993), 32.

12. Herbert Spencer, *Education: Intellectual, Moral, and Physical* (Boston: Small, 1886; New York: Appleton-Century-Crofts, 1927), 101.

13. Ibid., 17.

14. Ibid., 17–18.

15. Ibid., 283.

16. Ibid., 107–9.

17. New York: Harper & Brothers, 1886.

18. Chambliss, *Origins*, 36. Partridge compiled Hall's various positions on education and published them under the title *Genetic Philosophy of Education* (New York: Sturgis and Walton, 1912).

19. *Essays on Education, 1830–1862* (Gainesville, Fla.: Scholars' Facsimiles & Reprints, 1960).

20. Perry Miller, *The Transcendentalists* (Cambridge: Harvard University Press, 1950), 6–15.

21. James P. Wickersham, *Method of Instruction* (Philadelphia: J.B. Lippincott, 1865; New York: Arno Press, 1969).

22. William T. Harris, *Introduction to the Study of Philosophy* (New York: D. Appleton, 1890); and Harris's translation of and introduction to Johann K.F. Rosenkranz's *The Philosophy of Education* (New York: D. Appleton, 1886). Harris called Rosenkranz's book a genuine philosophy of education (p. vi).

23. Chauncey Wright, *Philosophical Writings*, edited by Edward H. Madden (New York: Liberal Arts Press, 1958).

24. New York: Macmillan, 1912.

25. New York, 1886.

26. Cincinnati, 1887.

27. Boston, 1887.

28. Terre Haute, Ind., 1893.

29. Chicago, 1897.

30. New York, 1898.

31. Boston, 1902.

32. Philadelphia, 1903.

33. New York, Macmillan, 1927.

34. Boston, 1907.

35. New York, 1910.

36. "Original Papers in Relation to a Course of Liberal Education," *The American Journal of Science and Arts*," 15 (January 1829): 297–351.

37. The breadth and depth of his thought is illustrated well in Peter R.L. Brown, *Augustine of Hippo: A Biography* (Berkeley and Los Angeles: University of California Press, 1967).

38. Lawrence A. Cremin's *The Transformation of the School: Progressivism in American Education, 1876–1957* (New York: Alfred A. Knopf, 1961) is the standard account of progressive education. William C. Bagley's (1874–1946), *Education and Emergent Man* (New York: T. Nelson and Sons, 1934), is probably as representative of essentialism as any of the books on the subject.

39. Kaminsky, *A New History of Educational Philosophy*, 62.

40. For a brief but illuminating account of idealism, see Herman H. Horne, "An Idealist Philosophy of Education," in *Philosophies of Education*, National Society for the Study of Education (NSSE), forty-first yearbook, Part I (Chicago: University of Chicago Press, 1942), 139–95.

41. In an effort to reverse idealism's demise, the philosophy was liberalized and modernized. For example, see Theodore M. Greene, "A Liberal Christian Idealist Philosophy of Education," in *Modern Philosophies and Education*, NSSE, fifty-fourth yearbook, Part I (Chicago: University of Chicago Press, 1955), 91–136.

42. John P. Lynch, *Aristotle's School: A Study of a Greek Educational Institution* (Berkeley and Los Angeles: University of California Press, 1972).

43. Lord Kames's *Elements of Criticism* (Edinburgh and London: 1762; New York: Johnson Reprint, 1967); and *Essays on the Principles of Morality and Natural Religion* (Edinburgh: R. Fleming, 1751; New York: Garland Publishing, 1983) contain the fundamentals of his thought.

44. Herbert W. Schneider, *A History of American Philosophy*, 2d edition (New York: Columbia University Press, 1963), 216.

45. Ibid., 217.

46. For a general account of American philosophy, into which prominent realists fit, see George P. Adams and William P. Montague, eds., *Contemporary American Philosophy*, 2 vols. (New York: Macmillan, 1930).

47. Frederick S. Breed, "Education and the Realist Outlook," in NSSE, *Philosophies of Education* 93.

48. On this point see, ibid., 116–18; and John Wild, "Education and Human Society," in NSSE, *Modern Philosophies and Education*, 34–36.

49. See John Patrick Diggins, *The Promise of Pragmatism: Modernism and the Crisis of Knowledge and Authority* (Chicago: University of Chicago Press, 1993).

50. Joseph Brent, *Charles Sanders Peirce: A Life* (Bloomington: Indiana University Press, 1993); and George Cotkin, *William James, Public Philosopher* (Baltimore: Johns Hopkins University Press, 1990).

51. J. Donald Butler, *Four Philosophies and Their Practice in Education and Religion*, rev. ed. (New York: Harper & Row, 1957), 433. See, too, Manley H. Thompson, *The Pragmatic Philosophy of C. S. Peirce* (Chicago: University of Chicago Press, 1953).

52. In his delightful chapter, "An Experimentalist Approach to Education," in *Modern Philosophies and Education*, 137–74, George R. Geiger confirms these components, although he prefers to call pragmatism experimentalism. He grants that it might seem to be overstatement to say that education is the "final testing ground" for philosophy "only if 'education' is artificially restricted and caricaturishly portrayed" (137).

53. In ibid., 141, Geiger calls knowledge a transaction: "what something may be when totally independent of any knower or frame of reference is a scientifically meaningless question."

54. Ludwig Wittgenstein, *Tractatus Logico-Philosophicus*, translated by D.F. Pears and B.F. McGuinness (New York: Humanities Press, 1961), 4.003.

55. Jean-Paul Sartre, *Being and Nothingness*, translated by Hazel E. Barnes (Paris: Gallimard, 1943; New York: Washington Square Press, 1956, 1966), 500.

56. Few late twentieth-century existentialists have done more to supply these explanations and definitions than Van Cleve Morris, *Existentialism in Education: What it Means* (New York: Harper & Row, 1966). Despite recognizing Morris's prominence, one should call attention to Donald Vandenberg's criticism of his work in a brief historical sketch of existentialism in education in "Existential and Phenominological Influence in Educational Philosophy," *Teachers College Record* 81, no. 2 (Winter 1979): 168–73.

57. Owen's educational views are reported in various books, but one convenient and dependable source is R. Freeman Butts and Lawrence A. Cremin, *A History of Education in American Culture* (New York: Henry Holt, 1953), 192–93.

58. Karl Marx and Friedrich Engels, "Manifesto of the Communist Party," in Carl Cohen, ed., *Communism, Fascism and Democracy: The Theoretical Foundations* (New York: Random House, 1972).

59. Walter B. Kolesnik, *Humanism and/or Behaviorism in Education* (Boston: Allyn & Bacon, 1974), 9–23.

60. See Ivan Illich, *Deschooling Society* (New York: Harper & Row, 1971), for a plea for deschooling.

61. New York: Alfred A. Knopf, Inc., 1971.

62. See, for example, Lester Frank Ward, *Dynamic Sociology* (New York: D. Appleton, 1883).

63. National Society for the Study of Education, eightieth yearbook, Part I, *Philosophy and Education*, Jonas F. Soltis, ed. (Chicago: University of Chicago Press, 1981).

64. Ibid., 7.

CHAPTER 6

EDUCATIONAL PHILOSOPHY'S SEARCH FOR DISCIPLINARY IDENTITY

Educational philosophy, as we have seen, lived a long time in the library where scholars either absorbed its wisdom or added to its weight. But its most striking growth occurred in the friendly halls of colleges and universities where it was studied by students and cultivated by professors.[1] Determined to set themselves apart from normal schools that had sprung up throughout the nation in the second half of the nineteenth century limiting their programs, for the most part, to the preparation of teachers for elementary schools, colleges and universities that invested in the study of education were careful to make educational philosophy a prominent subject in their courses of study.

Normal schools paid almost no attention to any theory without direct connection to pedagogic technique. But the colleges, and for reasons they thought good, refused to follow suit. They were at pains to find ways to distinguish themselves from normal schools, whose standards they thought inferior. But more to the point, they were likely persuaded that a theoretical base to the discipline of education is essential to its purpose, status, and academic integrity. A theoretical foundation for education sustained an argument that intellectual credentials qualified it for a place in the company of college courses.

We have seen how a rich legacy of philosophizing about education could be mustered to support an assertion that the two conditions for disciplinary status were present: an organized body of dependable knowledge and a special method of inquiry. From Plato to Herbert Spencer, the epistemological condition was strikingly evident. And traditional philosophy itself supplied the method that educational philosophers used in their speculative enterprise. So behind college gates educational philosophy gained a secure foothold and, it would seem, although it could not claim intellectual equality with the staples of the college course, looked forward to a promising future. After all, who was rash enough to declare that schooling the children of the nation is an unimportant matter or that in connection with schooling a theory of education is inconsequential?

The logic wedding theory to practice and giving the educational philosophers a prominent role in setting the direction of American education was compelling: it persuaded college professors and their students. But it seldom satisfied persons associated with the schools who were philosophically insensitive or who pointedly eschewed theory and, infatuated with practice, refused to listen to echoes from theory's reservoir. And it never satisfied a revolutionary fringe of college professors who were looking for a platform from which to preach economic and social reform or, in rare cases, anarchy. They wanted action, not analysis. In consequence of the rashness of the avant-garde, educational philosophers in the colleges had to fight a rear-guard action to protect their flanks from colleagues who thought them radicals and called them unpatriotic. Under such auspices as the radical fringe supplied, educational philosophy was a long way from being a speculative enterprise.

A divorce of educational theory from pedagogical practice has a long American history. Most scholastic associations formed in the early nineteen hundreds had little time for theory, and few of their leaders believed that the solution to any of the nation's scholastic problems could be found in books on educational philosophy. It was characteristic, then, for the children and grandchildren of these early associations—the National Education Association and the Progressive Education Association, for example—to do as their forebears had done: pay educational philosophy scant heed and exhibit a studied indifference to educational philosophers.

The National Education Association's neglect of theory turned into outright distrust when men like John Dewey, Harold Rugg (1886–1960), William Heard Kilpatrick (1871–1965), and George S. Counts (1889–1974) began to invest curriculum with a theory that was both progressive and reconstructionist. Calling upon the schools to change the social order and upon teachers to lead the march for social and economic reform was too radical for both the leaders and the rank and file of the National Education Association. Many of the most outspoken educational theorists had, in the opinion of the association, stripped speculative appurtenances from educational philosophy and turned it into a political enterprise, and a radical one at that.

Yet it is fair to debate Kaminsky's assertion that when the National Education Association rejected the progressive ideology of the reconstructionists, it embraced the conservative academic politics of educators such as Isaac Kandel (1881–1965), Robert Hutchins, Mortimer Adler, Jacques Maritain, and Arthur Bestor (b. 1908).[2] The evidence that the National Education Association paid attention to these essentialists is either hard to find or, if found, far from persuasive and, in any case, the association was not interested in adopting any philosophical stance. Its interest was in maintaining the public schools and saving public education from erosion threatened by partisan politics, radical educational theory, private-school proponents, and Marxists. The National Education Association turned a deaf ear to the activist rhetoric of these avant-garde educational philosophers. If not exhibiting direct hostility to education philosophy, they did nothing to encourage it.

The story is different with philosophy of education vis-à-vis the Progressive Education Association. The association was founded in 1918 with an agenda filled to overflowing with a theory of the child-centered school that its leaders thought was lodged in John Dewey's theory of experience. They might have been close to the truth when they claimed philosophical affinity with Dewey's stand on experience, although they went far beyond Dewey in expressing its pedagogical implications. But Dewey's coolness toward the Progressive Education Association was not so much a matter of his displeasure with its carrying the theory of experience too far, but in neglecting almost entirely a program of social and political reconstruction that was fundamental to Dewey's social and educational philosophy. In the end, the Progressive Education Association discovered it could not reconcile the social and educational aspirations of the progressive disciples of Dewey and the cautious political policies of its pedagogically sensitive members. Both factions were well-represented in the association. The result was friction that led first to a change of name from Progressive Education Association to the American Education Fellowship, and then, in 1955, to its dissolution. In any event, although the Progressive Education Association flirted with philosophical issues, it did little to cultivate interest in or advance the cause of educational philosophy.

Before its dissolution, though, the Progressive Education Association began to stray away from the classroom to countenance social, possibly radical, commitments. To the extent that this ideology gained more and more favor, some early converts to progressive education charged it with being unfaithful to its original commission and began to defect. Defection for this reason, however, was slight compared to the force of another allegation: political subversion. Radical change, Counts never tired of saying, is essential to democracy's vigor, and this preaching of radical change left progressive educators vulnerable to broad, unspecific indictments of disloyalty to the country and to allegiance to communism.

Factions in progressivism's camp might have given an appearance of tolerance within the association, but it could lead to confusion as well. Progressive education spoke with so many voices that it was hard to be sure which ones were credible. Even the publications of the association left readers in a quandary: What did the association stand for? Its original purpose was to introduce scholastic reform to the United States, but in 1955 even its most eloquent admirers admitted failure, while at the same time pointing to ephemeral triumphs in the country's elementary and secondary schools. Colleges and universities, with the exception of teachers colleges, were largely untouched by progressive education, although places like Bennington College and the General College of the University of Minnesota showed signs of progressive theory in their programs.

Progressive education and its ally, the Progressive Education Association, were accorded a level of support and attention that could come only in a country where progressive attitudes toward life and society were embraced. Historians might say that progressive education survived, although with a lower level of notoriety, but they are entitled to wonder why the association's life was so brief. Lawrence Cremin's explanation that it disappeared with the waning of interest in progressive education is likely the best.[3] Cremin found evidence of disarray in progressive education before World War II: Harold Rugg's recommendation on curriculum took it in one direction; Kilpatrick's infatuation with projects in another; and Counts, tempted to turn his back on pedagogy altogether, stressed social reform or revolution. Each had adherents, and zealous ones at that, so it is reasonable conjecture that internal warring siphoned away the inspiration that in the early years had turned the movement into a crusade, but this is only part of the story.

The original progressive educators had stressed the contribution their movement could make to American education, while their successors were mesmerized with criticism to heap on traditional pedagogy and went on to saturate their discourse with slogans. Francis Parker (1837–1902), for example, called attention to the accomplishments of progressive practices in the schools of Quincy, Massachusetts. But progressives who followed in his wake liked to heap scorn on old-fashioned schools without showing how the methods they endorsed were superior. Imprudence coupled with excessive zeal tempted the new breed of progressives to make their case by resorting to cliché and exaggeration. This drained off an abundance of good will that progressive education had earned.

When progressive education was at its best it was an ornament to educational efficiency, but this required teachers with extraordinary talent and students with high motivation and ability. Many teachers who enlisted in the ranks of progressivism lacked ingenuity and art to fulfill the promise of the new pedagogy. Their students were indisposed to take charge of their own learning. The kind of education suited to genius is very likely the worst kind of education for the rank and file. In the end, progressive education might have been swamped by an excess of ambition.

Progressive education was an ideology only partly reflected in educational activity, and it was cultivated by a progressive spirit in the nation. So long as this spirit remained intact, progressive education was helped. With the end of World War II, however, progressive spirit was replaced by a shift toward conservatism. This shift affected education, although its effect might have been less had progressive education remained a genuine educational movement rather than a cult where "educationists" alone were welcome. Excluded were members of the lay public and educators whose approach to schooling was traditional. All these factors, Cremin wrote, accelerated the demise of progressive education and with it the expiration of the Progressive Education Association. In the last analysis, both died of old age.[4]

Without adopting the thesis that educational philosophy "as we know it"[5] originated with and in the John Dewey Society, it can be conceded that the society was instrumental in helping educational philosophy attain a stature superior to what it would have been had it been only an intramural collegiate enterprise. Early in 1935 a group composed of public school administrators and college professors, apprehensive about the dire predictions of drastic decline in Western society's standards, undertook to form an organization designed to take the vanguard for social and economic reform. The principal weapon for such reform was education and the new society was commissioned to redefine it. This commission had the effect of redirecting philosophical discourse from traditional metaphysical and epistemological issues to social and ethical problems.

Conventional philosophy, in the opinion of most of the charter members of the society, refused to tackle the burning questions of the day; it allowed the field to lie fallow when the seed to plant a crop of social, economic, and political reform was at hand. Educational philosophy should, according to the members of this group, rechart its course and begin to redress the failure of the schools by conducting an intense study of the relationship between school and society.

Dewey had of course written about this very commission in *The School and Society*.[6] But it was supposed that Dewey's words, directed mainly at an academic audience, would not alter public opinion or penetrate to the level of the public schools. At the same time, as it turned out, Dewey's assertions were somewhat milder than those of his more zealous colleagues in the John Dewey Society. When their views were published, they sounded partisan, socialist (or Marxist), and radical. There is no telling where their ideas might have led educational philosophy had World War II not intervened to silence or at least to dampen criticism of the social and educational status quo. And when the war ended, the philosophers' thirst for radical change and partisan ideology was quenched: thereafter educational philosophy was pursued along more conventional and abstract lines. This, though, is something to be illustrated later.

It took some time for educational philosophy, as it was handled by the professional associations, to wean itself from radical politics and to set its compass in the direction of genuine philosophizing about education. We have seen how educational philosophy was manipulated by the Progressive Education Association and the John Dewey Society. In the end, the record seems to assert, the discipline had enough internal vigor to reject the seductive maneuvers of both and at almost the same time, one could argue, persuade some members of these groups to engage in a more genuine philosophical industry. Despite encouragement from the John Dewey Society, educational philosophy was neither strong nor attractive enough to succeed when it came face to face with the social and political intransigence of the persons who, in 1934, were responsible for founding *The Social Frontier*. Having a good deal in common with their colleagues in the Progressive Education Association, social frontiersmen eschewed what James Giarelli and J.J. Chambliss call "technical professionalism" to adopt an approach to educational philosophy that can be characterized as befitting "democratic citizens and amateur educators."[7]

When the Progressive Education Association and the John Dewey Society took stands too mild to suit their political and economic appetite, a fringe group of extremely radical educators—most of whom would not have called themselves philosophers—established *The Social Frontier*, a periodical intended as a vehicle for their criticism of capitalism and one allowing them to fan the flames of class warfare. George Counts was selected as editor. Two graduate students from Teachers College, Columbia—Mordecai Grossman and Norman Woelfel—signed on as his associates. Together they controlled a policy that conspired to mobilize the educational community— teachers and students alike—to reform American society. It seemed not to matter to them whether this reform was achieved with or without violence.

Although *The Social Frontier* carried the articles of many educators who shied away from the extreme preached by the editors—even John

Dewey, never a radical, wrote for the journal—its main thrust bordered on a revolution for crushing all kinds of injustice. Despite some sympathy for the basic reforms recommended by the *Frontier*'s editorial policy, a majority of professors of education, whether or not philosophically inclined, refused to enlist in the crusade to build a new social order. Revolution lacked appeal to all but the zealots who were not found in college classrooms but in union halls and politically radical (or subversive) organizations. In the end, even socially sensitive members of the new Philosophy of Education Society refused to embrace the activist principles pronounced by leaders of *The Social Frontier*.

The original members of the Philosophy of Education Society came largely from the John Dewey Society. In their new surroundings, they toned down their social and educational pronouncements to a point where interested outsiders might have wondered whether they were listening to extracts from educational or pure philosophy. This preoccupation with academic-historic philosophy was likely a reaction to what R. Bruce Raup (1888–1976), a professor of education at Teachers College, Columbia, discovered when he used part of a 1938–1939 sabbatical leave to visit colleges across the country to see how philosophy of education courses were faring. In many colleges the quality of their syllabi was suspect and professors responsible for them appeared unprepared to do much more than offer personal reminiscences about long careers in education. In other schools, however, he is said to have found educational philosophy handled with the respect and diligence it deserves, and frequently by professors schooled in philosophy as well as education.

Macmillan relates the scars Raup found, but tells, too, of praiseworthy conditions surrounding educational philosophy at Teachers College, Columbia; Ohio State University; the University of Pennsylvania; Saint Louis University; the University of Notre Dame; Marquette University; New York University; Harvard University; and some teachers colleges in Massachusetts, New York, and Maryland. Still, conditions surrounding the subject were so often distressing that Raup almost at once sought their redress by urging his colleagues to cooperate in forming a professional and technical philosophy of education society. The Philosophy of Education Society was founded in 1941 with thirty-four charter members.[8] An early preoccupation with philosophy, while discounting without forgetting education entirely, tended in later years to become so intense that at meetings of the Philosophy of Education Society one might endure several sessions hearing barely a word about pedagogy and theory's implications for it. The tragic irony to all this is evident if it is conceded that educational philosophy was yearning for maturity at the expense of the very objectives its nature recommended.

The Philosophy of Educational Society membership came from public and private colleges and universities alike. Shortly after the national association was in place, regional societies were established to maintain among members a more intimate academic relationship than the one annual national meeting afforded. And as membership increased it became more diverse, so the radical fringe that had transferred from the John Dewey Society with a strong urge to politicize educational philosophy was less and less influential. Men like John L. Childs (1889–1985)[9] and George S. Counts,[10] although members of the Philosophy of Education Society, were not posted among its leaders. Only the charming and intelligent Theodore Brameld (1904–1987), whose background certified him to the radical left, was able to overcome the excesses of his past to become and remain a leading, active, respected, and influential member of the Philosophy of Education Society until his death. For the most part the society resisted close ties with educational practice and was cool to all attempts to turn the philosophy it espoused into an applied discipline. The early issues of *Educational Theory*, the official journal of the society, amply illustrate this. Although such a philosophically antiseptic stance was later abandoned, in the 1980s one could peruse an issue of *Educational Theory* and wonder how it could represent a society that claimed to make a formal investment in philosophy and education.

During World War II the Philosophy of Education Society was inactive, although philosophers of education who remained in the colleges maintained a collegial relationship with their counterparts across the country. The education industry enjoyed a period of quiet during the war years. With the war's end the Society came to life and by 1951, through the joint efforts of the Philosophy of Education Society, the John Dewey Society, and the College of Education at the University of Illinois, established *Educational Theory*, a journal that was to serve as the official organ of the Philosophy of Education Society. The early issues of *Educational Theory* illustrate the interest of the society's members in questions with genuine philosophical import. So it would not be too much to say that educational philosophy in the 1950s and 1960s followed the conventional route of philosophizing about education. Sometimes, as a matter of fact, the articles might better have appeared in journals devoted to pure philosophy. There was little evidence that the members of the Philosophy of Education Society considered themselves cultivators of an applied rather than a speculative philosophy. Toward the end of the decade of the sixties, though, a change occurred and the content of *Educational Theory* reflected it. The articles became less and less philosophical, surely they were not highly speculative, and more and more sociological. Of course there was the exception, but the editorial policy and the preference of the readership appeared to be on the side of application, of pedagogy and of social issues. Philosophy of education, according to this preference, was expected to sail in the mainstream rather than in the tributaries of educational discourse.

Yet, neither in connection with classroom practice nor social issues was educational philosophy tempted to return to the days when social reconstruction was nailed to its masthead. Quite the opposite was, in fact, the case: educational philosophers who had led the march for rebuilding American society according to a socialistic paradigm were silenced by political threat. Their prewar appeal for social and economic justice could, in the postwar era, sound like anarchy. Instead of listening for echoes from the past that could conjure up visions of communist conspiracy, the educational community, with its philosophers at the head of the column, tried to be socially neutral by pretending that educational philosophy could somehow be purely scientific. And for a time this illusion appears to have been satisfying. At any rate, it allowed educational philosophy to regain the equilibrium it had lost and the respect it had bargained away in its fleeting liaison with radical politics.

Still, for all its effort to achieve and maintain respectability in the college curriculum and to gain standing extramurally in its societies, associations, and periodicals, educational philosophy was unable to maintain a cordial relationship with the discipline of philosophy. Some members of philosophy departments viewed educational philosophy with disdain. They characterized educational philosophers as academic interlopers or, worse, imposters. During these years philosophy had lost curricular ground to the social sciences. Many philosophers considered educational philosophy to be a social science rather than genuine philosophy, so its feet were thought to be planted in an enemy camp. Besides, philosophers supposed most educational philosophers, often unschooled in conventional philosophy, lacked the credentials qualifying them as genuine philosophers.

It might well have been true that a majority of American philosophers in colleges and universities either refused to consider or failed to understand philosophy's kinship with education. Despite the fact that philosophers were themselves teachers and educators who could benefit from having an educational theory to sustain them in their work, they were generally indifferent to or unsympathetic with what was going on in departments of education. And it would have horrified professors of philosophy to have been invited to offer courses in educational philosophy. They were overqualified for such work. Yet, one can go too far in stressing a general indifference of philosophers to education and to educational philosophy. The best evidence here is found in the fifty-fourth yearbook of the National Society for the Study of Education, Part I, *Modern Philosophies and Education.*[11]

Some philosophers, and among them some of America's best, contributed chapters to the yearbook expressing their understanding of the natural compact between philosophy and education. One can do no better than go to the yearbook itself. But for now it should be said that the following scholars wrote chapters for the yearbook: Kenneth Burke, Bennington College, on linguistic analysis; Robert S. Cohen, Wesleyan University, on Marxism; James K. Feibleman, Tulane University, on ontologism; Herbert Feigl, University of Minnesota, on logical positivism; George R. Geiger, Antioch College, on experimentalism (pragmatism); Theodore M. Greene, Yale University, on idealism; Ralph Harper, director of the Council for Religion in Independent Schools, on existentialism; Jacques Maritain, Princeton University, on Thomism (Christian humanism); and John Wild, Harvard University, on realism. Educational philosophers, who functioned as consultants, were: Robert H. Beck, University of Minnesota (logical positivism), Kenneth Benne, Boston University (linguistic analysis), Harry S. Broudy, University of Illinois (realism), J. Donald Butler, Princeton Theological Seminary (idealism), William F. Cunningham, University of Notre Dame (Thomism), Lawrence G. Thomas, Stanford University(experimentalism), Robert Ulich, Harvard University (existentialism), and James E. Wheeler, University of Alabama (ontologism).[12]

Despite the ornamental scholarship portrayed in the yearbook's chapters, as well as the intimate intellectual connection between philosophy and educational philosophy illustrated by philosophers of recognized stature, close bonds between philosophy and educational philosophy could not be kept intact. Philosophy departments were not disposed to reward professors who undertook to interpret the relationships between philosophy and education, or to raise genuine pedagogical issues in the context of philosophical speculation. Only the rare philosopher strayed from a safe reservation to engage in sorting out the enigmas in the enterprise of educational philosophy. Occasionally, and sometimes with spirit, the American Philosophical Association discussed educational issues at its general meetings and special seminars. But this was not enough the thaw the ice that encrusted philosophy and educational philosophy about equally. In the end, perhaps, neither discipline could be absolved from blame.

EDUCATIONAL PHILOSOPHY AFTER THE FORTY-FIRST YEARBOOK

Long before the middle years of the twentieth century, educational philosophy had made an indelible mark on intellectual history. Besides, especially in the United States, it was a staple in curricula organized to prepare teachers for the schools. Its reputation as a trustworthy guide for educators was nearly impeccable. To neglect a subject expected to elaborate educational ends and means would have been unthinkable. Its language, moreover, while now and then resorting to philosophy's technical rhetoric, belonged mostly to a lexicon familiar to teachers and students. It eschewed the argot or cant that had settled like blight on much pedagogical oral and written discourse.

Yet with the dawning of the decade of the 1950s American education was an industry: enrollment on all scholastic levels, but especially in colleges and universities, burgeoned as schools and colleges multiplied. Most telling for educational philosophy, graduate programs in education leading to doctoral degrees grew by leaps and bounds. Within these programs new specialties flourished, educational philosophy among them. In the upshot, for two decades after 1950 educational philosophy lacked assurance about its academic direction. Should it invest in the instruction of undergraduate students who expected to enter the nation's classrooms and who, although shying away from philosophical sophistication, wanted a fundamental theoretical grasp of education's meaning? Or should it spend its resources on graduate, mainly doctoral programs, where pure theory could be cultivated with hardly any thought about its application to scholastic policy and pedagogical practice? Was educational philosophy jeopardizing its practical professional appeal by promoting its disciplinary independence and logical purity to an unrealistically speculative level? In a period of extraordinary academic optimism, such questions went unasked. With the study of education prospering in the nation's colleges, graduate students could complete scholarly, sometimes erudite, dissertations and obtain appointments in education departments and schools and colleges of education the country over. Programs in education were thriving and the enterprise of educational philosophy, despite what should have been an urgent need to clarify its purpose, was a contented beneficiary of unearned increment.

The irruptions of the 1960s further muddied the water flowing in educational philosophy's mainstream. At the outset its worth went undisputed, but unrest on the campus and uncertainty in the syllabus put educational philosophy in an unenviable position. Why should students spend time on a subject about which questions of worth were being raised? What if any relevance was there to an educational theory mined from ancient reservoirs or hammered out on an anvil of symbolic logic? Could it speak directly to the burning social and academic problems of the day? By whom and where were these problems being confronted? Faced with threat to its stability and suffering indecision about its legitimate content and purpose, educational philosophy turned its back on its past, retreated from promise implied in analytic technique, and aspired to nothing more noble than customer satisfaction. The customers (the students) were unequipped to write the syllabus for a field of knowledge whose threshold they were about to cross.

Educational philosophy in some colleges was vigorous enough to withstand assault and maintain a place as a required course in programs of teacher education. But as often as not these victories were ephemeral: in the end the war was lost. Yet in the schools where educational philosophy was able to hang on, it was far from clear what its content should be. Many of the philosophy professors' colleagues professed not to see the worth of educational philosophy. Wanting the credit hours for their own subjects in the curricular slots philosophy occupied, they conducted active campaigns against it. Too often these academic guerrilla tactics succeeded. When they failed, professors who had custody of educational philosophy tried to organize the content of their courses in ways to attract students or to satisfy the ones they had. Some courses were organized around the traditional schools of philosophical thought, some became histories of educational thought, some were composed of the doctrines of great educators, some were organized around contemporary literature in education, some, incredibly, became exercises in sensitivity training, and others, sad to say, were group discussions about current social and educational issues which, while weighed down with opinion and ideology, had nothing in them resembling respectable academic stature.

With the discipline itself exhibiting uncertainty about its content, it turned out to be a hard task to persuade prospective teachers—the consumers in an age of consumerism even in the colleges—and college professors that the most ancient subject in the discipline of education contained a message too important to miss. And among the generation of students who flocked to the colleges in the 1960s, some were infected with a revolutionary academic doctrine that declared rational discourse and logical demonstration irrelevant and emotional commitment profound. The very nature of educational philosophy, despite its ornamental legacy, made it vulnerable to attack.

This, though, was only part of a story of academic anguish. Reflective educators and all educational philosophers know that only some educational questions are philosophical. Still, when genuine philosophical questions are asked, the public has a right to expect the philosophy of education to explain how they affect schooling. Genuinely philosophical questions have considerable range and are bound to be lodged somewhere in decisions on education's aim, on principles of permanence and change in shaping curricula, in coordinating pedagogic technique, in executing research, and in responsible and effective administration. Educational philosophy and educational philosophers, however, have no commission to intrude on the science of education to supply answers to questions that the science of education alone can answer. Put directly, educational science should not be expected to wrestle with philosophical issues, and philosophy should not pretend to be a substitute for science. To identify those problems or questions with a philosophical dimension is, Harry Broudy maintained in the eightieth yearbook, one of educational philosophy's most important functions.[13]

In any case, when educational philosophers speak to educators, their audience has a right to expect the discourse to be conducted in language stripped from technical rhetoric and linguistic obfuscation. Analytical philosophers have gone out of their way to stress this deficiency in all of philosophy, but especially educational philosophy: an inability to communicate meaning in educational discourse and practice. Yet, one should be careful about climbing too far out on this precarious limb: some discourse requires complex construction and complicated language to render meaning. Ideas cannot always be expressed clearly and fully in simple declarative sentences. Technical vocabulary, moreover, can be useful. So when an interested and educated public makes a legitimate demand upon educational philosophy for clarity and precision in idea and language, educational philosophy, on the other side of the coin, has a right to expect basic philosophical literacy from its audience. It is not too much to ask educators to have some knowledge of educational philosophy and the general philosophical propositions that sustain it. Educational philosophers are usually in agreement that educational philosophy should be a required professional experience.

If educators are right to seek direction from educational philosophy on issues that belong to philosophy, they are entitled also to expect from educational philosophy a careful analysis and responsible interpretation of disputed points in education: affirmative action, accountability, religion in education, and equality of educational opportunity, for example.[14] This is ground to which analytic philosophy, especially linguistic analysis, laid claim. Because of its investment in clarifying meaning in educational discourse, the claim had merit. Yet, one should understand that philosophy has always aspired to analysis, to distinction, to interpretation, and to clarification of meaning. Linguistic analysis was on the right track emphasizing the need for clarity of meaning in educational discourse, but emphasis cannot be translated as monopoly.

There are times, also, when educational philosophy extends its range to embrace what are called policy studies. Here philosophers of education can become mired in the quicksand of politics, economics, and ethics. The point is that solutions to educational problems such, for example, as affirmative action, have consequences extending beyond the schoolhouse. And to reverse the pendant, political and economic public policy and judicial decisions impinge upon education. Educational philosophers have a responsibility to explain their intended and unintended consequences for educational practice.[15]

How much more educators had a right to expect from philosophy of education as the discipline entered the last half of the twentieth century is hard to say. It was reasonable to suppose that some educational philosophers would undertake to present a comprehensive view of educational philosophy, say, a survey of the field, and some did. But when they made this professional decision, it seldom slowed the determination of specialists to till their own disciplinary garden. In the hands of specialists the likelihood of theoretical coherence in educational philosophy was slight. But neither the discipline itself nor its public could require scholars in the field to abandon their specialties and become generalists, although philosophical generalists performed a more useful service to educational philosophy than their specialist colleagues.

Most of all, though, educational philosophy was faced with this stark reality: to claim a place in the syllabus of education it had to achieve and maintain intellectual, academic, and philosophical respectability. A field without perspective, without purpose, and without commitment is useless. It must have been depressing for scholars who had spent their professional lives cultivating a discipline to discover their assumptions about its stability, maturity, and independence were undependable. Compared to other ancient disciplines with permanent and respected positions in the college curriculum, educational philosophy was clearly in trouble. After all this time, debate about its legitimate function and proper content should have been over. The record appears to confirm that it was not: educational philosophy was once again on probation.

It was one thing when intelligent outsiders fired verbal fusillades at both philosophy and educational philosophy, despairing of their penchant for living in an ivory tower; it was quite another thing when philosophers themselves began to discharge volleys in the direction of their own discipline. Educational philosophy, no less than general philosophy, could be indicted for a preoccupation with esoteric questions that no one was asking and whose answers, if there were answers, whose worth escaped reasonable men and women. Philosophy, moreover, had become sterile and, its critics said, was nothing short of preposterous. Surrounded by problems in urgent need of resolution, philosophers stuck to their traditional but inconsequential lasts. In addition, there was the allegation that questions of worth, of value, of moral standard, are outside philosophy's province because the answers to them depend upon time, place, and situation. If there are critical ethical issues in or out of education, philosophy is helpless to illuminate them.

Criticism of philosophy was not new and educational philosophy, when it came of age as an independent discipline, had no special dispensation. Yet, to the dispassionate observer with the advantage of a forty-year perspective, such criticism, while containing elements of truth, was much too harsh. First, critics withheld from philosophy a speculative commission and charged it, and especially educational philosophy, with investing all its resources in unraveling the conundrums indigenous to social crises. In a word, they seemed not to want educational philosophy to be philosophical at all. The principal complaint, though, was directed at the philosophers' inability to communicate and the tendency of so much philosophical discourse to confuse platitudes with expressions of profound thought. The clear and orderly prose of some nineteenth-century philosophical writers, William James and Josiah Royce, for example, was sorely missed.[16]

Anxiety among educational philosophers about the nature of their study was evident before the troubled decade of the 1960s and can be taken as an ominous sign that educational philosophy was laboring under an inferiority complex. Reading the forty-first yearbook of the National Society for the Study of Education, *Philosophies of Education* (1942), persuades one that the path ahead is clear and that the discipline can be entirely sanguine about its future. Debate would of course continue about which philosophy of education filled the bill or where some educational philosophies were deficient, but this had nothing to do with the essential nature of the the subject itself.[17] This confidence must have been genuine; it was also fleeting, a point well illustrated in the spring 1956 issue of the *Harvard Educational Review*.[18]

Twenty-five scholars were invited to write essays reacting to two questions raised by Harry Broudy and Kingsley Price in the *Journal of Philosophy*: How philosophical can the philosophy of education be, and is a philosophy of education necessary?[19] In an introductory editorial note, the assistance of Israel Scheffler in selecting the stable of authors to comment on the philosophical respectability and educational adequacy of philosophy of education is acknowledged.[20] One is entitled to inquire into the stature of a discipline with a half-century history in American colleges when it makes what must have been a serious effort to have its academic credentials checked by a jury composed of seventeen professors from philosophy departments and eight from the field of educational philosophy. Were there too few educational philosophers to empanel a jury or did they lack professional and scholarly qualifications? What would scholars in other academic disciplines think of a subject so timid and insecure as to ask outsiders to pare away doubt about its identity or tell it what to do? Would other subjects in the college curriculum so publicly confess to uncertainty? On their face, moreover, the questions posed by Broudy and Price might have been thought insulting and demeaning had it not been for the background of debate producing them in the first place.

After having been closely allied with philosophy for centuries, educational philosophy, determined to declare its independence and confirm its maturity, began to sever traditional ties with philosophy. For a long time the practice was fairly common for students to enroll in courses in basic moral and intellectual philosophy (often thought to be the heart of the curriculum) before studying educational philosophy. On the graduate level, students specializing in educational philosophy would spend, or had spent, much of their time in philosophy departments. When the long-standing cordial relationship between philosophy and education departments became frosty, undergraduate students lacking decent philosophical literacy began to appear in philosophy of education courses; graduate students in educational philosophy not only shied away from philosophy departments but were told courses in pure philosophy had nothing to offer them. If this were the case, how philosophical could philosophy of education be?

Finally, as some philosophers of education were declaring, their subject was a social science drawing its substance from empirical data not a humanity whose motherhouse was logic and reason. Correctly understood, Broudy's question was inoffensive. He wanted to know whether educational philosophy could be "philosophically genuine or educationally helpful" if the gulf between philosophy and educational philosophy were not spanned.[21] And along the same line, can educational philosophy function either as a "theory builder" or an "evaluator of theory" (both pursuits, although legitimate, are different) without the insights only genuine philosophy can supply?

Price's inquiry followed a slightly different route and called upon educational philosophy to decide whether it was to be a thoughtful assessment of a process that takes place mainly in the schools, or should it ascend to a level of theory and take for its audience an initiated few who might wrestle with technical and erudite issues touching the educational enterprise. Should educational philosophy stay on the level of theory and essay to translate metaphysical, epistemological, and ethical principles to educational practice, it would almost certainly be found wanting. Prospect for this kind of educational philosophy, Price thought, was dim unless agreement were reached on the fundamental principles whereupon metaphysics, epistemology, and ethics stand. Price stops short of saying that educational philosophy is unnecessary if it follows this latter course, but concedes that it will be a long time before agreement is reached upon principles. Yet, even educational philosophers who like to think of themselves as theory builders should cling to the hope that by working diplomatically they might engineer a consensus. Put bluntly, does educational philosophy belong to the library or the classroom? If educational philosophy ignores the schoolhouse, its claim to essential standing in a syllabus of teacher education is unpersuasive.

Looking back, it is only slightly short of amazing why an inquiry into the relationship between philosophy and the philosophy of education should have been mounted in the aftermath of the fifty-fourth yearbook, which had so explicitly confirmed their high degree of consanguinity. And why, too, ask a question about the necessity of educational philosophy when scholars the country over had certified its place in undergraduate programs of teacher education, a point left unstated in the yearbook but certainly implied? Besides, what illumination did the authors who wrote for the Harvard Educational Review supply? Did they, in the end, do what was asked of them? How would they have graded the essays they themselves wrote had they been turned in by their students to complete a similar assignment?

An observation that the authors of the essays were professors in colleges and universities whose education programs had only little more than a fringe commitment to the preparation of teachers might conjure up suspicion that the wrong people were invited to participate in the symposium. In much the same vein, only five were faculty members from public institutions and none of the contributors was from a school located west of the Mississippi River. With the exception of Tulane, the University of Michigan, and the University of Puerto Rico (where Theodore Brameld, on leave from New York University, was visiting professor), the schools represented were located in the northeast. The composition of this jury might give us pause were it not for the extraordinary range of (and frequently conflicting) opinion expressed in the essays: diversity of reaction to the two questions posed, when they were in fact alluded to, makes it almost impossible to believe the assets of a genuine discipline were being counted by sober, prudent scholars.

The general message from the twenty-five essays falls far short of an encouragement for educational philosophy to proceed in one or another direction or, for that matter, to proceed at all. And in connection with educational philosophy's purpose and essential nature, the verdict is mixed, muddled, and unenlightening. A few authors were confident in their assertion that educational philosophy is necessary on all levels of responsible educational practice, whereas others scoffed at the notion that educational philosophy has anything of consequence to say to teachers and administrators.

Some alleged that educational philosophy, indeed the entire educational enterprise, is helpless unless it translates to practice the metaphysical, epistemological, and ethical principles revealed in pure philosophy, only to be faced with the rejoinder that it is utter nonsense to maintain that philosophical principles have any logical implications for educational theory and practice.

If educational philosophy is first cousin to philosophy, authors friendly to a wedding of philosophy and educational philosophy argued, it is essential that educational philosophers be highly skilled in philosophy and, perhaps, more the products of philosophy than educational departments. On the reverse side of the coin, if educational philosophy is nothing more than teachers thinking about educational problems, the philosophical training, so much admired by some, is pointless as a professional credential. Probably a majority view, but one justified in a variety of ways, was that educational philosophy, with or without the assistance of philosophy, must be an analytical, evaluative, and synthetic enterprise. A few professors were amenable to the position that educational philosophy is responsible for setting goals and norms in education. One bold essayist, taking the bull by the horns, refused to acknowledge disciplinary dignity for educational philosophy and implied that it is an academic imposter.

Considering the lack of unanimity among persons who should have been in a position to know what philosophy of education entails, it comes as no surprise that the 1956 symposium appears to have exerted slight influence, if one is to base a judgment upon the attention paid its pronouncements over the years following immediately upon its appearance. But this is not a critical matter. More important is why, after all the years it enjoyed as a staple in college curricula, was the disciplinary status of educational philosophy suddenly on probation, and why was its maturity as a standard subject in programs for teacher education in limbo? Would the answers come over the next twenty-five years?

An exaggerated and cynical assessment of educational philosophy's condition during these years might call educational philosophers their own worst enemies who, rather than laboring to establish solid foundations for the discipline they pretended to represent, intentionally or unintentionally poisoned their own well. A more plausible argument might be advanced to explain the deflation of educational philosophy during the last forty years of the century, especially if one begins with the assumption that its apex of influence and popularity was reached between, say, 1940 and 1960. To a considerable extent the historical record indicates, this eminence was almost a direct result of the cordial reception accorded the forty-first and the fifty-fourth yearbooks of the National Society for the Study of Education. Both yearbooks, in addition to being widely consulted by all scholars in the field, were frequently adopted as textbooks in graduate courses in educational philosophy and, moreover, were regularly quoted in textbooks, monographs, and articles on educational philosophy.

When Burbules asked for a recitation of educational philosophy's literary canon, one could hardly do better than to begin by citing the two yearbooks.[22] Not an author in either yearbook, although certainly acknowledging substantial philosophical differences from one to another system, was ever tempted to intimate, much less assert, that the content of educational philosophy is fabricated by a subscription of opinion: one is as good as another, and none can be demonstrated to be right. But if this was a high point for educational philosophy, it was also a bad omen for the discipline itself and for the Philosophy of Education Society.

Raup could be excused for weeping had he been aware of Giarelli's and Chambliss's account of what the Philosophy of Education Society had become, and by extension educational philosophy as well. The society, they wrote, was not a professional organization devoted to the assertion of distinctiveness and authority, but a forum for dialogue across differences, open to all voices.[23] Equally distressing was the statement related by Burbules that "philosophy of education is nothing more than what philosophers of education decide it is."[24] Raup wanted educational philosophy and the Philosophy of Education Society to make a difference. Besides, he wanted the society whose birth certificate he signed to help define the nature of the discipline and give it stability as well as academic stature by establishing definite boundaries between it and other educational and philosophical organizations.[25] He, likely, would have recoiled in horror at the recommendation, one clearly stripping from educational philosophy academic respectability, that the nature of the subject repudiates the notion of professors who believe the achievement of students in their classes could or should be assessed. In a strange twist of fate some educational philosophers became addicted to the myth, declaring educational philosophy bereft of an objectively constituted body of knowledge.

But there is more to the record of the past thirty years than a litany of failure and false promise: the rise of analysis, valiant and zealous effort to rehabilitate (or elevate) existentialism, a reinterpretation, without any taint of revisionism, of the influence of John Dewey, and the invention of policy studies as a way of rescuing educational philosophy from the oblivion of the ivory tower. And as a sign of the times, likely without any direct relationship to or encouragement from the discipline itself, was the appearance of an impressive cadre of women scholars who began to invest their considerable talent in the subject.[26]

Anticipating the appearance of the eightieth yearbook of the National Society for the Study of Education, *Philosophy and Education* (1981) by two years, the *Teachers College Record* devoted its winter 1979 issue to articles on the general topic of "Philosophy of Education Since Mid-Century" with Jonas F. Soltis as general editor.[27] Without pretending to be systematic history, the articles nevertheless reported on the principal emphases in educational philosophy and the main shifts in its direction in the aftermath of the fifty-fourth yearbook. Analytic philosophy headed the list as educational philosophy began to stake out promising claims. By no means a novelty in general philosophy, analytic philosophy had only infrequently (and mainly in England) applied its techniques of elucidation and evaluation to education with Charles D. Hardie,[28] D.J. O'Connor,[29] and John Wilson[30] as a second generation of analysts leading the way. When the educational prescriptions of analysis crossed the Atlantic, they were read by Israel Scheffler and B. Othanel Smith, whose heraldry for analysis was joined later by Jonas F. Soltis. Richard Pratte is likely correct in declaring that the main contribution of analysis to educational philosophy during these years was its success in encouraging, rather than forcing, careful thought about educational problems.[31]

With the near abandonment of philosophical systems sometime after the fifty-fourth yearbook, the sole survivor was existentialism. This was an unusual occurrence largely because existentialism's application to education, to any practical pursuit for that matter, was feeble and underdeveloped. It might be said, then, that its survival was due to the fact that so much was yet to be done in converting it into a genuine philosophy of education. Despite extraordinary effort by Van Cleve Morris and George F. Kneller, to name the most energetic interpreters of existentialism, attempts to rehabilitate existentialism by making its educational message clear were doomed to failure. The same verdict, Donald Vandenberg maintains, can be rendered in connection with phenomenology.[32]

During the same years, Burnett alleges, Dewey's influence began to decline. From the preeminent position of high priest for educational philosophy for much of the first half of the century and a scholar who attracted a large cadre of disciples, his stature dipped to the point where finding fault with Dewey was not only acceptable but a sign of scholarly independence or boldness. This indulgence of fault finding was due partly to the failure of Dewey's followers to embrace unequivocally the philosophical principles he had endorsed. Too often their enthusiasm led them to reinterpret Dewey, an always dangerous undertaking, and in consequence introduce distortion and confusion to Dewey's original script. Then, too, Dewey had detractors who complained that his prose was incomprehensible and much of his philosophy unintelligible. Sometimes readers upon finishing *Democracy and Education* wondered whether the master was out of date or had hitched his wagon of social and economic reform to a burned out educational star.[33]

Amid these vexing conditions was educational philosophy's struggle to find practical and persuasive justification for maintaining an important position in education's collegiate syllabus. Under assault for being too theoretical, for standing too long in the shadow of irrelevance, some educational philosophers decided to add a new dimension to their study: issues of public policy as they touched upon education were added to the menu. While this strategy might have portrayed a melding of philosophy and policy study as contemporary and relevant, it appears to have had the effect of siphoning off the heavy investment in theory conventionally endemic to any subject commissioned to philosophize about education. And to add further length to the detour educational philosophy was being forced to take as it made a valiant effort to achieve maturity, the professors responsible for policy studies freely acknowledged that philosophy was not likely to contribute much to public policy, although they were sanguine about policy's ability to improve educational philosophy. Green might have put the last nail in the coffin burying public policy studies' effort to be helpful in increasing educational philosophy's prospect for maturity when he wrote that educational policy decisions "are practically never" based upon grounds of educational theory.[34]

The hope of some educational philosophers that the eightieth yearbook would at long last defuse the land mines in educational philosophy's path and allow it to assert itself as not only an independent discipline but a mature one at that was very likely genuine. Yet, although the yearbook illustrates the ability of its contributors to elaborate complex, abstruse sides to educational theory, it illustrates, also, the inability of educational philosophers to resist the temptation to shrink the focus of their special interest to a point where educational philosophy becomes a subject without an objective epistemological base, without a corpus of knowledge upon which a community of scholars can agree. So long as this condition persists, and the yearbook appears to attest it, disciplinary maturity is hardly more than a fond, faint hope. A similarly pessimistic diagnosis of educational philosophy's condition, if not explicit, is at least implied in the commentaries of Paul Hirst, Michael Apple, Allen Graubard, and C.A. Bowers on the eightieth yearbook.[35]

Educational philosophy was sentenced to navigate rough water after mid-century: if its port of call was disciplinary maturity, the port was missed by a fairly wide margin. This failure, though, was not entirely fatal, for an old topic, educational reform, appeared suddenly and unexpectedly. It was one whereupon men and women equipped to philosophize about education, without adopting the formal designation of educational philosopher, now turned their attention. Evidence of declining standards in American education, they said, was persuasive. So essentialistic arguments were reintroduced to the debate and to some extent were responsible for altering the traditional character of educational philosophy.

PHILOSOPHY'S CORRESPONDENCE WITH ESSENTIALISM'S REVIVAL

Essentialism in American education was not an invention of the 1980s. So to appreciate the thrust of its revival in the last years of the century and, in consequence its courtship with educational philosophy, a review that begins in the 1940s is useful background. Various professional organizations committed to the advancement of educational philosophy and the journals either sponsored by or friendly to them had enlisted early in progressive education's ranks. Although it lacked the disciplinary status of philosophy, progressivism called the pedagogic tune to which most American educational philosophers danced. Yet a variety of factors blocked a progressive domination of the schools. Principally, it was an indigenous conservative American temperament that led people who, hearing of the allegations lodged against progressive educators and their crusade to reconstruct society, gave modest but firm support to essentialists.

Essentialism was born of a strong antipathy to progressive school practice and benefited from a general indictment of progressive education for soft pedagogy. This indictment, although not fatal, turned out to be a permanent blemish on the image of progressivism, and one promoting a kind of learning catering solely to children's interests while exhibiting disdain for the validity, stability, and dependability of knowledge. Essentialist critics praised pedagogic techniques that capitalized upon interest, individualism, and freedom. But they condemned progressive practice for neglecting discipline, authority, truth, and tradition.

Progressive education, we know, was highly critical of American schools. It essayed to reconstruct them along with a reconstruction of society. Essentialists averred that American schools, having lost their way, needed redirection but not reconstruction; and by redirection they meant raising the quality of instruction in connection with those school subjects contributing directly to a common core to basic culture. They meant, too, raising standards of teacher preparation, which included a sharp distinction between training and education. Schools should be turned into pleasant academies where teaching and learning could occur in an environment of optimism and happiness, and where the learning process and the hard work inevitably associated with it would be respected. Essentialists endorsed pedagogic technique that made students principal agents in the educational process and counseled teachers to remember the central role activity plays in learning. These amendments to pedagogy, essentialists were confident, would redress the weaknesses of American schools and return them to their main mission of cultural transmission.

Surrounded by progressive educators of first rank at Teachers College, Columbia University, William C. Bagley emerged as essentialism's leading spokesman and one of progressive education's severest critics. That essentialism could survive in the hotbed tilled by Columbia's progressives is surprising. More surprising still is the influence it gained from Bagley's promotion and from the journal, *School and Society*, which he founded and edited. It would be exaggeration to allege that essentialism stunted progressivism's growth in American education. But it would be fair to say that essentialism was instrumental in blunting its appeal. And this was due in large part to the voice of *School and Society*, which, as a periodical of considerable stature, regularly carried articles reminding readers of the shortcomings in progressive school practice. It is easy to conclude that essentialism made its reputation by adopting a negative and hostile posture with respect to progressive education, and the conclusion contains elements of truth. But essentialism stood for something too: a decent and academically solid educational program for the nation's youth, a fundamental curriculum consisting of reading, writing, arithmetic, history, and English, and a scholastic setting where manners, discipline, and obedience are nurtured.

On another scholastic avenue, Nicholas Murray Butler (1862–1947), for years the president of Columbia University, complained of a decline in academic standards and indicted progressive education's indifference to achievement and its commitment to the regular promotion of students as the chief causes. But Bagley went beyond this charge to declare that the faults in progressivism did not stop with the schools. They infected national life, manner, and morals. The country's jails were filled with the products of schools that were heedless to discipline, indulged selfishness at the expense of the common good, and promoted the perpetuation of curricula that were feeble and vacuous. Essentialists conducted surveys to assess scholastic standards and reported that such things as national history, geographic knowledge, basic science, and fundamental mathematics were underdeveloped among the students of the country. All this, they claimed, was due to the contaminating effect of progressivism, a contamination needing quick and drastic remedy. Fortunately, essentialists said, remedy was close at hand: a return of scholastic objectives to a mastery of the essentials, stripping the schools of all signs of soft pedagogy, and reviving the schools' first and foremost purpose, a transmission of the cultural inheritance.

The case built by essentialists was strong but inconclusive and progressives fought back. Still, parents and teachers were anxious and could hardly have been expected to abandon the contest over education's integrity to a cadre of educators who fancied themselves qualified to set the direction schools should take. Evidence, not argument, was needed to settle the dispute. But evidence, frequently difficult to obtain, was exceptionally hard to interpret. For example, J.W. Wrightstone's 1938 study, *Appraisal of Newer Elementary School Practices*,[36] in a comparison of progressive and traditional school practice, seemed to say that progressive schools were better at teaching reading, whereas traditional schools were superior for their instruction in spelling and arithmetic. So when all was said and done, the differences between the two pedagogic techniques could have been judged inconsequential, and this verdict was disappointing to progressives and dissatisfying to essentialists. But where did it leave parents and teachers who were naturally solicitous about the instructional opportunity afforded oncoming generations of students? Mistakes could be costly, if not fatal.

The depression progressives suffered was mitigated somewhat by the results of an experiment conducted by the Progressive Education Association's commission on the relation of school and college, reported in five volumes under the general title *Adventure in American Education*,[37] and summarized in W.M. Aikin's book, *The Story of the Eight-Year Study*.[38] The experiment, popularly known as the eight-year study, involved thirty progressive secondary schools and three hundred colleges. The point was to compare the collegiate performance of graduates from the thirty schools with the collegiate performance of graduates from traditional high schools. Without adverting to details of the experiment's design, the cumulative four-year record of graduates from the thirty schools was reported as being superior to that of graduates from traditional high schools. The margin of superior performance was attributed to the instructional opportunity afforded in the thirty progressive schools. The progressive triumph, though, was brief and, essentialists declared, illusory. Both the design of the experiment and its objectivity were challenged by essentialists so that in the end things stood much as they had before. Conclusions relative to the efficacy of progressive school practice, on the one hand, or to the worth of traditional schooling, on the other, should, likely, be put on probation.[39]

Probation, however, was about the last thing essentialists had in mind. Educational decency, they said with supreme confidence, is not defined by experiments, studies, and research reports. It is lodged in the self-evident proposition that society's health depends upon an educational program where intellectual and moral achievement are primary goals, and is based upon an assumption where a mastery of the essentials basic to culture is an instructional imperative.

World War II, we know, interrupted debate over educational priorities, not because education was judged inconsequential, but because survival of Western democracy was at stake. With war's end and with hundreds of thousands of discharged soldiers and sailors returning to high schools and colleges, education soon regained its place as a critical issue in American society. And progressive education, in the prewar years preoccupied with elementary schools, now turned its attention to secondary education.

It is hard to find anything genuinely philosophical in the direction the progressives took, but unquestionably they concentrated upon "life adjustment education." All levels of schooling, but especially secondary education, should assume as its principal mission the creation of an instructional program ensuring in students an ability to make wise choices in connection with the demands of contemporary life. Critics of life adjustment education wondered what was novel about an educational program that set its sights upon preparing students for life in society, but, at the same time, were offended by the tendency on the part of this progressive movement to strip from the secondary schools their long-standing commitment to strict academic achievement. Life adjustment education, it appeared, was about to abandon the school's academic objective. In the end, though, life adjustment could not breathe enough new life into progressive education to ensure its survival as a vital force in America.

Sensing a weakening of progressive education's appeal, essentialists, who, too, had been either soft-spoken or silent during the war years, renewed their attack on what was considered especially vulnerable in progressivism: life adjustment theory. They stressed the points that life adjustment neglected clear academic objectives and replaced them with visionary or illusory statements about producing active and creative family members, workers, and citizens. While it was too early for the word *accountability* to have a place in education's vocabulary, it was clearly accountability the American public was demanding in the schools. What was the education dollar buying? Many of the books written by essentialists make for good reading today, for their authors were usually eloquent writers quite capable of arguing what they perceived as a strong case.

The litany of books condemning progressive and life adjustment education is too long for these pages, but a representative sample can be supplied. Bernard Iddings Bell, in *Crisis in Education: A Challenge to American Complacency*,[40] indicted the schools for their failure to promote sound learning and for their coddling of students. The consequence of such failure, Bell wrote, was scholastic mediocrity. The entire educational system, moreover, was overburdened by responsibilities belonging properly to other social agencies. Whether the fault for this displacement of responsibility was society's or the school's, Bell left unresolved, but at all costs it should be redressed. By being asked to do almost everything, schools were unable to do anything well. Bell's general prescription to right what had gone so wrong was for the public to regain control of schools from educationists.

Adopting a similar thesis, Mortimer Smith, in *And Madly Teach*[41] and *The Diminished Mind: A Study of Planned Mediocrity in Our Public Schools*,[42] charged the educational establishment with intellectual myopia and moral nihilism. He went on to allege that educationists followed a pedagogical party line. Smith wrote:

> If anyone will take the trouble to investigate, it will be found that those who make up the staffs of the schools and colleges of education, and the administrators and teachers whom they train to run the system, have a truly amazing uniformity of opinion regarding the aims, the content, and the methods of education. They constitute a cohesive body of believers with a clearly formulated set of dogmas and doctrines, and they are perpetuating the faith by seeing to it, through state laws and rules of state departments of education, that only those teachers and administrators are certified who have been trained in the correct dogma.[43]

Following Bell and Smith, Albert Lynd, *Quackery in the Public Schools*,[44] Arthur Bestor, *Educational Wastelands: The Retreat from Learning in Our Public Schools*[45] and *The Restoration of Learning: A Program for Redeeming the Promise of American Education*,[46] Robert Hutchins, *Conflict of Education in a Democratic Society*,[47] Paul Woodring, *Let's Talk Sense*

About Our Schools,[48] and Hyman Rickover, *Education and Freedom*[49] added fuel to the fire. They admonished schools to reject progressive pedagogical mythology and return to the serious business of instructing students in the recognized academic disciplines; to conduct scholastic programs where all citizens are taught the essentials of reading, writing, and mathematics; and to recruit candidates to teaching who are decently and liberally educated. In a final blow at the educational establishment, they called upon parents to regain control of American education from professional educators and therewith to rewrite state certification requirements for teachers to promote scholarship and sound learning rather than pedagogical techniques and life adjustment objectives.

From the 1960s to the early 1980s, American educational philosophy abandoned its liaison with systems or schools of thought—idealism, realism, pragmatism, are examples—and became infatuated with analysis. Likely this infatuation was never so intense as to undermine the compact between American pedagogical practice and the pragmatism indigenous to progressive education. But it had the effect of weakening it by siphoning off attention from the systems approach that had concentrated upon ends and means to methods of investigation and precision in discourse. The storm signals that had been raised by the essentialists shortly after World War II were still up. Now and then educators fretful about the standards in American schools adverted to them. Yet, it is fair to say, essentialists' warnings were heard but not heeded. An impasse was the result as the issue of educational standard on all scholastic levels was debated. But times changed as did the tone of educational discourse.

A first warning came from the National Commission on Excellence in Education in its report to the nation and the federal Secretary of Education in 1983: *A Nation at Risk; The Imperative for Educational Reform.*[50] Almost at once following the appearance of *A Nation at Risk* several reports, proposals, and documents, all aimed at educational reform, were published. Most prominent among them were: the Education Commission of the States' *Action for Excellence,* [51] The Twentieth Century Fund's *Making the Grade*,[52] Ernest Boyer's *High School: A Report on Secondary Education in America, The Carnegie Foundation for the Advancement of Teaching,*[53] John Goodlad's *A Place Called School: Prospects for the Future,*[54] Mortimer J. Adler's *The Paideia Proposal*,[55] and Report of the Holmes Group, *Tomorrow's Teachers.*[56]

Spurred on by the public's appetite to entertain criticism of American education and schools on all levels, Allan Bloom and E.D. Hirsch, Jr., led off with books that, although they could hardly fit the mold for formal philosophical discourse, were certainly able to raise the issue of educational quality in the United States to a philosophical level. Both Bloom in *The Closing of the American Mind*[57] and Hirsch in *Cultural Literacy: What Every American Needs to Know*[58] continued the message that essentialists had been preaching for a half-century. Bloom's emphasis was on the status of college standards and Hirsch's attention was riveted on secondary education. Neither Bloom nor Hirsch saw much good in progressive education. Both were vigorous in their complaint of low standards of achievement in American schools and for the inability of the American public to come to terms with a common core to basic culture, which would assure a solid foundation for communication. In the absence of an ability of citizens to communicate, American society is almost certain to deteriorate. Bloom more than Hirsch deplored the moral nihilism that, he declared, had permeated American education and rendered meaningless any moral distinction between right and wrong.

Neither Bloom nor Hirsch was read without rejoinder. While conservative and essentialist scholars tended to applaud their declarations, others put little stock in their dire prognoses.[59]

Analytical in style and never intemperate in tone, yet apprehensive about the quality and character of American education, especially higher education, was Ernest L. Boyer's *College: The Undergraduate Experience in America*.[60] Hardly a discourse on educational philosophy, *College* nevertheless raised questions about the place and purpose of American higher learning. Much like Boyer in sober temperament, but clearly intended as a philosophical interpretation was Jaroslav Pelikan's *The Idea of the University— A Reexamination*.[61] Taking themes in John Henry Newman's *Idea of a University* as points of departure, Pelikan undertook to reinterpret and apply them to contemporary higher education. As with all of Pelikan's work, readers are treated to sound scholarship and brilliant presentation without any hint of rancor. In a somewhat more sensitive vein, and an issue likely to be debated for years, Arthur M. Schlesinger, Jr., spoke out on the issue of cultural unity and diversity in *The Disuniting of America: Reflections on a Multicultural Society*.[62]

Still, there was more to come, but it is hard to be sure where philosophical utterance stopped and where diatribe began. The tone of discourse is easy to discern, although the philosophical ancestry from which it proceeds is far from clear. Yet, almost surely, there were philosophical dimensions to this literature. A few illustrations will do: Martin Anderson's, *Impostors in the Temple*,[63] Roger Kimball's, *Tenured Radicals: How Politics Has Corrupted Our Higher Education*,[64] and Charles J. Sykes's *Profscam:*

Professors and the Demise of Higher Education[65] and *The Hollow Men: Politics and Corruption in Higher Education*[66] fired live ammunition mainly at faculty in colleges and universities. Dinesh D'Souza's *Illiberal Education: The Politics of Race and Sex on Campus*,[67] and Page Smith's *Killing the Spirit: Higher Education in America*[68] were aimed principally at the curriculum which, they alleged, turned in one direction to abandon the main current of Western culture and replace it with a variety of minority cultures and, in another direction, to introduce to the curriculum a large number of studies without any disciplinary foundation.

In the wake of reform literature, if it can be taken as an accurate assessment of the status of American education, scholarship, learning, and standard of achievement in the schools and colleges have not benefited from examination, interpretation, experimentation. Nor has educational philosophy had a penetrating influence in the entire enterprise.

While recommendations for reform were made and broadsides were aimed at the cost and character of American education, educational philosophers stayed close to their scholastic last, although the craft they practiced in the last thirty years of the twentieth century was unconventional. Philosophical systems had lost most of their earlier appeal and, except perhaps for existentialism, were rarely discussed. In existentialism's case its camouflage was romantic humanism. In their place, and superseding existentialism as well, were logical positivism, illustrating an inevitable association with science, and linguistic analysis, exhibiting a partnership with logic and grammar. Neither had credentials as systematic educational philosophies. On the fringe of philosophical discourse stood a novel and not altogether unproductive way of interpreting education issues by introducing social criticism. Often in step with Marxist theory without being wedded to it, critical theory began to find its voice.[69]

This voice with its materialistic and socialistic timbre was heard less in connection with educational policy than with an analysis of practice, and could easily be confused with analytical philosophy were it not for its fundamental ideology. So when one meets critical theory as it wrestles educational issues, there is nothing to remind us of conventional educational philosophy, nor does it represent any traditional approach to general philosophy. The topic sentences in the discourses issuing from it are likely to be historical, sociological, and economic. A leading example of critical theory at work and, at the same time, one illustrating its affinity to Marxism, is *Schooling in Capitalistic America: Educational Reform and the Contradictions of Economic Life*, by Samuel Bowles and Herbert Gintis.[70]

Immensely popular for several years after its appearance, *Schooling in Capitalistic America* was critical of both progressive and essentialistic educational theory. Neither theory, the authors alleged, detected the fundamental flaw in American educational policy: its subservience to the capitalistic economic system. Both theories pronounce allegiance to equalization in educational opportunity and to the realization of personal gifts, but such pronouncements conceal the fact that schools are producing workers by imitating the conditions of the workplace. In the last analysis, the education enterprise is nothing more than a shill for an acquisitive economic system whose sole ignoble motive is profit. Schools are commissioned to cultivate one of the four factors of production—labor—and at the same time instruct their students to comply with those social rules and regulations that benefit a capitalistic economic structure. Approval of Marxism is barely concealed in the authors' veiled allegation that capitalism makes slaves of us all and that the nation's educational enterprise is a willing dupe. So the verdict is almost unavoidable: the issues controlling educational policy belong not to the province of educational theory but to politics.

The therapy prescribed for America's educational illness, according to these authors, is a peaceful socialist revolution to which the right kind of education can make a contribution by sponsoring a democratic, revolutionary socialist movement. Such a movement should aim toward equipping the people to reform oppressive economic institutions and turn them into cooperative enterprises where men and women are liberated. Although not a driver of this economic bandwagon, education occupies a prominent front seat.

Noteworthy and amazing was the popularity of this economic interpretation of one dimension to American education. For almost a decade, Bowles and Gintis were regarded as authoritative pathfinders. Their diagnosis might not have been understood, and their therapy might not have been fully endorsed, but they benefited from a restlessness that was felt about educational policy and its posture vis-à-vis economics. A feeling of economic disenfranchisement and an urge for reform, rather than the intrinsic cogency of the message, made the message appealing to hundreds of teachers in educational philosophy classrooms and to thousands of students who sat at their feet.

A striking anomaly in critical theory, sometimes resisted by those persons most enamored of it, is its indifference to philosophy, while it is, in fact, philosophy. Critical theorists are tempted to adopt Marx's complaint that philosophy is an introspective undertaking intent on analyzing the world itself rather than wrestling with the world's social and economic problems. But this in itself is hardly a novel indictment of philosophy's penchant for indulging theory while turning its back on the burning issues of the day. In connection with critical theory, however, its most active practitioners have turned away from philosophy to apply their analysis in the disciplines of history, sociology, and economics.

Critical theory is illustrated well in the history of education by the strident revisionism of Clarence Karier who charges American education, including John Dewey's progressive pragmatism, with an agenda of social control and a rejection of humanitarianism, all the while pretending to support social reform. In sociology, Madan Sarup and Michael Apple have applied Marxist perspective to a critical theory urging education to deal directly with the problems of race, division of labor, and class, and, finally, to redress American educational practice which preserves gender stratification and social privilege. Martin Conroy and Henry Levin examine the policies of American education and maintain that the elimination of poverty and inequality is either unlikely or impossible within the boundaries of economic capitalism.

More in step with conventional philosophical analysis, although promoted by the promise of critical theory, is the work of Walter Feinberg, when he recommends a reconstuction of educational inquiry that is informed by some Marxist principles. At the same time his work is a vivid illustration of the conviction of critical theorists that for the work of educational analysis to reap good results the analysts must use a variety of disciplines to inform educational discourse.

Sometimes with philosophical disposition and temper, the dilemma of democratic education, equality of opportunity, cost and control of education, teacher education and quality, alternative education, affirmative action, and standard of achievement on elementary, secondary, and higher scholastic levels were called up for appraisal by scholars who in other times might have called themselves educational philosophers, but now declared their commitment to educational policy studies.[71] In addition, questions about religion in education and moral education that for years had been simmering in political forums began to attract attention from academicians. The vocabulary of their answers tend to remind us that such questions have a substantial philosophical side. Still, philosophy was either too erudite for students and professors or academically barren and unbearable for educators uncomfortable with theory (or who considered theory irrelevant). So these topics found their way into educational philosophy's syllabus, and into its literature as well, with this tepid characterization: contemporary issues in education.

1. This observation differs sharply from James S. Kaminsky's thesis in *A New History of Educational Philosophy* (Westport, Conn.: Greenwood Press, 1993), 54–73, that educational philosophy achieved disciplinary status only after professional societies and associations began to husband it. It appears he is stressing the social reform and political-economic reconstructionist dimensions of educational philosophy rather than its traditional standing as a speculative enterprise. The point here is that such a delineation of educational philosophy's function neglects almost all its antecedents. It is, indeed, difficult to concur with the statement: "But in the United States it was not until the Philosophy of Education Society was organized that a suitable infrastructure for an academic version of philosophy of education was in place" (62).

2. Ibid., 51.

3. Lawrence A. Cremin, *The Transformation of the School* (New York: Alfred A. Knopf, 1961), 348–51.

4. Ibid.

5. Kaminsky, *A New History of Educational Philosophy*, 54.

6. Chicago: University of Chicago Press, 1900.

7. James M. Giarelli and J.J. Chambliss, "The Foundations of Professionalism: Fifty Years of the Philosophy of Education Society in Retrospect," *Educational Theory* 41, no. 3 (Summer 1991): 265–74.

8. Ibid., and C.J.B. Macmillan, "PES and The APS—An Impressionistic History," *Educational Theory* 41, no. 3 (Summer 1991): 275–86.

9. For a biography of this energetic and influential educator, consult Lawrence J. Dennis, *From Prayer to Pragmatism* (Carbondale: Southern Illinois University Press, 1992).

10. For an account of Counts' views, see Gerald L. Gutek, *The Educational Theory of George S. Counts* (Columbus: Ohio State University Press, 1970).

11. Chicago: University of Chicago Press, 1955.

12. John S. Brubacher of Yale University served as chairman of the yearbook committee.

13. National Society for the Study of Education, eightieth yearbook, Part I, *Philosophy and Education*, Jonas F. Soltis, ed. (Chicago, 1981), 34.

14. How educational philosophy in the last years of the twentieth century has endeavored to fulfill this expectation is recited in chapter seven.

15. Thomas F. Green relates the melding of public policy with educational theory in departments that adopted new nomenclature, such as, educational policy studies, in order to introduce a greater degree of relevance to their work. He concedes, though, that philosophy of education, or any philosophy for that matter, is not likely to improve public policy, but that by paying attention to public policy, educational philosophy will be improved. "Philosophy and Policy Studies: Personal Reflections," *Teachers College Record* 81, no. 2 (Winter 1979): 213.

16. For a fuller recitation of the age's evaluation of philosophy in American higher education, one might consult Brand Blanshard et al., *Philosophy in American Education* (New York: Harper and Brothers, 1945). It appeared to the authors of this volume that philosophy might be in danger of losing control over its own subject matter and become only an arbiter of scientific data. One should be precise: this book is not about educational philosophy, which is given a mere two-page treatment.

17. Arthur E. Murphy, "Special Courses and Programs of Study," in Brand Blanshard et al., *Philosophy in American Education*, 243.

18. *Harvard Educational Review* 26, no. 2 (Spring 1956): 94–202.

19. H.S. Broudy, "How Philosophical Can Philosophy of Education Be?" *Journal of Philosophy* 52 (Oct. 27, 1955): 612–22; and K. Price, "Is a Philosophy of Education Necessary?" *Journal of Philosophy* 52 (Oct. 27, 1955): 622–33.

20. *Harvard Educational Review* 26, no. 2 (Spring 1956): 93.

21. Broudy, "How Philosophical Can Philosophy of Education Be?" 613.

22. Nicholas C. Burbules, "Continuity and Diversity in Philosophy of Education: An Introduction," *Educational Theory* 41, no. 3 (Summer 1991): 261.

23. Giarelli and Chambliss, "The Foundations of Professionalism," 274.

24. Burbules, "Continuity and Diversity," 259. Fairness to Burbules requires this notation: he is only reporting his perception of educational philosophy's contemporary condition.

25. C.J.B. Macmillan, "PES and The APA—An Impressionistic History," *Educational Theory* 41, no. 3 (Summer 1991): 275–86.

26. See Mary S. Leach, "Mothers of In(ter)vention: Women Writing in Philosophy of Education," *Educational Theory* 41, no. 3 (Summer 1991): 287–300.

27. These articles were reprinted in book form: Jonas F. Soltis, ed., *Philosophy of Education Since Mid-Century* (New York: Teachers College Press, 1981).

28. *Truth and Fallacy in Educational Theory* (Cambridge, Eng.: Cambridge University Press, 1942).

29. *An Introduction to the Philosophy of Education* (London: Routledge & Kegan Paul, 1967).

30. *Educational Theory and the Preparation of Teachers* (Windsor, Eng.: NFER, 1975; Distributed in the United States by Humanities Press, Atlantic Highlands, N.J.).

31. Richard Pratte, "Analytic Philosophy of Education: A Historical Perspective," *Teachers College Record* 81, no. 2 (Winter 1979): 144–65.

32. Donald Vandenberg, "Existential and Phenomenological Influence in Educational Philosophy," *Teacher College Record* 81, no. 2 (Winter 1979): 166–91.

33. Joe R. Burnett, "Whatever Happened to John Dewey?" *Teachers College Record* 81, no. 2 (Winter 1979): 192–210.

34. Green, "Philosophy and Policy Studies: Personal Reflections," 220.

35. "Symposium on Philosophy and Education," *Harvard Educational Review* 51 (August 1981): 415–31.

36. New York: Teachers College Press, 1938.

37. New York: Harper and Brothers, 1942.

38. New York: Harper and Brothers, 1942.

39. See, for example, W.H. Lancelot, "A Close-up of the Eight-Year Study," *School and Society* 42 (1939): 141–44.

40. New York: Whittlesey House, 1949.

41. Chicago: Henry Regnery, 1949.

42. Chicago: Henry Regnery, 1954.

43. Smith, *And Madly Teach*, 7.

44. Boston: Little, Brown, 1953.

45. Urbana: University of Illinois Press, 1953, 1985.

46. New York: Alfred A. Knopf, 1955.

47. New York: Harper and Brothers, 1953; Westport, Conn.: Greenwood Press, 1972.

48. New York: McGraw-Hill, 1953.

49. New York: Dutton, 1959.

50. National Commission on Excellence in Education, *A Nation at Risk; The Imperative for Educational Reform: A Report to the Nation and the Secretary of Education* (Washington, D.C.: Government Printing Office, 1983).

51. Denver: The Commission, 1983.

52. New York: The Twentieth Century Fund, 1983.

53. New York: Harper & Row, 1983.

54. New York: McGraw-Hill, 1984.

55. New York: Macmillan, 1982.

56. East Lansing, Mich.: Holmes Group, 1986.

57. New York: Simon & Schuster, 1987.

58. Boston: Houghton Mifflin, 1987.

59. See Robert L. Stone, ed., *Essays on the Closing of the American Mind* (Chicago: Chicago Review Press, 1989).

60. New York: Harper & Row, 1987.

61. New Haven: Yale University Press, 1992.

62. Knoxville, Tenn.: Whittle Direct Books, 1991.

63. New York: Simon & Schuster, 1992.

64. New York: Harper & Row, Publishers, 1990.

65. Washington, D.C.: Regnery Gateway, 1989.

66. Washington, D.C.: Regnery Gateway, 1990.

67. New York: Free Press, 1991.

68. New York: Viking, 1990.

69. Critical theory is an expression of the main views of the Frankfurt School of Western Marxism. It melds the philosophical theory of Kant, Hegel, and Freud with the dialectical materialism of Marx and employs Marxism's method of examining ideologies and demonstrating their shortcomings. Promient figures of the Frankfurt School are Max Harkheimer (1895–1971), Theodor Adorno (1903–1969), Herbert Marcuse (1898–1979), Jürgen Habermas (b. 1929).

70. New York: Basic Books, 1976.

71. Green sets the stage for this scholastic genre in "Philosophy and Policy Studies: Personal Reflections," 211–24.

CHAPTER 7

EDUCATIONAL PHILOSOPHY'S CONTEMPORARY STATUS

In or out of school, education is a principal means for preserving an intellectual inheritance and maintaining a social structure to ensure the realization of civility. Amid frequent idealizations of education, zealous, missionarylike, and sometimes unrealistic assertions are sprinkled. Sober reflection rejects hyperbole as necessary to persuade anyone of the importance of education. So when we stop to ponder the stature of education in contemporary American society, its fundamental worth becomes self-evident. At this point agreement is easy. More difficult to achieve, even on a level of compromise, is consensus with respect to education's nature and purpose. This is particularly so when educational philosophy is construed as analysis or an educational policy study.[1]

Stating the nature, the purpose, and the means for education, and then translating these principles into policies to implement them, has been the business of educational philosophy for the greater part of its history. Educational philosophy's reservoir of pedagogic wisdom is worth the attention of educators. But it would be saying too much to declare that philosophical literacy is high or that philosophical principles penetrate every analysis of the broad mission of American education. So, while philosophy is important, probably essential, to the smooth operation of the educational enterprise, it is not always able to muster a kind of eloquence that will tempt people to follow its admonitions.

It might be, then, that the voice of the philosopher is not strong or persuasive enough to give schools, teachers, parents, and students the guidance they need. And it might be, as well, that some of the considerations driving our philosophical forebears are dated and incoherent in the face of current educational problems. If this is the case, it goes a long way toward explaining why the following contemporary issues have gained high visibility in the field of educational philosophy, while the traditional topics have begun to recede, without disappearing, in the philosophical syllabus. It is worth our while to examine the most prominent among them.

DILEMMA OF DEMOCRATIC EDUCATION

From the first years of the American common school, public education in the United States was put in a dilemma. Its principal purpose was to ensure the realization of social solidarity by conducting school programs preparing citizens to shape public policy through the medium of public opinion. At the same time, public education was expected to contribute to social unity by directing citizens toward common objectives. The nation's strength and, as well, its political virtue were to be incubated in a society working resolutely toward a common goal. All this, indeed praiseworthy, had competition from a social and educational goal that is best described as individual development. An instructional program with sights set on social cohesion almost surely neglects or, at least slights, the development of talent that takes persons outside the circle of social unity.[2]

One horn of the dilemma, then, social solidarity, is an obstacle to individual development, the other horn. Clearly, however, both goals are eminently worthwhile and both should be countenanced in a democratic society. While certainly recognized by educational philosophers for at least a century, the dilemma was given less attention than it deserved. In consequence, American education assumed a posture where attention was riveted upon average students, when above-average and superior students, on the one hand, and below-average and slow learning students, on the other, were neglected. Safe to say, educators were not totally indifferent to the dilemma described here—programs were sometime mounted across the country to resolve it—but it was seldom recognized as a critical educational issue.

The same dilemma, however, with slightly different dimensions, became not only important, but controversial, in the late years of the twentieth century. Then, in place of individual development of special talent, attention was focused upon cultural and linguistic differences among students in the schools. Social solidarity, still a desirable objective in a democratic society, was often made to play second fiddle to cultural pluralism. Cultural and linguistic diversity were promoted as principal strengths of American society, reversing a long-standing policy where solidarity took precedence over distinctive, and sometimes socially rewarding, differences.[3]

It should be noted, though, that the subordination of solidarity to diversity is hardly central to educational philosophy: the diversity bandwagon was, and is, driven by social philosophers, politicians, and avant-garde members of the judiciary. Without much guidance from educational philosophy, educators were tempted to follow a seemingly popular creed rather than weigh the dangers to society in abandoning the mainstay of solidarity: a common medium of communication. Despite its lack of cultivation by contemporary educational philosophers who have relinquished the field to sociologists, the dilemma of democratic education must be acknowledged as an important plank in the repertoire of educational philosophy.

Some of the questions educational philosophy might be expected to answer can be recited: Is cultural pluralism a middle ground between segregation and assimilation? Should schools pay allegiance to the dominant culture? Is cultural diversity or, better, multiculturalism, a national asset? Is the assertion accurate that some minority groups are intimidated by *assimilation* schooling and should therefore be absolved from it? Does pluralism lead to social polarization, to lower academic standards, to fragmentation of the curriculum, and to moral disunity and anarchy?

Not a paragraph in any philosophy of education discounts instruction in languages (in the case of the United States) other than English. While it is probably true that interest in foreign-language instruction in American schools has declined as the English language has achieved near ubiquity throughout the world (and this in the face of a world that because of transformations in communication and commerce is becoming more compact), it must be observed that practice has driven curricular policy. In the absence of demand for foreign-language instruction, and in the absence, too, of a language requirement for college admission, the syllabus of language instruction has shrunk. Despite this decline, educational theorists have been called upon to support or oppose a different approach to language instruction in the schools: bilingualism.[4]

Population shift and immigration have increased the number of students in the schools whose native language is not English. While this phenomenon was common enough in earlier decades of our history, it is alleged that historical literacy among educators has declined so sharply that the nineteenth-century American experience with language instruction is neglected, misunderstood, or unknown. In the nineteenth century no educator was rash enough to say that English might not be the official language of the schools and of public discourse as well. As a result, educational policy directed that English should be taught, sometimes to the exclusion of the language that students brought to school with them. Although a policy prohibiting foreign-language instruction in the schools was rejected as being unconstitutional, neither court decision nor educational policy countenanced the slighting of English.[5]

Contemporary proponents of bilingual education, however, and sometimes with the support of the federal courts, declare that students for whom English is not a native language have a constitutional right to be instructed in their native language. Some supporters of bilingual instruction intend that instruction in a foreign language be ephemeral: that it continue until students have a fluency in English equipping them to employ it as the language of instruction. At the same time, it is understood that students have the opportunity to continue to study their native language and literature.

This sensible policy, though, is by no means adopted universally. Some bilingual-education advocates want to foreclose instruction in English altogether. This approach, say educational philosophers who accord primacy of place to social solidarity and see a common language as its chief support, is antithetical to the principles of democratic education. They go on to declare that without competence in English, students are sentenced to failure. But, bilingual proponents argue, the melting-pot hypothesis is culturally and linguistically indefensible in a democratic society.[6]

Educational Equality

Etched into the portrait of democratic education, and wedded to the dilemma just mentioned, are policies pertaining to educational equality. For decades the temptation was almost irresistible to declare for a policy of equality of educational opportunity, a policy intended to protect all citizens from irrelevant discrimination and, at the same time, enable them to realize their native talent. Equality of educational opportunity, moreover, is intended to interdict ancient policies based upon social status or the privileges afforded by wealth. On its face and, likely, popularly understood, equality of educational opportunity is evenhanded when as a matter of principle it discounts artificial and irrelevant discriminating factors and allocates society's educational resources solely on the basis of talent.[7]

Still, even in a society where education is recognized as an essential foundation for a republican form of government—where public policy is shaped by public opinion—an obvious fact arises: society's resources are limited and decisions must be made in distributing educational opportunity. To whom should society's educational resources be assigned and what kind of talent has priority in allocation? Judgments vary about the kind of talent most needed by society and, therefore, most in need of support. More difficult to handle on a policy level is the allegation that decisions with respect to the identification of talent are invalid and that allocation of resource for the kind of talent that society considers most beneficial are undemocratic. These issues worry educational philosophers and test their wisdom.

Despite the protest of extreme egalitarians, the empirical fact is that inequality among persons is a reality, and the opportunity afforded to one person might, if afforded to another, be wasted. Policy decisions must be based, careful educational philosophers aver, upon a common acknowledgment about inequality among persons and that opportunity should be offered to those who can profit from it. Prudence and, some would add, justice require that society invest its resources in ways that return the highest social dividend. When capacity to achieve is unequal, inequality in the allocation of opportunity is both prudent and just. Still, there is difficulty. The definition and identification of talent is not an easy exercise. Some kinds of talent are obvious, so dispute does not arise, but not all talent reaches this level: some talent is buried by social and educational disadvantage. Boys and girls should be given a fair chance to develop their talent in the early years of their schooling. And, in consequence, they should be entitled to claim an unequal allocation of educational resources later.

If this were the whole story on allocation of resource according to talent, with the proviso added that compensation is made early in life for a variety of social and educational disadvantage, the case for a policy of equality of educational opportunity could be closed. But this is not the whole story. Philosophy provides us with one point of view; psychology with another. On the psychological side are hereditarians and environmentalists. Talent is lodged, hereditarians declare, mainly in genetic endowment. It is amenable to some refining and honing, but not to substantial amendment. What anyone becomes, regardless of the amount of opportunity for development offered, depends upon a native, and nearly immutable, deposit of talent.

Environmentalists declare that the pendant has another side and, although loathe to discount genetic endowment and individual difference, are quick to declare that neither plays more than a part in the realization of talent. The environment with all its multiple forces must be equalized, they aver, if disadvantage among persons is to be eliminated. In the end, then, genetic capacity might determine talent's level. Without the chance to cultivate native endowment, a chance contained only in the environment, there is no reason to believe that equality of opportunity is anything more than myth.

In the last analysis the outcome of a policy of equality of educational opportunity might not be equality. As a policy it intends to ensure fairness in extending to all a chance to develop their talent. But when talent is shaped and refined, it will disclose differences in achievement among persons and therefrom inequality in education, social status, and economic standing. This is the logical outcome of the policy. Can it be embraced as a just policy for education in a democratic society? The policy's defenders maintain that procedures will be employed to select persons in such a way that those factors other than talent will be discounted (or compensated for) and equal resources will be allocated to equal talent.

Despite the generally accepted assumption that equality of educational opportunity is a decent and fair public policy, there are demurrals coming from the fringe: educational and social theorists freely admit to the fact of inequality among persons. Declaring that racial, religious, ethnic, and gender characteristics cannot be taken as evidence of inequality, they go on to acknowledge differences in ability to learn. None of these differences, they maintain, can be used to shape a policy on the allocation of society's educational resources. Nor is it fair or just for social policy to embrace one type of talent as being more beneficial and socially useful than another. Justice demands, say these theorists, that society's resources be distributed on a share and share alike policy. No one, and no type of talent, is justified in asserting a preferred claim.

Affirmative Action

Although it is hard to touch every aspect of equality of educational opportunity, and some might not have been forwarded, affirmative action is one to be noted. To say that it is a contemporary issue in education as well as other sides of life in American society is understatement: its controversial status is evident. Limiting our inquiry to education, it appears that except for the employment of school personnel (teachers and others), elementary schools are relatively free from grievances involving affirmative action.

But on more advanced educational levels issues of representation for women and minorities have been raised, not only in connection with faculties and opportunity for employment on them, but in connection with students as well. The issue has a special impact upon the admission of students to professional schools, where places are limited and where standards for admission are often hard for some minority-group students to meet.

Should students and teachers in the schools and colleges be admitted or employed on a basis that mirrors the composition of the total population? Should access to employment and instruction in the schools be based upon a system of artfully disguised quotas? Should appointment to positions and admission to schools take into account the disadvantages certain groups in the population have suffered over the past several generations? Does justice and fairness require that preference be given to members of certain groups (with, it might be argued, discrimination against those who do not belong to these groups) or does it do nothing more than demand that impediments to success be eliminated, that discrimination against persons on any artificial basis be rejected, and that persons of equal talent be treated equally? And does a just and fair society seek to eliminate disadvantage visited upon certain minorities by offering compensatory opportunity?

All these questions are important, and some are philosophical. Yet educational philosophers often search in vain for adequate or acceptable answers.[8] Without undertaking here to supply the answers to these vexing questions, it should be said that in the distribution of educational resources, the burden of proof should be shifted. Currently, the disposition among politicians and sociologists, as well as some philosophers, is to assume that persons who do not meet the established norms are entitled to the positions they seek unless it can be demonstrated that they are not. Properly applied in these cases involving affirmative action, the principle of equality of educational opportunity requires those whose intellectual performance is below the norm to show that their performance is only an apparent indication of their capacity, one relating to contingent factors, but not to real intelligence. At the same time, even for those whose intellectual ability is obvious, there must be a public justification when they share unequally in society's educational resources.

This principle, however, is not universally endorsed. Distributive justice requires, some argue (as we have illustrated above), that in the distribution of society's resources for education (and all others as well) various classes of persons be given a share proportionate to their number in society. On the other side of the coin, exponents of compensatory justice maintain that society's resources be given to persons in such a way as to redress any deprivation they might have suffered from the distribution of resources in the past.[9]

There are, though, social philosophers who declare against compensatory justice as a dangerous principle. They allege that it can be extended indefinitely and thus make for endless trouble. Who, they ask, is to determine what is proper compensation for various minorities? Nathan Glazer wrote:

> When it is established that the full status of equality is extended to every individual, regardless of race, color, or national origin, and that special opportunity is available to any individual on the basis of individual need, again regardless of race, color, or national origin, one has done all that justice and equity call for and that is consistent with a harmonious multigroup society.[10]

Having a nominal historical authenticity, but lacking contemporary standing in practice and policy, is the educational myth that local jurisdictions possess autonomy in both the support and control of public schooling. There is, besides, the perception common among many members of the education community that most if not all of the critical issues facing education in the United States disappear when money is plentiful. Whether money comes from the local, state, or federal sources seems not to matter, so far as solving education's ills is concerned, although it matters a great deal both on the level of policy and practice. Policy identifies the level of government with responsibility for supporting education. The practical question is concerned with deciding which of the various jurisdictions is most capable of bearing the burden of supporting education? Issues of policy and practice are a good deal easier to express than to resolve.

In some states, California for example,[11] courts have declared that the common practice of supporting local schools largely from levies on real property offends the constitutional guarantee of citizens' equal treatment before law. The force of these decisions was blunted severely when the United States Supreme Court refused to endorse them.[12]

When a local school district is unable to raise enough money to meet its projected budget, it appeals to the state for help. And for several decades, states have used equalization formulas to ensure that a minimum level of support is available to local schools. When states lack the resources to support public education, the federal government becomes a source of last resort. But for a long time, federal aid to education was resisted out of fear that federal control would follow the federal dollar. Besides, opposition came from private and religious schools who alleged that federal aid to education, if not offered to them, is discriminatory. After a long time while the issue simmered, federal aid became a reality. The opposition that had been generated against it from private and religious sources declined without disappearing.

Despite a softening of opposition to local school districts and states accepting money from the federal government, the issue of educational control remains prickly. Educational authority is vested in the state, although now and then local action challenges it. Whatever tug of war existed in the past between local communities and states over the location of educational authority, policy is now entirely clear and final. Yet, when states and local communities accept money from the federal government for general or special educational programs, federal authority intrudes. This creates tensions, that while usually manageable, make responsibility for conducting educational programs clumsy. The political dispute centers on the volatile question of states' rights.

Educational theorists are quick to admit that the issues of support and control are more political than philosophical. Yet they have to do with policies that are bound to affect the conduct of school programs. State and local educational communities worry that the imposition of federal control undermines local and state initiative, and ends up as an impediment to the realization of sensible scholastic standards. Clearly, federal aid to education is followed by elements of federal control. It seems unlikely that this reality will ever be amended. So the policy issue for educators who labor in the field of educational theory is one of finding a reasonable way to accommodate the interests of the various jurisdictions while maintaining a solid tradition that specifically rejects both national control of education and a national system of education.

THE EDUCATION AND STATUS OF TEACHERS

Although license is evident in calling the education and status of American teachers a contemporary issue with genuine philosophical standing, the preparation of teachers, the conditions of their work, and their image as professional persons are certainly elements affecting the educational process. Additionally, teachers enliven the curriculum, the materials of instruction, and the instructional facilities of the school, making them more effective for students, the principal agents in the educational process.

Self-education, while difficult, is possible, although one should be careful about employing the illogical expression *self-teaching*. (To teach, the knowledge to be communicated must be possessed, but when this is the case, teaching is unnecessary; when it is not the case, teaching is impossible.) Analogous to self-education is the restoration of health and the growth of crops: both physicians and farmers are cooperative artists. No one claims that students cannot learn without teachers, that health cannot be maintained or restored without physicians, or that plants wither in the absence of farmers' cultivation. The point is that students learn more efficiently with the help of good teachers, that illness is intimidated by the intervention of doctors, and that crops are more bountiful when nurtured by husbandmen.

Educational philosophers and methodologists share common ground when they agree that all learning is a matter of discovery, and when they acknowledge, as well, that were life long enough and capacity for achievement equally distributed, unaided discovery might be superior to aided discovery. But had we been required to discover everything we know without help, we should soon realize how slim our repertoire of knowledge and skill would be. Considering the human condition, aided discovery—that is, teachers' instruction—is essential. And in this connection, teachers function as cooperative artists. They aid nature in achieving an entirely natural end. As has been said, the principal agents in the educational process are students, but teachers are important—better, essential—auxiliaries, so various techniques are employed to assess their performance.

Throughout the greater part of American educational history, professional status commensurate with that of lawyers, physicians, engineers, and clergy was withheld from teachers. Usually for public employees, excellence was seldom expected. When teachers were mainly hearers of lessons rather than genuine educators, and when the public demanded nothing more, chances for improving their condition were slim. But schooling matured as the decades passed. By the advent of the twentieth century attitudes with respect to the quality of teaching and the qualifications of teachers were altered sharply. Qualifications for teachers were raised and the public once satisfied with teachers who had been exposed to a normal school regimen now began to believe that teachers should not only be decently educated but should be skillful in directing instruction as well. Largely in consequence of their own effort, teachers improved their image before the public and were more generally regarded with the respect that should be accorded to such important work. Yet, genuine professional recognition is more a fond hope than a reality. With few exceptions teachers labor under a public perception that they are engaged in an occupation rather than a profession.

The complexities of teaching and learning, the work of teachers as cooperative artists assisting nature, make precision in an assessment of their pedagogical performance exceptionally hard. Yet teachers have felt a need to record their productivity as professional persons. This has led, in recent years, to the introduction of accountability: a way of determining, with scientific precision it is alleged, the effectiveness of their cooperative artistry. On the practical side, one should not be surprised to learn that accountability is something the public and school boards who represent it are prepared to embrace. They want to know the level of teachers' performance. On the side of theory, however, the matter is somewhat more complicated. Is it possible to determine the level of skill teachers possess by measuring the performance of their students? If teachers were operative rather than cooperative artists, say cobblers, shaping the material at their disposal, then all the assessments used to measure performance might be justified. But as cooperative artists teachers are not shaping their students like little lumps of plastic.[13]

An application of all their skill does not guarantee a standard level of accomplishment. There is, one should acknowledge, considerable enthusiasm for accountability in education, much of it generated by favorable evidence from industry. Yet, it is important for the educator, and especially for educational philosophers, to weigh accountability carefully. They should decide whether it is a useful, even praiseworthy, instrument for raising the level of teaching and learning, or just another example of pedagogical humbug.[14]

A moment of sober reflection confirms the public's right to know how the money appropriated for education is being used and with what result. So from one perspective it can be acknowledged that accountability is not only possible but desirable. And for exponents of accountability the foregoing acknowledgment rests upon three assumptions: the proper outcome of instruction can be determined; the pedagogical elements required for the attainment of the outcome can be identified; and the critical pedagogical element in connection with the realization of the outcome is the teacher. If the expected outcome is not obtained, teachers or teaching are at fault.[15]

For those who either oppose the notion of accountability or are lukewarm to it, the assumptions with respect to accountability go too far. The public has an unquestioned right to know how public money for education or anything else is being spent, and with what result. But, they go on, as presently conceived accountability is a mechanistic and unrealistic approach to so complicated an undertaking as learning and so artistic an enterprise as teaching. Many factors are involved in the learning process, and the skill of teachers, while certainly important, is not the controlling one. It is not only unfair to teachers, but a simplistic conception of the educational process to declare that if learning does not occur, or if the right kind of learning does not occur, it is the teacher's fault.

Put another way, and perhaps more directly in connection with the assumptions, is it fair to ask who is to determine the outcomes of learning? Are the students' freedom to learn and the teachers' freedom to teach impaired in this process? Who has the authority to set the goals? And is it fair to ask what part each of the pedagogical elements plays in the instructional process? Are teaching and learning deterministic situations wherein variables will function according to a set pattern? If it is not deterministic, then who or what assesses the influence of each variable? And if teaching and learning are not exact or positive in their operations, why pretend that they are? Finally, can accountability ignore the capacity and willingness of students to learn? The whole theory, opponents aver, converts teachers from humanists to technicians. It appears to take the position that even if all of the various elements in teaching and learning cannot be measured, they should be measured anyway.

Whether contemporary American teachers are better educated than their counterparts of earlier generations is a curious condundrum. Clearly, contemporary teachers have more schooling and, likely, are more fluent in varieties of pedagogic technique. This issue might be amenable to an empirical solution. But there remains a philosophical issue, one pondered for decades in educational philosophy: Should teacher-education programs maintain a commitment to liberal culture and to knowledge itself, or should they be strictly professional and technical with a preoccupation for the development of the skills teachers must have if they are to conduct pedagogically sound programs of instruction?

For centuries teachers were prepared by an exposure to liberal studies. The assumption was evident that a well-schooled person should be able to teach others. We should recall that in the first universities of the Western world, the degree of master of arts was a license to teach. With the advent of the nineteenth century, however, the science of pedagogy had made considerable progress and the old assumptions about knowing what to teach is what counts were amended to give precedence to knowing how to teach. Knowledge was, of course, never sold at discount, but it was becoming clearer that it was subordinate to pedagogic skill. Doubtless, the philosophy of teacher-education should form part of the educational philosopher's syllabus. But it is evident from a perusal of the current literature pertaining to the education of teachers and reforms connected therewith that philosophy of education has paid it scant heed. One is tempted to believe that when philosophy of education ignores a burning question of the day, its relevance becomes hard to defend.

ALTERNATIVE EDUCATION

What is meant is not an alternative to education, which, it would seem, is totally unrealistic, but an alternative to traditional schooling. Persuaded that contemporary schooling is unsatisfactory because it is mainly irrelevant, a cadre of educators posing as philosophers argues, without much precision or agreement, for a different kind of education. One alternative is the private school. Operating outside the boundary of strict public control and support, it should have the flexibility to permit the introduction of the radical amendments these reformers have in mind. But private schools, except in rare instances, are seldom disposed to abandon the traditional and substantial features of schooling to ride a bandwagon that appears to have no driver.[16]

Alternative education, whether tested in the schools or only recommended by avant-garde educators, implies nonacademic instruction. Its promoters maintain that an effective life in society is rarely inspired by language, literature, mathematics, and science. Such subjects, they declare, have little to do with life's realities. What is needed is a scholastic program putting students in direct contact with the art of living. When the school's curriculum is designed to meet the exigencies of genuine life, students shall be better served.

A mature grasp of educational philosophy, however, teaches us that scholastic programs are not amenable, nor is the total climate of the school, to instructional tinkering that makes nondirective social experience grist for the instructional mill. When this lesson is learned, the architects of reform undertake to introduce extramural experience to the educational program by depending heavily upon community resources. The community becomes one great school and the traditional school is neglected or rejected. However much this might satisfy the reformers, it tempts the majority of school patrons to wonder why school buildings should be constructed and maintained, why teachers should be employed, and why education should be so expensive if students are going to be offered nonacademic experiences by and in their community?

Still, with unusual zeal these ardent reformers refuse to surrender. Some go on to recommend an abandonment of compulsory attendance laws, if not for all educational levels, at least for secondary schooling. Even when this brand of alternative education is made attractive and elicits support, it suffers from a lack of structure and is susceptible to the charge of being anything students want to make it. Can such an educational program qualify students for an effective and productive life in society? And this question can be asked alongside the concession that much out of school experience is, indeed, consequential and should be encouraged: for all the good it does, the school is not the sole custodian of decent educational experience.[17]

Further support for alternative education comes in recommendations that tax credit be given to parents who pay tuition to private schools, and for a voucher program allowing parents to select schools for their children with the public treasury allocating to the schools chosen the money to pay for their instruction. Both recommendations introduce voluntarism—a kind of alternative plan—and display a tendency to rupture a public education monopoly. Yet, both recommendations illustrate in convincing fashion the prominence of political and fiscal considerations in the conduct of popular education. Philosophy, for all its traditional eminence among intellectual disciplines, might not in the end be the final arbiter of dispute in education.[18]

An abundance of oral and written commentary upon American education has called attention to lower standards among students in the schools. The complaint is registered with amazing regularity that the meaning of a high school diploma is mainly mystery. There is, though, another side to the coin. The absence of a common level of achievement might not be a sure sign that the quality of American schooling is low. Standards, one might argue, are different from those of the past when the population of American schools was homogeneous, but this is not proof that they are lower.

For decades the goal of American educators was to standardize their product (instructional outcome), and they counted upon a definition of objectives, a choice of curricula, and a command of method to achieve the goal. They could claim a precise knowledge of what a high school diploma or a college degree represented. With the encouragement of progressive educational philosophy, though, common standards were abandoned in favor of educational programs assumed to be personally satisfying and socially contemporary. As stability receded into the educational background, innovation was promoted in its place. This shift, or drift, toward doing something different, innovative, and up to date has not been immune from criticism. Teachers, parents, and educational philosophers have railed against an attitude that idealizes change and takes as dogmatic the proposition that change and progress are identical. They go on to allege that innovation in most educational programs is introduced at the expense of decent standards of achievement.

In the last analysis, however, careful educators and perceptive educational philosophers should want to know whether these complaints of lower standards of achievement represent educational reality. Are general assessments good enough? Should a more precise and scientific assessment of achievement and of scholastic quality be demanded before any tinkering is done with standards in American schools? Is there a case to be made for testing the competence of students (and of teachers)?[19]

If educational policy is to be guided by precedent, assessment of competence (or achievement) stands on solid ground: throughout the history of education, it has been a standard practice, although, admittedly, one exercised in a variety of ways. Now, however, there is dispute about the validity of tests. Educators favoring the use of tests for assessing competence vouch for their validity and go on to declare that unless they are used the survival of public education is in jeopardy. Educators who oppose competency testing are uncertain about the validity of tests and, moreover, introduce an issue of fairness.

Yet fairness, a many-sided affair, can be illuminated somewhat by questions such as these: Who sets the standard to be met? Is it fair to judge students on skills they have not been taught? Do all the children in the school or the school system lack these skills? Is it fair to society to graduate students who have not met a minimum standard? Is it fair to high school students who are qualified to graduate when unqualified students are allowed to graduate? While it might be possible to establish the level of basic knowledge for professional and technical fields, what knowledge and skill are essential for good citizenship? Does the granted right to an education impose upon those who use the right a duty to meet a standard? Who is responsible for justifying the standard? Do justice and fairness require that standards from one to another school be allowed to vary?

The list can be lengthened as the questions multiply: Is it fair, right, and just to judge teacher competence on the basis of student achievement? If too much attention is visited upon test results, is there a danger than teachers will teach for the test? But unless teaching for the test is narrowly conceived (just answering the questions on a test), what is wrong with teaching for a test? Do tests create more pressure than students can handle or should be expected to handle? Is one outcome of competency testing a narrowing of educational goals? Do children go to school to be tested or to be educated? Is it fair to require children to attend school and then fail them? Should different kinds of diplomas be awarded to indicate different kinds of achievement? Since individual difference in talent is evident, why not regard individual difference in achievement in schools and in society as nothing more than a concession to reality?

Educational philosophy might not play a large role in the solution or resolution of the issues that surround standard of achievement. But it is hard to understand, or endorse, an approach to educational philosophy that is indifferent to them. At the same time, should an educational philosophy be responsible, it will inevitably undertake to apply the principles embraced to educational policy and practice.[20]

RELIGION IN EDUCATION

American law and tradition have combined to establish a policy, characterized as separation of church and state, where public institutions assume a neutral stance vis-à-vis religion. Public schools, in consequence, are proscribed from including in their courses of study any matter judged to be sectarian. But the Bible as literature and religion in history are authorized as being essential to a complete and competent view of the world.

Stating the policy is fairly easy; interpreting and enforcing it is considerably more difficult. When does religious neutrality become official secularism? Why are parents ignored who believe their children should be afforded a complete education (including religious instruction) under public auspices? As citizens, do they have as much right to claim religious instruction for their children as those who oppose the introduction of religious teaching in the schools? Is the rejoinder sound that parents who want religious instruction for their children can obtain it by sending them to private schools? In a country where a majority of citizens profess religious belief and belong to religious denominations, and where religion has played a huge role in the foundation and development of the nation, is a public policy excluding religious instruction from the schools equitable and rational? And if religious instruction is allowed in public schools, can it be conducted without an expression of denominational preference?

Public policy with respect to religion in education is based upon an interpretation of the United States Constitution. The courts have spoken with respect to religion in education. And in the face of judicial interpretation limiting the place of religion in the schools, a movement to amend the Constitution to allow religious teaching in the schools has failed to garner enough public support for anyone to be optimistic that public policy is on the verge of being changed. Still, it is hard to justify a curriculum which is so silent about religion in the evolution of world history and American life as to give the impression that it neither existed nor exists. Religion has played an enormous role in the civilization and culture of the West. Is an educational program that ignores it one that deserves public support? There is, moreover, the belief that the most secure foundation for morality is religion, and that any effort to promote moral education in the schools is bound to fail without this foundation.

There is much to debate on the issue of religion in education, but there is little that is genuinely philosophical. Still, it would be hard to believe that anyone who philosophizes about American education could be justified in ignoring the issue, whatever level of philosophical sophistication might be claimed for it.

MORAL EDUCATION

For almost as long as philosophers have speculated about education, various statements of educational objectives have stocked their lexicon. Besides, they have tended to distinguish education both from schooling and erudition. Education's scope extends beyond schooling (an undebatable point) to involve total personal development, whereas erudition aims at the cultivation of literary ability. One part of total formation is the preparation of men and women for life in society and equipping them to make a civic contribution. So almost from the outset of educational history, moral philosophy counseled educators to pay attention to the development of civic virtue. And for most of the history of education in the West, moral education was accorded a prominent position on a hierarchy of educational objectives.

We need not stop to debate whether our forebears were right or wrong or, for that matter, what place on a scale of objectives moral education should have. We need only embrace the notion that some kind of moral education, some view of the difference between right and wrong, some sensitivity for the proposition that good is preferable to evil, and that an education in living a responsible life in society is worth our attention and, moreover, should be accorded a place in educational programs. It might be admitted, of course, that scholastic programs should neither be assigned total responsibility for moral formation nor be allowed to pretend that by themselves they can achieve everything that needs to be done in the development or moral virtue.[21]

Before proceeding beyond a general and impressionistic appeal for character formation, this point should be made: without an affirmation of freedom, any discussion of moral education is pointless. Theories of moral education seldom advert to philosophical principles of freedom, but buried in them is the assumption that persons are capable of exercising choice. And if there is no point to any discussion of moral education without an affirmation of freedom, there is no logic in an assignment of personal responsibility without an acknowledgment of freedom: that choice from among various courses of action is possible. If different courses of action are impossible, if only one course can be followed, there is no reason to speak about choice and freedom to choose. Unless moral agents can control their behavior or accept one alternative and reject others, discussions of freedom are largely a waste of time.

In expressions of moral philosophy where free will is stipulated, rejoinders return ranging all the way from classical physical determinism, to random determinism, to internal (environmental) determinism explaining how men and women function either as captains of their fate or victims of unknown but immutable forces. In the vocabulary of classical determinism, behavior follows the prescript of dogmatic natural physical law. Alternatives for moral agents are foreclosed and elements of control are absent, because only one outcome is possible, the one dictated by a physical cause. Personal responsibility, moreover, is an empty phrase.

The theory of random determinism (or indeterminism) maintains that natural causes produce natural effects, with a chance, within narrow limits, that something might occur to alter a natural effect slightly. Like flipping a coin, moral action might have a statistical regularity, but this is a long way from freedom to choose. In any case, the outcome, given the causes, will be fixed. The agent has no control and, as with classical determinism, there is no talk of personal responsibility.

Internal determinism, a theory of more recent vintage than classical and random determinism, had its most prominent sponsorship in the custody of John Broadus Watson's (1878–1958) behaviorism and, more recently, in the research and writing of Burrhus Frederic Skinner. All of our experiences affect us but, behaviorists say, our conditioning (behavioral programming) is mainly social and emotional. Conditioning prescribes how we act. Understood on its basic level, we are the products of our environment. Once the environment has made its imprint upon us, once it has shaped us, that is the way we will behave. Alternative courses of action might present themselves, but if they do, we will act in only one way, the way we have been conditioned to act.

In connection with moral education, the behaviorist, in affirming its worth, declares that whether we like it or not we are the products of planned or unplanned social engineering. If the environment is chaotic, behavior is unpredictable. But if the environment is planned and if we are conditioned to act in certain approved ways, we and society shall be the beneficiaries. We might think we are free but, behaviorists say, if we knew more about the calculus of cause and effect, and the dynamics of behavior, we would know that freedom is an illusion, a joke, and a bad one at that.[22]

Proponents of freedom reject opposing arguments. An empirical case for freedom, although possible, they admit, is hard to make, but then they go on to declare that testimony from internal experience is persuasive. We know one rather than another course of action is possible. We experience freedom. Experiencing freedom, though, has nothing to do with the existence of alternatives from which to choose. Sometimes there are none. So to be free means neither that choice is always possible nor does it eliminate the possibility of habitual behavior. It certainly does not mean that behavior occurs in a vacuum where men and women are immunized from external influence. It means only that choice is possible, even in those cases when it is not exercised, but it does not mean that we can do anything we choose, because coercion by events and persons can occur. It should be stressed, as well, that a theory of freedom does not mean that behavior will always meet an objective moral standard. Bad choices are possible. In the last analysis, when we are functioning in normal circumstances, the theory of freedom declares, men and women are responsible for their behavior.

In considering the prominent theories of moral education (values clarification, cognitive-developmental, cognitive-analytic, and traditional),[23] a distinction should be drawn between moral standard—that is, what ought to be done—and the ability of a moral agent to exercise choice in relation to the content of the standard. Put another way, knowing what ought to be done belongs to a different order from doing what ought to be done. Both sides of the pendant involve education: the former implies that there is a body of moral knowledge or, at the very least, a body of accepted standards of conduct that can be communicated. When it is communicated responsibly and effectively, persons are instructed in accepted courses of behavior. The latter involves a kind of education, training, or habit that disposes a moral agent to do what is perceived to be in line with an objective moral good or an accepted standard of conduct. This distinction is acknowledged by moral educators who adopt the theses of traditional moral education. At best, other theories keep it on probation. Finally, traditional theory maintains, the purpose of moral education is to understand the rules of good behavior, not to write them.

Values clarification, cognitive-developmental, and cognitive-analytic theories try to avoid the establishment of standards of moral conduct. Such standards, whatever their genesis, are bound to be arbitrary when they ignore the situations where action is required. To declare that one kind of behavior is right while another kind is wrong borders, many contemporary moral educators aver, on indoctrination or coercion. There may or may not be an objective good, a good which can be certified by moral philosophy, but theories of moral education, except for the traditional theory, find no profit in conducting a debate along these lines. Their emphasis is on instruction that pays attention to how to think about what ought to be done, not what to think. The purpose of moral education, in addition to preparing persons to analyze and assess their conduct and practice in choosing, is to promote the "examined life."

FREEDOM, DISCIPLINE, AND RIGHT IN EDUCATION

A long tradition in educational philosophy has recognized intellectual and moral autonomy as education's ultimate purpose. The same line of reasoning makes freedom a condition allowing for the realization of this purpose. Students in schools, though, are at various maturational levels and few are qualified for autonomous status. Put another way: autonomy is at the end of educational effort, not at the beginning. Besides, society has organized a system of schools with the express purpose of introducing succeeding generations to public bodies of knowledge. The educational effort is intended to prepare youth to take its place in society. And all societies, like it or not, make certain demands upon their members, demands perilous to ignore.

Despite the durability and some would declare the good sense of this tradition, it lacks unanimous support. The core to critical theory, and certainly the heart of Marxist educational philosophy, rejects, not the notion of freedom, but the right of society to intrude on educational programs in such a way as to perpetuate the conditions that have kept a majority of men and woman in an unenviable position of subordination and subjection. In company with Marxism, critical theory excoriates capitalism and what it perceives as society's domination by the industrial-educational complex. The missed mark, however, is that in those countries where the principles of critical theory and Marxism have been applied in practice, neither the educational nor political freedom of citizens has been ensured.

In addition to these theories, American educational philosophy has flirted both with progressivism and romantic humanism where freedom, according to their enemies, has been redefined as license. The progressives of earlier days and contemporary romantic humanists say that freedom in education, like any freedom, is grounded in nature where growth must be allowed to occur without interference. A rejoinder to what could be called naive naturalism, though, coming from essentialists and others with a conventional notion of freedom, maintains that children do not just grow to become what their nature intends, any more than plants in a garden if left alone just grow and become what they ought to be. Neglected gardens will soon be overrun with weeds. Productive gardens are cultivated. Analogously, students' development will be retarded or misdirected if talent is left uncultivated. An unplanned and unplanted plot can hardly be said to be a garden, and a chaotic, unregulated scholastic program does not result in decent education.

To sustain nothing more subtle than good order in society, it is reasonable to suppose that some restraint upon freedom must be accepted by all members of a society. Freedom is something all persons ought to have, yet in individual instances it might conflict with the responsibility of other persons and institutions. For example, are children free to do what they want when their parents are responsible for them? Are children free to be instructed as they like when society provides teachers for them? So, conventional educational theory maintains, freedom should be regarded not as if it were total and comprehensive, but rather as something students should have commensurate with their level of maturity and responsibility. Freedom in education, put another way, is something about which its promoters must be precise and specific.

Finally, in connection with any view of freedom, confusion should be removed between being free and being able. Persons free to act might be hindered from action because they lack knowledge or skill. Conversely, they might be able to do something but be blocked from acting. Freedom without ability is only forlorn hope; yet one should understand that limitations upon freedom might sometime be necessary if ability is to be achieved.

Little can be achieved without discipline, and discipline, essential to any degree of excellence, makes achievement possible. Here there is usually agreement among thoughtful men and women. But the genesis of discipline is a matter for dispute. Does discipline originate with respect for authority and when, in scholastic settings, students understand why rules are stated and enforced? And should children, everyone for that matter, be introduced to the experience of following rules? Responsible educators have a favorable attitude toward discipline and appreciate the worth of external support and pressure to keep students on a steady course. Few, however, suppose that discipline appears spontaneously or suddenly: it is developed gradually as part of the educational process. To the extent that an educational process in and out of school neither encourages nor promotes the development of discipline, that educational process is deficient. Points of view differ: no doubt there are attitudes associated with the development of discipline that are hard or impossible to measure, but empirically, the development of discipline takes into account and involves the systematic following of rule. Schools without rule might not be schools at all.

Finally, in most analyses of educational perspective the issue of right is introduced, even at the risk of trivializing the concept of right by extending it too far. Some philosophers have used the phrase *natural right* in connection with education and put it on the same level as "life, liberty, and the pursuit of happiness." So one must tackle this question: Does the right to education belong to the category of natural right? And in this connection, it should be noted, a distinction between education in its fundamental meaning and schooling is important. Even when an assertion of right is made, or when a right is granted according to some legal or political rule, neither assertion nor granting of right translates into justification for the right.

If the right to an education is a granted right or an entitlement can certain qualifications for it be imposed? This is a much debated question. If there is a granted right to schooling, must all schools be open to everyone? Is there, then, a right to fail? Or can right to schooling be granted only to students who are in the best position to benefit from it? Granted right to schooling leaves an open, often unanswered, question: Does it mean an offer of schooling without interference—that is, without intruding upon the performance of others—or does it mean intervention to improve the performance of those who otherwise might gain slight benefit from the scholastic opportunity extended to them?

CENSORSHIP AND INDOCTRINATION

Censorship and indoctrination are contemporary issues that only now and then boil in controversy, but under any circumstance are grist for educational philosophy's mill. Taking censorship first, dual meanings are stipulated: one, exercising control over experience presumed capable of undermining manners and morals; two, prohibition of publication or circulation of material alleged to be objectionable.

In the United States, public policy expressed in interpretation of the First Amendment sometimes limits (though seldom without acrimony) circulation of material considered objectionable. But prohibition of publication, rather than prohibition of circulation, is another matter. Publication would seem to be constitutionally protected. Yet, apart from constitutional guarantees in connection with free speech, which might or might not square with logic and moral philosophy, is there anything educational philosophers can say, or should say, about the kind of material (or experience) a morally responsible society should permit, restrict, or prohibit?

Unless the assumption is endorsed that standards with respect to experience are essential and that society should affirm allegiance to moral responsibility, there is hardly any need to introduce the issue of censorship. Should society adopt a laissez faire policy, implying that an objective moral code cannot be pronounced, or embrace moral relativism and nihilism, then neither experience nor behavior of any kind might be subjected to censorship. Men and women, it is sometimes maintained, are alone capable of determining the kind of experience they want or need. Nothing is right or wrong, true or false, offensive or inoffensive, formative or destructive except when weighed in the perspective of a strictly personal moral code. Yet, even with this relativistic view, an acknowledgment is usually forthcoming that men and women are largely, although not wholly, formed by their experience.

To a great extent, it can be said, we are what our experience has made us. We not only learn best from experience; we learn only from experience. Experience, though, is either direct or indirect, objective or vicarious, so what is experienced either directly or indirectly is responsible both for forming our minds and for shaping our moral standards. Morally and intellectually, then, we come to assign greater worth to the significance of one rather than another kind of experience.

What is read, heard, and seen is experience. Some experience, safe to say, is morally innocuous. Yet rich and various experience enables men and women to construct a frame of moral reference wherein judgments about worth are made, and gives them an intellectual, at least an experiential, foundation for assessing conduct. Why should I behave one way rather than another? And when, in fact, I do act, why do I do one thing rather than another? Behavior is guided by a standard whose origin is somewhere.

Instructions from moral and educational philosophers are unnecessary when it comes to protecting youth, or anyone else for that matter, from physical or intellectual experience that will almost certainly harm them. This is the common sense of the matter. When children engage in dangerous play, censoring their activity meets with approval. Censorship is likewise accepted when children are exposed to obviously false information. But the experience of children, relativists say, with what is plainly morally false or dangerous belongs to a separate category, because what is supposed to be morally false or dangerous does not matter or, as likely, the allegation that something is morally false cannot be supported by verifiable evidence.

If not the first, Plato was among the first Western philosophers to justify censorship. Yet when Plato censored the poets, he indicted them for lying when they used myth to recite the ideals of Greek life. He worried about intellectual rather than moral contamination, although it would be unfair to say that his addiction to truth translated into indifference to morality. There is no assertion that moral truth—what ought to be done—is unfathomable. Still, it occurred to Plato that life in society is itself the best moral teacher. Athenian citizens would learn to be moral, not by being told what to do, but by learning what ought to be done by doing what ought to be done. Teachers of morals were the citizens of Athens who, Plato declared, should act always for the good. And what the good is, although seldom easily discovered, can be discovered and justified rationally. Put otherwise, standards for intellectual truth must be established and justified rationally. Standards for moral truth—what is the good—can also be demonstrated and justified rationally. For society to be morally standardless, to allow or encourage men and women go to their own moral way, is to lay a foundation for social anarchy and moral license.

Scholastically, although it is conceivable that some literature should be subject to absolute censorship, it is more likely that it is a matter not of censorship but of selection and timing. Young children are prohibited from driving automobiles—clearly a way of censoring activity—and no one objects. Driving, for more mature youth, might be encouraged. For a student in the eighth grade a certain reading assignment might be judged inappropriate, but the same assignment might be on the required reading list for a college freshman. So in the last analysis, it appears that censoring literary experience might not be the critical element. It is, instead, a matter of coming to terms with who is either authorizing or suppressing curricular material. Who, it can be asked, should be the keeper of the public conscience?

Educators who knowingly or unknowingly engage in indoctrination are often found on the side of censorship. But, we should be careful: one can certainly oppose genuine indoctrination (rather than caricatures of indoctrination) and acknowledge the good sense in supervising and, if need be, restricting the experience of youth during formative years. Immunity is enjoyed by no one to the manners, morals, and standards practiced or observed in the social environment. And it is hard to avoid the conclusion that the contagion of social standard and convention—for good or ill—is insidious and probably inevitable.

Understandably, morally sensitive men and women maintain a stern posture in opposition to relativism and nihilism. They are tempted to employ indoctrination to ensure acceptance or rejection of what is socially acceptable or unacceptable. Still, when indoctrination is suspected or affirmed outright, one must be careful and not assume that persons who practice indoctrination, endorse it, or are victims of it, are morally reprehensible.

Within and without educational circles and sometimes among educational philosophers, as well, what is and what is not indoctrination is unclear. Educational philosophy as an analytic exercise can be of considerable help here. To teach as true something universally held to be true, and that can be demonstrated publicly and clearly to be true, is not indoctrination. Conversely, to maintain that something is true when at best it is on probation, and to assert its truth when evidence either contradicts or questions its truth is plainly indoctrination. Yet, linguistic precision is important: indoctrination has to do with doctrines or parcels of belief, not carefully crafted bodies of knowledge. Little can be added in the way of informed discussion by talking about indoctrination in the multiplication tables or, for example, geographic information or grammatical rule. These things, and others like them, are not matters of belief. Moreover, the discussion derives nothing from confusing indoctrination with narrow and uninspired instruction or teaching by rote.

To understand the meaning of indoctrination more fully, a distinction should be drawn between assertions of different orders. First, there is an assertion where disagreement among persons conversant with the matter involved about the kind of evidence that will support or reject the assertion is entirely absent. Second, there is an assertion where the evidence either to support or deny the assertion is disputed. How to obtain evidence and verify it is also a matter of dispute. Indoctrination comes into sight when the latter assertion is taught as truth.

Such assertions might be complex in their formation and articulation and, besides, have a high degree of internal consistency. Both tend to contribute to the appearance of truth. When these assertions are represented as true, teachers who advance them are practicing indoctrination.

On the other side of the coin, to declare that a point of doctrine is false because it cannot be tested scientifically and empirically is itself indoctrination. Good teachers encourage students to search for truth, to think for themselves, to assess the evidence, and arrive at a conclusion. But this is not the whole of the instructional process: there are many times, experienced teachers declare, when direct teaching, telling, and explanation are illustrative of good and economical instruction.

When controversial issues cannot be demonstrated to be true or false, where should teachers stand? As often as, not neutrality is counseled. But even in the best of circumstances neutrality is probably beyond teachers' reach, and in any case teaching is not the same thing as moderating a discussion. Teachers are responsible for teaching what can be taught. So they should teach what they believe, or are persuaded by evidence, is either true or good. And they should do so with fairness and an awareness of their ability to influence their students. Their aim should be to develop and open the minds of their students, not close them. Critics of conventional instruction who maintain that all teaching is nothing more than a form of indoctrination are guilty of imprecision in thought and language, and of conceptual confusion, too.

EDUCATIONAL PHILOSOPHY: A RECAPITULATION

Neither as an independent discipline nor as a subsidiary to politics and ethics has educational philosophy been regarded by intelligent insiders and outsiders as a useless exercise. Even when the recommendations of philosophy's expositors were rejected, their authors refused to abandon them or lose confidence in theory's ability to inform educational practice. Throughout the history of educational thought, and even when unsystematic ideas or a "general hang of things" masqueraded as educational philosophy, these questions were pondered at various levels of sophistication: What is the proper role of educational philosophy? Is educational philosophy necessary? Should educational philosophy have a part to play in the education of teachers?

The role of educational philosophy should be expressed without reference to a particular philosophy or philosopher. And we should begin by outlining the general direction educational philosophy has taken. First, euu-cational philosophy has had responsibility for determining the broad pur-pose of education, and then essaying to evaluate the pedagogic process lead-ing to its realization. When this was the expectation for educational philoso-phy, then, safe to say, it was a leader marching in the vanguard of educa-tional practice. As a leader, and if philosophy is complete, it is reasonable to suppose that it will answer the following questions: Who is being taught? Why is teaching undertaken in the first place? What should be taught? How should the instructional process be conducted? When educational philoso-phy assumes the role of leader, it functions as a directive doctrine and asks nothing more from practice than it be faithful to stated principles. When we recite the names of philosophers who have labored in the educational vine-yard over the past twenty-five hundred years, we must be struck by the large number who supposed educational philosophy to be nothing if it were not a directive doctrine. But this is only part of the story.

The other part, although for most of educational philosophy's life expressing a minority view, represents educational philosophy with a more limited role vis-à-vis practice—one never posting it to the vanguard of prac-tice. In this definition of purpose, educational practice follows various routes dictated largely by social, economic, and political reality. It lacks neither aim nor perspective, but both have their origin in the practical considerations of life in society rather than in the speculative discourse of scholars and aca-demicians. Education should fit its clientele for the tasks of life, and since these tasks are manifold and usually unpredictable, the business of educa-tion is to deal with them flexibly and imaginatively. Education, to paraphrase Herbart, should eschew philosophical speculation: it should do first what needs doing, and when what needs doing has been done, there is time for philosophy to interpret, justify, and rationalize practice.

Interrogatives about human nature are answered by educational phi-losophers only after they have observed children in the schools. Why are children being educated is an important question. But, it has been declared, is one that cannot be answered outside the context of a learning situation in a real, rather than a theoretical, educational and social environment. What should be taught is a question whose import cannot be gainsaid. But if the answer is given too early and without reference to the needs and interests of students who are expected to absorb the experience organized in the cur-riculum, it might be irrelevant. How is the educational process conducted to ensure the realization of worthwhile objectives? This question can be asked anytime, but a responsible answer can be given, say educators who accept educational philosophy as a liberal discipline and reject any assertion that it is a directive doctrine, only after the educational process begins, and when children in the schoolhouse are ready to articulate their needs and interests.

The story has a last chapter. In it we are told that educational philosophy is neither directive nor liberal: it is delegated to report on educational practice, to call attention to what has been done and to inform teachers of the success, or its lack, of various teaching strategies and methodologies. But this definition of role lacks appeal because of its unphilosophical and unacademic appearance, and has never commanded either a large or loyal following.

Despite evidence of philosophers' allegiance to different philosophies of education, the assertion is sometimes heard that too much attention is paid to philosophy. Classroom practice is what counts, and when talk about theory ceases, common pedagogic techniques are left. Philosophy aside, educational practice goes its own way. The argument can be put more directly. All teachers do the same things in their classrooms irrespective of the philosophies of education (if any) they embrace. If this is indeed the case, what need is there for educational philosophy? Or if educational philosophy is only a codification of common sense, is it reasonable to conclude that all philosophies of education end up with unanimity of purpose on teachers' desks?

Mustering persuasive argument to reject this discounting of philosophy is harder than it sounds. In any case, and with only minor exceptions, the best-known educational thinkers have rushed to the defense of philosophy and have declared that it makes a difference in the day-to-day practices of schooling. John Dewey, likely more than any of his predecessors or successors, was persuaded of the importance of educational theory and refused to countenance any shrinking of its stature.

Finally, in connection with the questions posed for philosophy, is it important in the education of teachers? Looking back, we see that for all their interest in philosophy (theory, educational thought and ideas), the philosophers with whom we are acquainted, with the exception of Herbart and Dewey, showed remarkably little interest in transporting their ideas from the library to the classroom or, moreover, in urging prospective teachers and teachers to adopt their ideas and make them permanent possessions in their professional repertoire. We need not recite detail here, but save for Herbart's seminar and Dewey's long career as a teacher of teachers, educational philosophy was seldom promoted as a necessary subject in a curriculum for teacher education. It might have been assumed, or hoped, that teachers, becoming aware of educational philosophy, would recognize it as essential; or that it would infect the intellectual outlook of educated persons and alter their approach to pedagogy. Yet, for whatever reasons, good or bad—and finding them would not be easy—educators appeared content to make their pronouncements about teacher education and then leave it entirely to chance, or to others, the matter of communicating them to schoolmasters. Teaching a science of education to prospective teachers was a plank in Herbart's scholastic platform. In the hands of John Dewey, however, educational philosophy attained a maturity that recommended it as a staple in programs of teacher education.

The cautious and conventional attitude long dominating educational thought rested on the assumption that an explicit philosophy of education was not only essential to but necessarily preceded educational practice. This assumption is weakened or demolished by a closer examination of history's record. Hardly any evidence bolsters the supposition that the theories of Plato or Isocrates were adopted in the schools of ancient Greece. It is not clear that the elaborate recommendations of Quintilian were followed in Rome during his lifetime, or for two or three centuries thereafter. Cassiodorus, a revisionist, could make only slight impression on the school practices of his time, although the innovations he recommended were followed faithfully in the monastic schools that came into existence in succeeding centuries.

So long as Alcuin remained on the level of pedagogic technique and undertook to teach an accurate Latin along lines most useful to the government of church and state, his work paid huge dividends. But when he began to invest in theory—which was seldom—he lost his footing and revealed an inability to appreciate the worth of theory or to organize it as a foundation for his instructional regimen. Despite apparent weakness in outlook, Alcuin was a pioneer whose pedagogic wisdom accelerated the development of medieval education. Besides, it is barely possible that Alcuin's practical pedagogy concealed an incipient theory, formulated in tradition, perpetuated by custom, and applied intuitively. But a habitual conformity to a highly theological view of men and women and their temporal welfare could hardly count as educational philosophy. Both in content and elaboration it missed the mark of adequacy.

Hugh of St. Victor and John of Salisbury, compared with Alcuin, were more decently educated and their agile minds led them to an understanding of the often subtle contributions educational theory could make to school practices. Yet, their involvement with theory was limited mainly to its use in opening classical literary vaults that their forebears with a tender Christian conscience had sealed. The were preoccupied with using the literary legacy of the past to fill the curriculum. Their method of selection and use of theory were centered on decontaminating classical literature or proving that decontamination was unnecessary. Textual exposition, improved and illuminated by Hugh of St. Victor and John of Salisbury, was a monumental achievement. Huge benefits accrued to education from its use. But for all their good work, both men depended so heavily upon reading that the educational process for their own and later days was severely limited. Their use of theory (convictions about education reaped from the work of ancient and early Christian writers) was hardly praiseworthy. For what they rejected was, in the long run, more significant than the points accepted. In some respects they were faultless, for the full corpus of classical pedagogical literature was as yet unavailable. Still, enough classical work on education was in the library, so it is hard to believe that their rejections were due to ignorance: they refused to use what they did not want. Despite their determination to preserve their grasp of the Christian educational tradition, and for all the good work they accomplished along lines of allegorical interpretation, the schools were little affected by their labor. The road running from theory to practice was long and filled with obstacles; not many teachers thought the journey worth making.

Erasmus was in a better position to speak with authority on the educational views of ancient authors and of the promise implicit in a complete classical education. An accomplished scholar, Erasmus found ways to achieve distinction. Enrolling early in the cult of fame, he was prepared to defend the proposition that talent is rewarded in all kinds of successful careers: scholars and artists should be accorded the same recognition for their accomplishments as soldiers and politicians. Moreover, Erasmus never disputed the notion that almost everything worth knowing can be found somewhere in the classics. So in studying and analyzing the classics, in making a heroic effort to remember everything in them, a superior education—that is, a full cultivation of the human abilities of thought and expression—is the result. Henceforth, in all his educational writing, he promoted a program of teaching and learning wherein the development of thought and expression had pride of place. His *pietas litterata* is remarkably thorough, despite being incomplete: Erasmus never left the classics nor understood why educators would want to. Despite the onesidedness of his educational plan and its tendency to perpetuate medieval pedagogical edicts, Erasmus's theory was attractive. When it was translated for practice during his lifetime, it was elevated to the status of a directive doctrine.

Comenius stood at the threshold of a new educational era. The luster of his reputation was due in no small part to his ability to accommodate his educational plan to a world in religious and political ferment. Like John Dewey, he arrived on the educational scene when educational practice was ready to follow a new trail. So a reforming educator with a philosophy amenable to change could find an attentive audience. His audience, however, listened to his advice when it was directed at practical pedagogical considerations, but tended to ignore both his philosophy of education and the psychological justification advanced as a foundation for his innovative natural method.

In the final analysis, then, schoolmasters were most impressed when he told them to use books that were written especially for school use and to remember that all learning begins with the senses. The historian can praise Comenius as a pioneer in the enigmatic field of educational philosophy, but cannot demonstrate that his philosophical propositions were heeded.

John Locke can be indicted for having a penurious spirit when he turned to education. He complained bitterly about the practices and doctrines of the past, and then went on to make vague recommendations about educating the sons of gentlemen. Evidence of interest in popular education is almost totally lacking. Teaching, he seemed to imply, was fully accounted for when tutors were engaged. Yet behind this veil of indifference was the suggestion that psychology—questions about the nature of learning and the learning process itself—contained the key to the educational puzzle box. Locke, though, left to others the trick of finding the box's keyhole.

Rousseau was no doubt familiar with Locke's work in philosophy and psychology, and he appeared to follow Locke, although not to explain his theory for which he was unequipped, but to counsel indifference to the large-scale educational problems that plagued his century. Even if schoolmasters had wanted to, they could not have taken anything in Rousseau's educational prescription in *Emile* and put it to work in schools. Rousseau knew his advice was impractical but, the argument goes, it contained a pedagogical message understood by Pestalozzi, who was responsible for translating Rousseau's naturalism to education. This might inflate Rousseau's stature and deflate Pestalozzi's, although both were intent upon reforming education. Where Rousseau wanted to achieve reform by dismantling education's formal structure, Pestalozzi wanted reform to begin within the boundaries of conventional educational systems. Put another way, he followed a path leading away from Rousseau's radical goal. So instead of a master-disciple relationship, it would appear that Rousseau inspired Pestalozzi to invent techniques of natural pedagogy to ameliorate distressing unfavorable social and educational conditions visited upon common people. In the long run Pestalozzi was successful, for a century after his death scholars recognized his accomplishments and praised them, but during his mature years friend and foe alike regarded him as a kind but disturbed eccentric who embarked upon a fruitless educational crusade.

After amateurs like Rousseau and Pestalozzi had tinkered with education and came close sometimes to subverting it, scholars thought it time for their intervention. When they intervened they were turning back the clock, or better, the calendar; the time had come for scholars to examine the basic pedagogical issues, make sense of them, organize them, and introduce pedagogy as a scientific discipline. This meant that questions asked before should be asked again, and that dependable answers be supplied. What is the purpose of education? What are its foundations in the fields of psychology, sociology, and philosophy? What should teachers teach, and how should techniques be used to make instruction most effective? Herbart set out to make pedagogy scientific; and to succeed on this mission he needed to demonstrate a sound theory guiding it and a dependable content informing it. In addition, it needed a reliable method. Yet, apart from a seminar he conducted for prospective teachers, Herbart rested confidently on the level of philosophical pronouncement: an academic platform, he thought, despite his highly quotable advice that education must not just be talked about but also must be practiced, was the best place to conduct an examination of education's most important questions. For the most part, except when his followers misinterpreted his views on method and codified them in five formal steps, Herbart's educational philosophy—his science of education—was a scholar's theory for a teacher-centered school.

If Herbart was not entirely practical in delivering an educational message, he nevertheless gave credence to the idea that education has vital social as well as individual significance, and that old, sometimes tired, generalizations, despite their validity, had not been effective in sponsoring changes in schooling. Teaching and learning are important human pursuits, and dependable knowledge is needed concerning their direction and practice. How is dependable knowledge to be obtained? Now we come to the stage where a science of education is played, and John Dewey is the principal actor. He ignored the distinctions usually made between theory and practice, and taught that theory's work is to report on the successes and failures of practice. Thus, educational theory or philosophy—what education should do, what teaching and learning should accomplish—cannot be jettisoned, on the one hand, or be allowed to remain aloof to validation in day-to-day practice in real schools with real children, on the other. With John Dewey educational philosophy came of age; from his time forward it wore an entirely new face. And for almost the first time in history, educational philosophy began to make a difference in scholastic practice.

While taking into account the attention paid educational philosophy (either as ideas about education, educational thought, or educational theory) for more than two millennia, the book recounting its history is unfinished. New theories or new interpretations of philosophy, revivals of old theories, or radical restructuring of educational philosophy's place and purpose appear more or less regularly. Deconstruction is an example of the radical and innovative. While it has penetrated literary criticism and has solicited attention in philosophy and educational philosophy, its prospects for affecting educational philosophy are far from clear. If there is danger to the status of educational philosophy, it is not likely to be lodged in an indifference to philosophizing about education, about wrestling with issues in educational policy and practice that seem to be critical, but whether the discipline will be taken seriously by the educators and the enterprise it is intended to serve.

The current preoccupation among educational philosophers is not with probing for the fundamentals of the educational act before beginning seriously to teach, but with making practice and an integration of practice into a caricature of educational philosophy. Dewey, probably more than anyone else in educational philosophy's history, made educational philosophy a respectable and necessary partner in the business of education, but his achievement along this line is in jeopardy. Contemporary educational philosophers should resist the temptation to ride every bandwagon of educational dispute and underscore the significance of their discipline by making it communicate to educators, prospective educators, and an intelligent and interested public the fundamental nature and goal of philosophy.

A genuine educational philosophy will not likely regain prominence in the academic arena or in the schools and, what is more, be regarded as relevant unless it abandons an observable contemporary tendency to follow the trail blazed centuries ago by rhetoric and philosophy: to invent and use a technical language in a pedantic and artificial way in connection with questions no one has asked and whose answers, if there are answers, no one understands. When educational philosophy is turned into an arsenal of rules recited in language incomprehensible to decently educated people, it will have foreclosed the reason for its existence in a scholastic syllabus and any allegiance it might elicit from a community of intelligent women and men.

NOTES

1. On this point, consult "Symposium on Philosophy and Education," *Harvard Educational Review* 51 (August 1981): 415–31.

2. Robert A. Carlson, *The Quest for Conformity: Americanization Through Education* (New York: John Wiley & Sons, 1975), 90–93.

3. See, for example, Arthur M. Schlesinger, Jr., *The Disuniting of America: Reflections on a Multicultural Society* (Knoxville, Tenn.: Whittle Direct Books, 1991).

4. For perceptive and well-reasoned analyses, see Keith Baker, ed., *Bilingual Education: Time for a Second Look* (Bloomington, Ind.: Phi Delta Kappa, 1990).

5. Meyer v. Nebraska, 262 U.S. 390.

6. For what is often considered to be the classic account, see Israel Zangwill, *The Melting-Pot, Drama in Four Acts* (New York: Macmillan Company, 1909). A quicker and shorter representation of the melting-pot idea, minus Zangwill's dramatic features, is Maurice Wohlgelernter's *Israel Zangwill: A Study* (New York: Columbia University Press, 1964), 175–86.

7. See Walter Feinberg, *Reason and Rhetoric: The Intellectual Foundations of 20th Century Liberal Educational Policy* (New York: John Wiley & Sons, 1975), 93–133.

8. Michel Rosenfeld, *Affirmative Action and Justice: A Philosophical and Constitutional Inquiry* (New Haven: Yale University Press, 1991), 282–336, offers a philosophical and constitutional, and often persuasive, justification, for affirmative action.

9. Robert D. Heslep, "Preferential Treatment and Compensatory Justice," *Educational Theory* 26 (Spring 1976): 147–53.

10. Nathan Glazer, *Affirmative Discrimination: Ethnic Inequality and Public Policy* (New York: Basic Books, 1975), 201.

11. Serrano v. Priest, 96 *California Reporter* 601–26 (1971).

12. San Antonio Independent School District v. Rodriguez, 411 US 1, 58 (1973).

13. Edward A. Ross, *Social Control* (New York: Macmillan, 1906), 168.

14. Raymond Callahan's, *Education and the Cult of Efficiency: A Study of the Social Forces That Have Shaped the Adminstration of the Public Schools* (Chicago: University of Chicago Press, 1962), 42–64, refers to the middle years of the twentieth century, but many of his criticisms are thought applicable to contemporary educational practice.

15. Albert Shanker, "Accountability: Possible Effect on Instructional Programs," in Leon M. Lessinger, and Ralph W. Tyler, eds., *Accountability in Education* (Worthington, Ohio: C.A. Jones, 1971), 66–74.

16. For a more comprehensive treatment of educational purpose, consult Henry J. Perkinson, *Teachers Without Goals, Students Without Purposes* (New York: McGraw-Hill, 1993).

17. Paul Goodman, *Compulsory Mis-education* (New York: Horizon Press, 1964), 31–34.

18. Thomas F. Green, "Philosophy and Policy Studies: Personal Reflections," *Teachers College Record* 81, no. 2 (Winter 1979): 211–24.

19. This old debate is joined again in the work of Banesh Hoffman, *Tyranny of Testing* (New York: Crowell-Collier Press, 1962); and B.F. Skinner, *Beyond Freedom and Dignity* (New York: Alfred A. Knopf, 1971).

20. John Wilson, *Fantasy and Common Sense in Education* (New York: John Wiley & Sons, 1979), 15–26.

21. William James in *The Moral Philosophy of William James*, edited by John K. Roth (New York: Crowell, 1969), 197–201, asserts that knowledge should precede action, but then concedes that moral behavior rests also upon the development of good habits.

22. B.F. Skinner takes this position throughout *Beyond Freedom and Dignity*.

23. Howard Kirschenbaum and others have popularized values clarification (Sidney B. Simon, Leland W. Howe, and Howard Kirschenbaum, *Values Clarification* [New York: Dodd, Mead, 1978]). Lawrence Kohlberg was responsible for the success of cognitive-developmental theory (Lawrence Kohlberg, *The Philosophy of Moral Development* [New York: Harper & Row, Publishers, 1981]). And John Wilson has elabo-

rated the principles of cognitive-analytic theory (John Wilson, *Reason and Morals* [Cambridge, Eng.: Cambridge University Press, 1961]). Traditional theory, wherein freedom is dogmatically assumed, has a list of exponents too long to recite here.

BIBLIOGRAPHY

Adams, George P., and William P. Montague, eds. *Contemporary American Philosophy*. 2 vols. New York: Macmillan, 1930.

Adamson, John W. *Pioneers of Modern Education: 1600–1700*. Cambridge, Eng. : Cambridge University Press, 1905; New York: Teachers College Press, 1972.

Adler, Mortimer J. *The Paideia Proposal*. New York: Macmillan, 1982.

Aikin, W.M. *The Story of the Eight-Year Study*. New York: Harper and Brothers, 1942.

Alcott, Bronson. *Essays on Education, 1830–1862*. Gainesville, Fla.: Scholars' Facsimiles & Reprints, 1960.

Alcuin. *Alcuin of York, c. A.D. 732–804: His Life and Letters*. Translated by Stephen Allott. York, Eng.: William Sessions Ltd., 1974.

Anderson, Martin. *Impostors in the Temple*. New York: Simon & Schuster, 1992.

Aristippus. *Aristippi et Cyreniacorum Fragmenta*. Edited by Erich Mannebach. Leiden: E.J. Brill, 1961.

Aristotle. *The Complete Works of Aristotle*. 2 vols. Edited by Jonathan Barnes. Princeton: Princeton University Press, 1984.

Aristoxenus. *Aristoxenus Elementa Rhythmica*. Edited by Lionel Pearson. Oxford: Clarendon Press, 1990.

Augustine, St. *A Select Library of Nicene and Post-Nicene Fathers of the Christian Church*. 14 vols. Edited by Philip Schaff. New York: Charles Scribner's Sons, 1886–1889.

———. *St. Augustine: On Education*. Translated and edited by George Howie. Chicago: Henry Regnery, 1969.

Bacon, Francis. *The Advancement of Learning*. Edited by Joseph Devey. New York: American Home Library, 1902.

———. *The Novum Organum*. Translated and edited by Peter Urbach and Joseph Gibson. Chicago: Open Court, 1994.

Bagley, William C. *Education and Emergent Man*. New York: Nelson and Sons, 1934.

Baker, Keith, ed. *Bilingual Education: Time for a Second Look*. Bloomington, Ind.: Phi Delta Kappa, 1990.

Baldwin, C.S. *Medieval Rhetoric and Poetic*. New York: Macmillan, 1928.

Barnard, Leslie W. *Athenagoras: A Study in Second-Century Apologetics*. Paris: Beauchesne, 1972.

Barnes, Timothy D. *Tertullian: A Historical and Literary Study*. New York: Oxford University Press, 1971, 1985.

Bell, Bernard Iddings. *Crisis in Education: A Challenge to American Complacency*. New York: Whittlesey House, 1949.

Bernstein, Richard. *Dictatorship of Virtue: Multiculturalism and the Battle for America's Future*. New York: Alfred A. Knopf, 1994.

Bestor, Arthur. *Educational Wastelands: The Retreat from Learning in Our Public Schools*. Urbana: University of Illinois Press, 1953, 1985.

———. *The Restoration of Learning: A Program for Redeeming the Promise of American Education*. New York: Alfred A. Knopf, 1955.

Blanshard, Brand, et al. *Philosophy in American Education*. New York: Harper and Brothers, 1945.

Bloom, Allan. *The Closing of the American Mind*. New York: Simon & Schuster, 1987.

Bode, Boyd H. *Fundamentals of Education*. New York: Macmillan, 1921.

———. *Modern Educational Theories*. New York: Macmillan, 1927.

———. *Progressive Education at the Crossroads*. New York: Newsome, 1938.

Boethius. *The Consolation of Philosophy*. Translated by Richard Green. New York: Macmillan, 1962.

Bogoslovsky, B.B. *The Ideal School*. New York: Macmillan, 1936.

Bolgar, R.R. *The Classical Heritage and Its Beneficiaries*. Cambridge, Eng.: Cambridge University Press, 1954.

Bowersock, G.W. *Hellenism in Late Antiquity*. Ann Arbor: University of Michigan Press, 1990.

Bowles, Samuel, and Herbert Gintis. *Schooling in Capitalist America; Educational Reform and the Contradictions of Economic Life*. New York: Basic Books, 1976.

Boyer, Ernest L. *College: The Undergraduate Experience in America*. New York: Harper & Row, 1987.

———. *High School: A Report on Secondary Education in America, The Carnegie Foundation for the Advancement of Teaching*. New York: Harper & Row, 1983.

Brameld, Theodore. *Ends and Means in Education*. New York: Harper & Row, 1949.

———. *Toward a Reconstructed Philosophy of Education*. New York: Dryden Press, 1956.

Brehaut, Ernest. *An Encyclopedist of the Dark Ages: Isidore of Seville*. New York: B. Franklin, 1912, 1964.

Brehier, Emile. *Chrysippe et Ancien Stoëcisme*. 9th edition. Paris: Presses Universitaires de France, 1951.

Brent, Joseph. *Charles Sanders Peirce: A Life*. Bloomington: Indiana University Press, 1993.

Broudy, Harry S. *Building a Philosophy of Education*. Englewood Cliffs, N.J.: Prentice-Hall, 1961.

———. "How Philosophical Can Philosophy of Education Be?" *Journal of Philosophy* 52 (October 27, 1955): 612–22.

Brown, Peter R.L. *Augustine of Hippo: A Biography*. Berkeley and Los Angeles: University of California Press, 1967.

Burbules, Nicholas C. "Continuity and Diversity in Philosophy of Education: An Introduction," *Educational Theory* 41, no. 3 (Summer 1991): 257–63.

Burnett, Joe R. "Whatever Happened to John Dewey?" *Teachers College Record* 81, no. 2 (Winter 1979): 192–210.

Butler, J. Donald. *Four Philosophies and Their Practice in Education and Religion*. Revised edition. New York: Harper & Row, 1957.

Butler, Nicholas Murray. *The Meaning of Education*. New York, 1898.

———. *The Place of Comenius in the History of Education*. Syracuse, N.Y.: C.W. Bardeen, 1892.

Butts, R. Freeman. *The American Tradition in Religion and Education* Boston: Beacon Press, 1950.

———. *A Cultural History of Education*. New York: McGraw-Hill, 1947.

Butts, R. Freeman, and Lawrence A. Cremin. *A History of Education in American Culture*. New York: Henry Holt, 1953.

Callahan, Raymond. *Education and the Cult of Efficiency: A Study of the Social Forces That Have Shaped the Administration of the Public Schools.* Chicago: University of Chicago Press, 1962.

Capella, Martianus. *Marriage of Philology and Mercury.* Edited by William H. Stahl and Richard Johnson, with E.L. Burge. 2 vols. New York: Columbia University Press, 1971.

Carlson, Robert A. *The Quest for Conformity: Americanization Through Education.* New York: John Wiley & Sons, 1975.

Carter, James G. *Letters on Free Schools in New England.* New York: Arno Press, 1969. Reprint of the 1824 edition, published under the title *Letters to the Hon. William Prescott, L.L.D. On the Free Schools of New England.* Boston: Cummings, Hilliard, 1824.

Cassiodorus. *An Introduction to Divine and Human Readings.* Translated by Leslie Webber Jones. New York: Columbia University Press, 1946.

Chadwick, Henry. *Boethius: The Consolations of Music, Logic, Theology and Philosophy.* New York: Oxford University Press, 1981.

———. *Early Christian Thought and the Classical Tradition: Studies in Justin, Clement, and Origen.* New York: Oxford University Press, 1966.

Chambliss, J.J. *The Origins of American Philosophy of Education: Its Development as a Distinct Discipline, 1808–1913.* The Hague: Martinus Nijhoff, 1969.

Chancellor, William E. *A Theory of Motives, Ideals and Values in Education.* Boston, 1907.

Childs, John L. *Education and Morals: An Experimentalist Philosophy of Education.* New York: John Wiley & Sons, 1950, 1967.

———. *Education and the Philosophy of Experimentalism.* New York: Century, 1931.

Cicero. *De Oratore.* 2 vols. Translated by E.W. Sutton and H. Rackham. Cambridge: Loeb Classical Library, Harvard University Press, 1942.

———. *On Oratory and Orators.* Translated by J.S. Watson. London: Bell, 1891.

———. *The Republic of Cicero.* Translated by G.D. Dardingham. London: B. Quartitch, 1884.

Clark, Donald L. *Rhetoric in Greco-Roman Education.* New York: Columbia University Press, 1957.

Clarke, John. *An Essay Upon the Education of Youth in Grammar-Schools. In Which the Vulgar Method of Teaching, and a New One Proposed, for the More Easy and Speedy Training Up of Youth to the Knowledge of the Learned Languages; Together with History, Chronology, Geography, etc.* Second edition. London, 1730.

Clarke, M.L. *Higher Education in the Ancient World.* London: Routledge & Kegan Paul, 1971.

Collins, James D. *The Teacher.* Chicago: Henry Regnery, 1954.

Comenius, John Amos. *The Analytical Didactic.* Translated by Vladimir Jelinek. Chicago: University of Chicago Press, 1953.

———. *Comenius.* Translated by M.W. Keatinge. New York: McGraw-Hill, 1931.

———. *The Great Didactic.* Translated by M.W. Keatinge. London: Adam and Charles Black, 1896.

———. *The School of Infancy.* Edited by Ernest M. Eller. Chapel Hill: University of North Carolina Press, 1956.

Commission on the Relation of School and College. *Adventure in American Education.* New York: Harper and Brothers, 1942.

Comte, August. *The Positive Philosophy.* Translation of the 1855 edition by Harriet Martineau. New York: AMS Press, 1974.

Conrad of Hirschau. *Dialogus super auctores sive Didascalion,* edited by C. Schepss. Würzburg: Beck, 1889.

Copleston, Frederick. *A History of Philosophy.* 9 vols. Westminster, Md.: Newman Press, 1946–1975.

Cotkin, George. *William James, Public Philosopher*. Baltimore: Johns Hopkins University Press, 1990.

Counts, George S. *Dare the School Build a New Social Order?* New York: John Day, 1932; New York: Arno Press, 1969.

———. *Education and the Promise of America*. New York: Macmillan, 1945.

Cremin, Lawrence A. *American Education: The Colonial Experience, 1607–1783*. New York: Harper & Row, 1970.

———. *American Education: The Metropolitan Experience, 1876–1980*. New York: Harper & Row, 1988.

———. *American Education: The National Experience, 1783–1876*. New York: Harper & Row, 1980.

———. *The Transformation of the School: Progressivism in American Education, 1876–1957*. New York: Alfred A. Knopf, 1961.

Cunningham, William F. *The Pivotal Problems of Education*. New York: Macmillan, 1940.

Darwin, Charles. *On the Origin of Species*. Photoprint edition of the 1859 edition. Cambridge: Harvard University Press, 1964, 1976.

Demiashkevitch, Michael. *An Introduction to the Philosophy of Education*. New York: American Book Company, 1935.

Dennis, Lawrence J. *From Prayer to Pragmatism: A Biography of John L. Childs*. Carbondale: Southern Illinois University Press, 1992.

Dewey, John. *Democracy and Education*. New York: Macmillan, 1916.

———. *Experience and Education*. New York: Macmillan, 1938, 1974.

———. *Reconstruction in Philosophy*. New York: Holt, Rinehart & Winston, 1920; Boston: Beacon Press, 1948.

———. *The School and Society*. Chicago: University of Chicago Press, 1900.

Diggins, John Patrick. *The Promise of Pragmatism: Modernism and the Crisis of Knowledge and Authority*. Chicago: University of Chicago Press, 1993.

Diogenes Laertius. *Lives of Eminent Philosophers*. 2 vols. Translated by R.D. Hicks. London: W. Heineman, 1925; New York: G.P. Putnam's Sons, 1925.

Döring, Klaus, von. *Der Sokratesschuler Aristipp und die Kyrenaiker*. Stuttgart: Franz Steiner Verlag Wiesbaden, 1988.

D'Souza, Dinesh. *Illiberal Education: The Politics of Race and Sex on Campus*. New York: Free Press, 1991.

Dudden, F. Holmes. *Gregory the Great: His Place in History and Thought*. 2 vols. New York: Longmans, Green, 1905.

Dunkel, Harold B. *Herbart and Education*. New York: Random House, 1969.

———. *Herbart and Herbartianism: An Educational Ghost Story*. Chicago: University of Chicago Press, 1970.

———. "Herbart's Pedagogical Seminar," *History of Education Quarterly* 7 (Spring 1967): 93–101.

Education Commission of the States. *Action for Excellence*. Denver: The Commission, 1983.

Emerson, Ralph Waldo. *Emerson on Education: Selections*. Edited with an introduction by Howard Mumford Jones. New York: Teachers College Press, 1966.

Erasmus, Desiderius. *Copia: Foundation of the Abundant Style*. In *Literary and Educational Writings*, edited by Craig R. Thompson. Translated and annotated by Betty I. Knott. Toronto: University of Toronto Press, 1978.

———. *On the Method of Study*. In *Literary and Educational Writings*, edited by Craig R. Thompson. Translated and annotated by Brian McGregor. Toronto: University of Toronto Press, 1978.

Farrell, Allan P. *The Jesuit Code of Liberal Education*. Milwaukee: Bruce, 1938.

Feinberg, Walter. *Reason and Rhetoric: The Intellectual Foundations of 20th Century Liberal Educational Policy*. New York: John Wiley & Sons, 1975.

Finney, Ross L. *A Sociological Philosophy of Education*. New York: Macmillan, 1928.

Fletcher, Joseph. *Moral Responsibility: Situation Ethics at Work*. Philadelphia: Westminister Press, 1967.

Fontaine, Jacques. *Isidore de Seville et la culture Classique dans L'Espagne Wisigothique*. 2 vols. Paris: Etudes Augustienes, 1959.

Fortenbaugh, William W., and Peter Steinmetz, eds. *Cicero's Knowledge of the Peripatos*. New Brunswick, N.J.: Transactions Publishers, 1989.

Franklin, Benjamin. *Benjamin Franklin on Education*. Edited by John Hardin Best. New York: Teachers College Press, 1962.

———. *The Papers of Benjamin Franklin*. 30 vols. Edited by Leonard W. Labaree and Whitfield J. Bell, Jr. New Haven: Yale University Press, 1959–1993.

Freeman, Kenneth J. *Schools of Hellas: An Essay on the Practice and Theory of Ancient Greek Education from 600 to 300 B.C.* 3d ed. London: Macmillan, 1932

Gaiser, Konrad. *Theophrast in Asso*. Heidelberg: C. Winter Universitätsverlag, 1985.

Giarelli, James M., and J.J. Chambliss. "The Foundations of Professionalism: Fifty Years of the Philosophy of Education Society in Retrospect," *Educational Theory* 41, no. 3 (Summer 1991): 265–74.

Gibson, Margaret, ed. *Boethius: His Life, Thought and Influence*. Oxford, Eng.: B. Blackwell, 1981.

Glazer, Nathan. *Affirmative Discrimination: Ethnic Inequality and Public Policy*. New York: Basic Books, 1975.

Gleason, John B. *John Colet*. Berkeley and Los Angeles: University of California Press, 1989.

Goodlad, John. *A Place Called School: Prospects for the Future*. New York: McGraw-Hill, 1984.

Goodman, Paul. *Compulsory Mis-education*. New York: Horizon Press, 1964.

Gould, Josiah B. *The Philosophy of Chrysippus*. Leiden: E.J. Brill, 1970.

Green, Thomas F. "Philosophy and Policy Studies: Personal Reflections," *Teachers College Record* 81, no. 2 (Winter 1979): 211–24.

Grendler, Paul F. *Schooling in Renaissance Italy: Literacy and Learning, 1300–1600*. Baltimore and London: Johns Hopkins University Press, 1989.

Gutek, Gerald L. *The Educational Theory of George S. Counts*. Columbus: Ohio State University Press, 1970.

———. *Pestalozzi and Education*. New York: Random House, 1968.

Gwynn, Aubrey. *Roman Education from Cicero to Quintilian*. London: Oxford University Press, 1926; New York: Teachers College Press, 1966.

Hardie, Charles D. *Truth and Fallacy in Educational Theory*. Cambridge, Eng.: Cambridge University Press, 1942.

Harris, William T. *Introduction to the Study of Philosophy*. New York: D. Appleton, 1890.

Haskins, Charles H. *The Renaissance of the Twelfth Century*. Cambridge: Harvard University Press, 1927, 1955; New York: New American Library, 1976.

Henderson, C. Hanford. *Education and the Larger Life*. Boston, 1902.

Henderson, Ernest N. *A Text-Book in the Principles of Education*. New York, 1910.

Herbart, J.F. *ABC of Sense Perception and Minor Pedagogical Works*. Translated by W.J. Echoff. New York: D. Appleton, 1903.

———. *On the Aesthetic Revelation of the World as the Chief Work of Education*. Translated by H.M. Felkin and E. Felkin. London: Swan Sonnenshein, 1892.

———. *Outlines of Educational Doctrine*. Translated by A.F. Lange. New York: Macmillan, 1901; Folcroft, Penn.: Folcroft Library Editions, 1977.

———. *The Science of Education: Its General Principles Deduced from Its Aim*. Translated by H.M. Felkin and E. Felkin. London: Swan Sonnenshein, 1892; Washington, D.C.: University Publications of America, 1977.

Heslep, Robert D. "Preferential Treatment and Compensatory Justice," *Educational Theory* 26 (Spring 1976): 147–53.

Hirsch, E.D., Jr. *Cultural Literacy: What Every American Needs to Know*. Boston:

Houghton Mifflin, 1987.

Hoffman, Banesh. *Tyranny of Testing*. New York: Crowell-Collier Press, 1962.

Hofstadter, Richard, and Wilson Smith. *American Higher Education: A Documentary History*. 2 vols. Chicago: University of Chicago Press, 1961.

Honeywell, Roy J. *The Educational Work of Thomas Jefferson*. Cambridge: Harvard University Press, 1931.

Hook, Sidney. *Education for Modern Man: A New Perspective*. New York: Dial Press, 1946; New York: Alfred A. Knopf, 1963.

Horne, Herman H. *The Democratic Philosophy of Education*. New York: Macmillan, 1932; Westport, Conn.: Greenwood Press, 1978.

―――. *Idealism in Education*. New York: Macmillan, 1910.

―――. *The Philosophy of Education*. New York: Macmillan, 1927.

Hugh of St. Victor. *Didascalicon: A Medieval Guide to the Arts*. Translated by Jerome Taylor. New York: Columbia University Press, 1961.

Hutchins, Robert M. *Conflict of Education in a Democrat's Society*. New York: Harper and Brothers, 1953; Westport, Conn.: Greenwood Press, 1972.

IJsseling, Samuel. *Rhetoric and Philosophy in Conflict: An Historical Survey*. The Hague: M. Nijhoff, 1976.

Illich, Ivan. *Deschooling Society*. New York: Harper & Row, 1971.

Isocrates. *Isocrates*. 3 vols. Translated by G. Norlin and LaRue Van Hook. Cambridge: Loeb Classical Library, Harvard University Press, 1928–1945.

Jaeger, Werner W. *Paideia: The Ideals of Greek Culture*. 3 vols. Translated by Gilbert Highet. New York: Oxford University Press, 1939, 1945; Oxford: B. Blackwell, 1954–1961.

Jagu, Armand. *Zenon de Cittium*. Paris: J. Vrin, 1946.

James, William. *The Moral Philosophy of William James*. Edited by John K. Roth. New York: Crowell, 1969.

―――. *Pragmatism*. New York: Longmans, Green, 1907; Cambridge: Harvard University Press, 1975.

―――. *Talks to Teachers*. Cambridge: Harvard University Press, 1983.

―――. *Variety of Religious Experience*. New York: Longmans, Green, 1916; Cambridge: Harvard University Press, 1985.

Jarrett, James L., ed. *The Educational Theories of the Sophists*. New York: Teachers College Press, 1969.

Jefferson, Thomas. *Notes on the State of Virginia, with an Appendix*. 26 vols. Boston: David Carlisle, 1801; New York: Harper & Row, 1964.

―――. *The Papers of Thomas Jefferson*. 25 vols. Edited by Julian P. Boyd, et al. Princeton: Princeton University Press, 1950–.

Jerome, St. *Select Letters of St. Jerome*. 24 vols. Translated by F.A. Wright. Cambridge: Loeb Classical Library, Harvard University Press, 1933.

John of Salisbury. *The Metalogicon: A Twelfth-Century Defense of the Verbal and Logical Arts of the Trivium*. Translated with an introduction and notes by Daniel D. McGarry. Berkeley and Los Angeles: University of California Press, 1955, 1962.

Kames, Henry Home, Lord. *Elements of Criticism*. Edinburgh and London, 1762; New York: Johnson Reprint, 1967.

―――. *Essays on the Principles of Morality and Natural Religion*. Edinburgh: R. Fleming, 1751; New York: Garland Publishing, 1983.

Kaminsky, James S. *A New History of Educational Philosophy*. Westport, Conn.: Greenwood Press, 1993.

Kandel, Isaac L. *William Chandler Bagley, Stalwart Educator*. New York: Teachers College Press, 1961.

Karier, Clarence J. *Shaping the American Educational State, 1900 to the Present*. New York: Free Press, 1975.

Katz, Michael B. *Reconstructing American Education*. Cambridge: Harvard University Press, 1986.

Kennedy, George A. *Classical Rhetoric and Its Christian and Secular Tradition From Ancient to Modern Times.* Chapel Hill: University of North Carolina Press, 1980.

Kimball, Bruce A. *The "True Professional Ideal" in America: A History.* Cambridge, Mass.: B. Blackwell, 1992.

Kimball, Roger. *Tenured Radicals.* New York: Harper & Row, 1990.

Kneller, George F. *Existentialism and Education.* New York: John Wiley & Sons, 1958.

Kohlberg, Lawrence. *The Philosophy of Moral Development.* New York: Harper & Row, 1981.

Kolesnik, Walter B. *Humanism and/or Behaviorism in Education.* Boston: Allyn & Bacon, 1974.

Kottje, Raymund, and Herald Zimmermann. *Hrabanus Maurus: Lehrer, Abt und Bischof.* Wiesbaden: Steiner, 1982.

Kuklick, Bruce. *Churchmen and Philosophers from Jonathan Edwards to John Dewey.* New Haven: Yale University Press, 1985.

———. *Josiah Royce: An Intellectual Biography.* Indianapolis: Bobbs-Merrill, 1972.

Lancelot, W.H. "A Close-up of the Eight-Year Study," *School and Society* 42 (1939): 141–44.

Laurie, S.S. *John Amos Comenius, Bishop of the Moravians: His Life and Educational Works.* Cambridge, Eng.: Cambridge University Press, 1884.

Leach, A.F. *The Schools of Medieval England.* London: Methuen, 1916; New York: Barnes & Noble, 1969.

Leach, Mary S. "Mothers of In(ter)vention: Women Writing in Philosophy of Education," *Educational Theory* 41, no. 3 (Summer 1991): 287–300.

Lessinger, Leon M., and Ralph W. Tyler, eds. *Accountability in Education.* Worthington, Ohio: C.A. Jones, 1971.

Levy, Daniel C. *Private Education: Studies in Choice and Public Policy.* New York: Oxford University Press, 1986.

Levy, Leonard W. *The Establishment Clause: Religion and the First Amendment.* New York: Macmillan, 1985, 1989; rev. ed., Chapel Hill: University of North Carolina Press, 1994.

Locke, John. *An Essay Concerning Human Understanding.* Edited by Peter H. Nidditch. Oxford: Clarendon Press, 1979.

———. *Some Thoughts Concerning Education.* Edited by John W. Yolton and Jean S. Yolton. New York: Oxford University Press, 1989.

Lynch, John Patrick. *Aristotle's School: A Study of a Greek Educational Institution.* Berkeley and Los Angeles: University of California Press, 1972.

Lynd, Albert. *Quackery in the Public Schools.* Boston: Little, Brown, 1953.

McGucken, William J. *The Catholic Way in Education.* Milwaukee: Bruce Publishing, 1934; Chicago: Loyola University Press, 1962.

Macmillan, C.J.B. "PES and The APS—An Impressionistic History," *Educational Theory* 41, no. 3 (Summer 1991): 275–86.

MacVannel, John Angus. *Outline for a Course in the Philosophy of Education.* New York: Macmillan, 1912.

Marx, Karl, and Friedrich Engels. "Manifesto of the Communist Party," in Carl Cohen, ed., *Communism, Fascism and Democracy: The Theoretical Foundations.* New York: Random House, 1972.

Mather Cotton. *Cares About the Nurseries. Two Brief Discourses. The One Offering Methods and Motives for Parents to Catechise their Children While Yet Under the Tuition of Their Parents. The Other, Offering Some Instructions for Children, How They May Do Well, When They Come to the Years of Doing for Themselves.* Boston, 1702.

———. *Corderius Americanus. An Essay Upon the Good Education of Children. And What May Hopefully Be Attempted, for the Hope of the Flock. In a Funeral*

Sermon upon Mr. Ezekiel Cheever. The Ancient and Honorable Master of the Free-School in Boston. Who Left Off, But When Mortality Took Him Off, in August, 1708, the Ninety-Fourth Year of His Age. With an Elegy and an Epitaph Upon Him. By one that was as a Scholar to him. Boston, 1708.

Mayer, Mary Helen. *The Philosophy of Teaching of St. Thomas Aquinas.* Milwaukee: Bruce Publishing, 1929.

Miller, Perry. *The New England Mind: The Seventeenth Century.* New York: Macmillan Company, 1939; Boston: Beacon Press, 1954.

———. *The Transcendentalists.* Cambridge: Harvard University Press, 1950.

Miner, John N. *The Grammar Schools of Medieval England: A.F. Leach in Historiographical Perspective.* Kingston, Ont.: McGill-Queen's University Press, 1989.

Monroe, Paul, editor. *A Cyclopedia of Education.* 5 vols. New York: Macmillan, 1911–1913.

Monroe, Will S. *Comenius and the Beginning of Educational Reform.* New York: Charles Scribner's Sons, 1900.

Morgan, Thomas J. *Studies in Pedagogy.* Boston, 1887.

Morris, Van Cleve. *Existentialism in Education: What It Means.* New York: Harper & Row, 1966.

National Commission on Excellence in Education. *A Nation at Risk; The Imperative for Educational Reform: A Report to the Nation and the Secretary of Education.* Washington, D.C.: Government Printing Office, 1983.

National Society for the Study of Education. *Modern Philosophies and Education.* Yearbook, vol. 54. Chicago: University of Chicago Press, 1955.

———. *Philosophies of Education.* Yearbook, vol. 41. Chicago: University of Chicago Press, 1942.

———. *Philosophy and Education.* Yearbook, vol. 80. Chicago: University of Chicago Press, 1981.

Neef, Joseph. *The Method of Instructing Children Rationally in the Arts of Writing and Reading.* Philadelphia, 1813.

———. *Sketch of a Plan and Method of Education Founded on an Analysis of the Human Faculties, and Natural Reason. Suitable for the Offspring of a Free People, and for Rational Beings.* Philadelphia, 1808.

Newman, John Henry. *The Idea of a University.* Garden City, N.Y.: Image Books, 1959. (There are dozens of editions of this classic.)

O'Connor, D.J. *An Introduction to the Philosophy of Education.* London: Routledge & Kegan Paul, 1967.

O'Donnell, James J. *Cassiodorus.* Berkeley and Los Angeles: University of California Press, 1979.

O'Shea, M.V. *Education as Adjustment: Educational Theory Viewed in the Light of Contemporary Thought.* Philadelphia, 1903.

Palmer, Francis B. *The Science of Education, Designed as a Textbook for Teachers.* Cincinnati, 1887.

Payne, William H. *Contributions to the Science of Education.* New York: Harper and Brothers, 1886.

Pelikan, Jaroslav. *The Idea of the University—A Reexamination.* New Haven: Yale University Press, 1992.

Perkinson, Henry J. *The Imperfect Panacea: American Faith in Education: 1865–1976.* New York: Random House, 1968, 1977, 1991.

———. *Teachers Without Goals, Students Without Purposes.* New York: McGraw-Hill, 1993.

Pestalozzi, J.H. *Leonard and Gertrude.* In Henry Barnard, *Pestalozzi and Pestalozzianism.* Syracuse, N.Y.: C.W. Bardeen, 1874.

Peters, Richard S. *Authority, Responsibility and Education.* 3rd edition. London: Allen and Unwin, 1973; New York: Eriksson, 1973.

Picket, Albert, and John W. Picket. *The Academician: Containing the Elements of Scho-*

lastic Science, and the Outlines of Philosophical Education, Predicted on the Analysis of the Human Mind, and Exhibiting the Improved Methods of Instruction. New York: C.N. Baldwin, 1820.

Plato. *The Dialogues of Plato.* 5 vols. Translated by Benjamin Jowett. New York: Oxford University Press, 1892.

Plutarch. *Plutarch's Lives.* 11 vols. Translated by B. Perrin. Cambridge: Loeb Classical Library, Harvard University Press, 1914–1926.

Pratte, Richard. "Analytic Philosophy of Education: A Historical Perspective," *Teachers College Record* 81, no. 2 (Winter 1979): 144–65.

Price, Kingsley. "Is a Philosophy of Education Necessary?" *Journal of Philosophy* 52 (October 27, 1955): 622–33.

Progressive Education Association. *Adventure in American Education.* New York: Harper and Brothers, 1942.

Quintilian. *The Education of an Orator.* 4 vols. Translated by H.E. Butler. Cambridge: Loeb Classical Library, Harvard University Press, 1921–1926.

Ravitch, Diane. *The Revisionists Revised: A Critique of the Radical Attack on the Schools.* New York: Basic Books, 1978.

———. *The Troubled Crusade: American Education, 1945–1980.* New York: Basic Books, 1983.

Report of the Holmes Group. *Tomorrow's Teachers.* East Lansing, Mich.: Holmes Group, 1986.

Riché, Pierre. *Education and Culture in the Barbarian West, Sixth Through Eighth Centuries.* Translated by John J. Contreni. Columbia: University of South Carolina Press, 1976.

Rickover, Hyman. *Education and Freedom.* New York: E.P. Dutton, 1959.

Rosenfeld, Michel. *Affirmative Action and Justice: A Philosophical and Constitutional Inquiry.* New Haven: Yale University Press, 1991.

Rosenkranz, Johann K.F. *The Philosophy of Education.* Translated by William T. Harris. New York: D. Appleton, 1886.

Ross, Edward A. *Social Control.* New York: Macmillan Company, 1906.

Rousseau, Jean Jacques. *Emile.* Translated by Barbara Foxley. New York: E.P. Dutton, 1911, 1938.

Russell, Bertrand. *Education and the Good Life.* New York: Boni & Liveright, 1926.

Ryan, Mary B. *John of Salisbury on the Arts of Language in the Trivium.* Washington, D.C.: Catholic University of America Press, 1958.

Sadler, John E. *J.A. Comenius and the Concept of Universal Education.* New York: Barnes & Noble, 1966.

Sartre, Jean-Paul. *Being and Nothingness.* Translated by Hazel F. Barnes. Paris: Gallimard, 1943; New York: Washington Square Press, 1956, 1966.

Scaglione, Aldo D. *The Classical Theory of Composition.* Chapel Hill: University of North Carolina Press, 1972.

Scheffler, Israel. *The Language of Education.* Springfield, Ill.: Charles C. Thomas, 1960.

Schlesinger, Arthur M., Jr. *The Disuniting of America: Reflections on a Multicultural Society.* Knoxville, Tenn.: Whittle Direct Books, 1991.

Schneider, Herbert W. *A History of American Philosophy.* Second edition. New York: Columbia University Press, 1963.

Shanzer, Danuta. *A Philosophical and Literary Commentary on Martianus Capella and the Seven Liberal Arts.* 2 vols. New York: Columbian University Press, 1971, 1977.

Shields, Thomas E. *Philosophy of Education.* Washington, D.C.: Catholic Education Press, 1921.

Simon, Sidney B., Leland W. Howe, and Howard Kirchenbaum. *Values Clarification.* New York: Dodd, Mead, 1978.

Skinner, B.F. *Beyond Freedom and Dignity.* New York: Alfred A. Knopf, 1971.

Smith, B.O., and Robert H. Ennis. *Language and Concepts in Education.* Chicago:

Rand McNally, 1961.

Smith, Mortimer. *And Madly Teach*. Chicago: Henry Regnery, 1949.

———. *The Diminished Mind*. Chicago: Henry Regnery, 1954.

Smith, Page. *Killing the Spirit: Higher Education in America*. New York: Viking, 1990.

Smith, Wilson, ed. *Theories of Education in Early America 1655–1819*. Indianapolis and New York: Bobbs-Merrill, 1973.

Soltis, Jonas F., ed. *Philosophy of Education Since Mid-Century*. New York: Teachers College Press, 1981.

Spencer, Herbert. *Education: Intellectual, Moral, and Physical*. Boston: Small, 1886; New York: Appleton-Century-Crofts, 1927

Stahl, William H., and Richard Johnson, with E.L. Burge. *Martianus Capella and the Seven Liberal Arts*. 2 vols. New York: Columbia University Press, 1971, 1977.

Stone, Robert L., ed. *Essays on the Closing of the American Mind*. Chicago: Chicago Review Press, 1989.

Sykes, Charles J. *The Hollow Men: Politics and Corruption in Higher Education*. Washington, D.C.: Regnery Gateway, 1990.

———. *Profscam: Professors and the Demise of Higher Education*. Washington, D.C.: Regnery Gateway, 1989.

"Symposium on Philosophy and Education," *Harvard Educational Review* 26, no. 2 (Spring 1956): 94–202.

"Symposium on Philosophy and Education," *Harvard Educational Review* 51 , no. 2 (August 1981): 415–31.

Tate, Thomas. *Philosophy of Education; or, The Principles and Practice of Teaching*. Syracuse, N.Y.: Bardeen, 1884.

Taylor, Jerome. *The Origin and Early Life of Hugh of St. Victor*. Notre Dame: Mediaeval Institute of the University of Notre Dame, 1957.

Tertullian. *On Prescription Against Heretics*. 3 vols. Translated by Peter Holmes, in *The Ante-Nicene Fathers*. Edited by Alexander Roberts and James Donaldson. New York: Charles Scribner's Sons, 1896–1903.

Theodore (Thierry) of Chartres. *Heptateuchon*, in A. Clerval, *Les écoles de Chartres*. Paris: Vrin, 1895.

———. *Commentaries on Boethius*. Edited by Nicholaus M. Haring. Toronto: Pontifical Institute of Mediaeval Studies, 1971.

———. *The Latin Rhetorical Commentaries*. Edited by Karin M. Fredborg. Toronto: Pontifical Institute of Mediaeval Studies, 1971.

Thompson, Manley H. *The Pragmatic Philosophy of C.S. Peirce*. Chicago: University of Chicago Press, 1953.

Tomkins, Arnold. *The Philosophy of Teaching*. Terre Haute, Ind., 1893.

Ulich, Robert. *History of Educational Thought*. New York: American Book Company, 1945, 1950, 1968.

Vandenberg, Donald. *Being and Education: An Essay in Existential Phenomenology*. Englewood Cliffs, N.J.: Prentice-Hall, 1971.

———. "Existential and Phenomenological Influence in Educational Philosophy," *Teachers College Record* 81, no. 2 (Winter 1979): 166–91.

Van Doren, Carl. *Benjamin Franklin*. New York: Viking, 1938.

Vincent, George E. *Social Mind and Education*. Chicago, 1897.

Vlastos, Gregory. *Socrates, Ironist and Moral Philosopher*. Ithaca: Cornell University Press, 1991.

Wadsworth, Benjamin. *The Well-Ordered Family; or, Relative Duties, Being the Substance of Several Sermons, About Family Prayer, Duties of Husbands & Wives, Duties of Parents & Children, Duties of Masters and Servants*. Boston, 1712.

Wagner, David L., ed. *The Seven Liberal Arts in the Middle Ages*. Bloomington: Indiana University Press, 1983.

Ward, Lester Frank. *Dynamic Sociology*. New York: D. Appleton, 1883.

Watts, Isaac. *Improvement of the Mind, To Which Is Added, A Discourse on the Edu-*

cation of Children and Youth. London, 1751.

Webb, Clement C.J. *John of Salisbury*. London: Methuen, 1932.

Weis, Lois, ed. *Class, Race, and Gender in American Education*. Albany: State University of New York Press, 1988.

West, Andrew F. *Alcuin and the Rise of Christian Schools*. New York: Charles Scribner's Sons, 1909; Westport, Conn.: Greenwood Press, 1969.

White, Emerson E. *The Elements of Pedagogy*. New York, 1886.

Wickersham, James P. *Method of Instruction*. Philadelphia: J.B. Lippincott & Co., 1865; New York: Arno Press, 1969.

Wilks, Michael, ed. *The World of John of Salisbury*. Oxford: B. Blackwell, 1984.

Wilson, John. *Educational Theory and the Preparation of Teachers*. Windsor, Eng: NFER, 1975: distributed in the United States by Humanities Press, Atlantic Highlands, N.J.

———. *Fantasy and Common Sense in Education*. New York: John Wiley & Sons, 1979.

———. *Reason and Morals*. Cambridge, Eng.: Cambridge University Press, 1961.

Wittgenstein, Ludwig. *Tractatus Logico-Philosophicus*. Translated by D.F. Pears and B.F. McGuinness. New York: Humanities Press, 1961.

Wohlgelernter, Maurice. *Israel Zangwill: A Study*. New York: Columbia University Press, 1964.

Woodring, Paul. *Let's Talk Sense About Our Schools*. New York: McGraw-Hill, 1953.

Woodward, William H. *Desiderius Erasmus Concerning the Aim and Method of Education*. Cambridge: Cambridge University Press, 1904; New York: Teachers College Press, 1964.

Wright, Chauncey. *Philosophical Writings*. Edited by Edward H. Madden. New York: Liberal Arts Press, 1958.

Wright, Esmond. *Franklin of Philadelphia*. Cambridge: Belknap Press of Harvard University Press, 1986.

Wrightstone, J.W. *Appraisal of Newer Elementary School Practices*. New York: Teachers College Press, 1938.

Yale Faculty. "Original Papers in Relation to a Course of Liberal Education," *The American Journal of Science and Arts* 15 (January 1829): 297–351.

Zangwill, Israel. *The Melting-Pot: Drama in Four Acts*. New York: Macmillan, 1909.

Zeno. *The Fragments of Zeno and Cleanthes*. Edited by A.C. Pearson. London: C.J. Clay, 1891.

INDEX